The Daily Telegraph

BOOK OF

GOLF

The Daily Telegraph
BOOK OF
GOLF
edited by NICK HOULT

Aurum

First published 2008 by Aurum Press Limited
7 Greenland Street
London NW1 0ND
www.aurumpress.co.uk

A catalogue record for this book is available from the British Library.

ISBN 978 1 84513 376 4

1 3 5 7 9 10 8 6 4 2
2008 2010 2012 2011 2009

Typeset in Spectrum by Saxon Graphics, Derby
Printed and bound in Great Britain by Cromwell Press,
Trowbridge, Wiltshire

CONTENTS

INTRODUCTION

BY NICK HOULT

Golf is about shared experience. The thousands of supporters lining the fairways at Royal Birkdale during the 2008 Open championship would have felt every swing, every putt and every palpitation endured by the golfers contending for the auld Claret Jug.

That is why golf's newspaper readership is probably the most informed of all sports audiences. As a writer, if you get your rescue club mixed up with your lob wedge then expect a letter through the post (invariably they are still letters these days), pointing out your error and (sometimes politely) asking you to check your facts in the future.

The *Daily Telegraph* has long been the favoured read in golf clubhouses up and down the British Isles and the newspaper has spent several generations building a loyal readership in a sport that demands certain standards.

One of those standards is honesty. A golfer is expected to remain honourable at all times. Cheating is the worst of all charges in a sport where a player's word remains his bond. With that in mind, the onus is on the *Daily Telegraph* to fire its shots straight down the middle of the fairway. No hook to the left or slice to the right. Through the years of Ryder Cup misery when the British Isles lagged like a sorry pack behind the dominant Americans, the *Daily Telegraph* was expected to point out the shortcomings and the demand for a change in the competition's rules. Likewise when the Ryder Cup was reborn with the formation of a European team inspired to victory at the Belfry in 1985 by Tony Jacklin, the *Daily Telegraph* remained a calming voice amidst a whirlwind of new-found pride in a team bearing the European standard.

The intention of this book is to give a peek into those great moments thanks to the vast library of cuttings that sit in the *Telegraph* archive and are dedicated to the sport of golf. The newspaper has reported on millions of drives, putts and the odd shank, dedicating acres of space to the reporting of the sport.

Unlike cricket, locating reports from the early days is difficult. There is no eyewitness to tell us how Young Tom Morris dominated the early Opens. There is no obituary to comb over a life cut short at the age of 24 when he died in bed on Christmas Day 1875. Instead we have to wait until the early 1920s for golf to take its place alongside cricket and horse racing as one of the major tenets of *Daily Telegraph* sports journalism.

Readers tend to resist radical change. They build up a relationship with a writer; share experiences; disagree and agree on major moments. There have been few *Daily Telegraph* golf correspondents. It is a job title that changes hands infrequently. As this book shows, different eras are seen through the eyes of consistent witnesses.

George Greenwood was the first powerful figure of golf journalism. His musings are contained in this book, but it is the writing of Leonard Crawley that shaped the *Daily Telegraph*'s coverage for a quarter of a century. A fine amateur sportsman, Crawley played first-class cricket for Essex and Worcestershire between the wars and was a direct contemporary of E.W. Swanton, the *Daily Telegraph*'s eminent cricket correspondent. Often the two would disagree over principles of their respective sports. Their correspondence would sometimes be contained on the letter pages of the *Daily Telegraph*. Through their ups and downs they remained firm friends and often shared a round of golf at Swanton's club, the glorious course at Sandwich.

Crawley was a member of a famous sporting family that dominated the 'post-Kaiser war years,' according to *Wisden*. He was to dominate golf writing in the same stylish manner, bearing witness to the exploits of Ben Hogan, Sam Snead, Henry Cotton and Bobby Locke.

Michael Williams succeeded Crawley, and his period as correspondent coincided with the domination of Tom Watson and Jack Nicklaus: names which still pass through the pages of the *Daily Telegraph* today, and it's the image of Nicklaus, teeing off at Augusta, that adorns the cover of this book.

Williams' final act as correspondent of the *Daily Telegraph* was to cover the 1997 US Masters championship. A seminal moment in major golf history. There Williams witnessed the emergence of Tiger Woods. His 12-shot victory was startling and Williams' closing words to his report were prescient: 'In four historic days they have been left feeling weak and inadequate, asking themselves, as the great Walter Hagen once put it many years ago, "Who's going to be second?"'

Williams passed away suddenly, just days after returning from Augusta. He collapsed on his home course, Chelmsford.

With the passing of Williams, the *Telegraph* appointed Fleet Street's first female golf correspondent. Eleven years later and Lewine Mair is now chief golf correspondent of both the *Daily Telegraph* and *Sunday Telegraph*. She has covered 13 major victories by Woods and witnessed the dominance of the European Ryder Cup team.

This is not the *Daily Telegraph*'s first venture into golf book publishing. In the mid-1990s an excellent chronicle of the sport was written by Ted Barrett, a former sports editor of the *Daily Telegraph*. Thanks to some of his research this book is able to reproduce some of the best golf writing to have appeared in the newspaper since it was first published in 1855.

The vast weight of material could fill several volumes, and the hardest task of any editor is to be ruthless in what you leave out.

Golf has provided so many dramatic moments, and *Daily Telegraph* writers have recorded scenes of great personal joy and desperate days of despair.

We witness Nicklaus returning to Augusta in 1986 to win the Masters at the age of 46, we experience the flamboyance of Severiano Ballesteros, the domination of Nick Faldo and the rise of Tiger Woods. But golf is not all about the joy of victory. Anyone who has seen a three-foot putt lip out on the 18th green will have at least a modicum of sympathy for golf's nearly men: the players who have grasped at glory only to throw it away in a moment of weakness.

The opening chapter charts those many magnificent moments but also lingers on the glorious failures of Jean Van De Velde at Carnoustie in 1999 and Doug Sanders' missed putt at St Andrews 19 years earlier, described as the 'agony that is the basis of nightmares'.

Passing through the history of golf, it is the names of its greatest exponents that linger in the memory, and chapter two sees a multitude of *Telegraph* writers, from Paul Hayward to Michael Parkinson, pay tribute to their feats, their humility and the legacy many have left behind.

One man is missing from the chapter. Tiger Woods is a golfing – sorry, *sporting* – phenomenon. Tapping his name into the *Daily Telegraph*'s electronic archive throws up thousands of results. Here we dedicate a chapter to one man. We experience some of his greatest achievements and lowest moments, as well as his emotional victory at St Andrews, just weeks after the death of his father. Woods was first introduced to *Telegraph* readers in March 1992. With Jack Nicklaus's haul of 18 majors now in sight, the *Telegraph* no longer refers to him as Eldrick Woods.

Writing about golf does not solely concentrate on the exploits of the professionals. It is that shared experience theme again. Many magazines are devoted to instruction. Helping us shave shots off a handicap spiralling out of control. The *Telegraph* has done its bit to help. In chapter four David Leadbetter, one of golf's great technicians, reveals how to improve your drive. The

Telegraph has long employed golfers as writers. Colin Montgomerie reveals his frustration at abuse from US crowds, while Justin Rose charts his amazing week at Birkdale in 1998.

Golf may be a solitary sport but once every two years men who are rivals on a weekly basis join together to play for the Ryder Cup. A competition that has grown from humble origins into a multi-million pound tourist industry. The penultimate chapter lingers on its relevance in today's game, while the book closes fittingly at the 19th hole. There it is time for Jasper Carrott to regale us with stories, jokes and anecdotes. Golf is not all about winning. For many that is its greatest attraction and one we can all share.

CHAPTER I
MAJOR MOMENTS

---

26 JUNE 1926

MR 'BOBBY' JONES THE NEW GOLF CHAMPION

A GREAT TRIUMPH: FAILURE OF HAGEN

George W. Greenwood

St Annes-on-Sea, Friday

Mr 'Bobby' Jones, the American amateur champion, won the Open golf championship on the Royal Lytham and St Annes links today with a total of 291, made up of scores of 72, 72, 73 and 74. This equals Braid's record score of 291 at Prestwick in 1908. All the leading places are occupied by United States players, Albert Watrous, of Grand Rapids, Michigan, being second with 293, and Hagen and Mr George Von Elm, of Los Angeles, a member of the American Walker Cup team, tying for the third place, each with 295. American players, therefore, have swept the board, and the British cup goes to the States for the fifth time in six years. This is by no means all, for less than a month ago Mr Jesse Sweetser won the British Amateur Championship, while the American team of amateurs once more captured the Walker Cup, which, so far, they have never lost.

To Mr Robert Tyre Jones we offer hearty congratulations on having won the world's premier golfing event in the face of the fiercest opposition on the part of both British and American professionals, whose business it is to win championships open to all and sundry. Mr Jones is the first amateur to win the British championship for 29 years, Mr Harold Hilton, at St Andrews in 1897, being the last of his kind to meet with success. Mr Jones is the most amazing golfer of all time. At the age of 24 years he is a dual champion and in America he is the most feared man of all, both among professionals and amateurs. Especially is this so in the score play, where you are fighting the invisible foe and not the man stalking at your elbow. Mr Jones' record in United States championships is an amazing one. In the space of four years he has either tied or been runner-up three times, and has won it on the other occasion.

Mr Jones is a worthy champion in every respect. He is extremely modest, hates to talk about himself and shuns all lime-light like he would the plague. When hailed the champion by 10,000 people he vanished into the clubhouse and shut himself up in a corner of the smoking room. Not only had the magnitude of the victory stunned him, but the manner in which it had been accomplished. As the fates ordained, he was engaged in a titanic fight with one man only, and that man happened to be his partner, Watrous. Both were on the verge of collapse; in fact, one man did collapse, and that was Watrous. Mr Jones kept his head and his nerve to the end.

It is a pretty story, with a very human side to it. Mr Jones and Watrous went out together on the last fatal round, accompanied by a vast crowd of people, and though they exhibited no outward signs of partiality, one had not to be a Sherlock Holmes to discover where the sympathies of the men and women lay. They were with Mr Jones, a quiet young man dressed in brown knickers and jersey, and wearing a cap which he pulled far over his eyes to keep away the fierce glare of the sun. When he played the shot he was swallowed up by thousands of excited people, who dashed madly forward to gain a point of vantage among the sand hills to see the next shot played. Watrous started with an advantage of two strokes, and these should have been enough if he had not broken down towards the end.

Mr Jones had caught his man at the fifth hole, but Watrous got his nose in front again at the seventh – 534 yards – where he played a great cleek shot to the green, while Mr Jones was in a bunker to the right. At the ninth Mr Jones went boldly for a putt of six yards and ran three yards past. He missed the putt back, and was thus two strokes to the bad again. Each was out in 36. Watrous maintained his lead with five holes still to play. Now came the great test of skill and nerve. On both the 14th and 15th greens Watrous took three putts, and it was clear that the strain had, in his case at any rate, begun to tell. The players were all square again, but when Mr Jones, at the dog-legged 17th, put his drive into the long stretch of sand and bents away on the left the position indeed looked black. But, after much study, Mr Jones played one of the finest shots ever witnessed in a championship, and one that will live in history. Taking a number four iron, he thumped the ball slap on to the middle of the green nearly 180 yards away. This was so unexpected a development that Watrous, who had visions of getting in front again, took three putts and was one stroke to the bad.

If there had been any doubt about his collapse hitherto there was no doubt at all now, for at the last hole he hooked his drive into a bunker, and in going for a long recovery shot, which he was compelled to do by sheer force of circumstances, he pulled into another bunker to the left of the green. With Mr Jones on the green and only five yards from the pin the drama was at an end. Dazed and shaken by the awful strain of the last three hours, Mr Jones disentangled himself from the crowd of admirers and sought the refuge of the clubhouse. In a chat afterwards, Mr Jones said that his putting very nearly brought about his downfall. He had taken 39 putts for the 18 holes, which was the worst putting round of his career, except the championship at Columbia five years ago, when in one round he had as many as 49 putts. 'Today,' he said, 'I completely lost confidence on the green; in fact, I was completely dazed.'

It was an unusual form of strain which Mr Jones was experiencing, due to the feeling that this was a personal duel between himself and Watrous. 'I felt that we were simply cutting one another's throats, and more than once I felt that I was desperately near cracking. Relief only came through the failure of Watrous near the end of the struggle, when he took three putts on three greens. Probably the shot that won me the championship was the one from the great heaps of sand at the 17th hole. I took great care to find the line over the hills, and I was lucky to strike the green. Then I felt I was safe.'

But there was Hagen still to be reckoned with. He started out like a lion, but he came in like a lamb. He was in many bunkers, and, moreover, he missed a putt of two feet on one green, a fact that greatly disgusted him. He came to the last two holes requiring a couple of 3s to tie with Mr Jones. Hagen was within a hair's breadth of getting the 3 at the 17th, the ball stopping on the lip of the hole. He now required a 2 at the last hole. I do not know whether Hagen tried to hole his second shot, a long mashie; but the fact is that the ball ran past the flag and plunged into a bunker at the back of the green. He failed to get out, and instead of a 2 there came a 6. If he had been content with a 4 he would have been second; but this was not good enough for Hagen, who was out to catch Mr Jones. A very gallant effort failed.

If the position overnight was dismal, it became tragic so far as British hopes were concerned when the third round was concluded, for Compston, the one and only man who had any chance of catching the Americans, was disqualified. The incident, entailing the imposition of this most severe penalty, occurred at the 12th hole, where Compston cut his drive into a bunker, not far from the green. The shot out was far too strong, the ball careering across the green into a plantation on the other side. Round the plantation is an improvised fence, indicating that beyond it is out of bounds. Compston was warned of the situation, and advised to go back and play another ball. Apparently, he listened to contrary advice of an unofficial character, and elected to play the ball in the wood and risk the consequences. The incident was reported by the marker to the committee, and Compston was disqualified. There can be no sort of question about the justice of the decision. But in any case it did not matter, as Compston had wrecked his chances, after a most brilliant start, by playing a succession of loose shots that met their proper deserts. The curious feature about his disqualification is that two years ago, in the northern championship on this same course, Compston suffered the same fate by turning up late.

With the dismissal of Compston the championship ceased to be an international contest; rather was it an American championship played on English soil. The only interest that remained was in witnessing a great triangular duel between Mr 'Bobby' Jones, Hagen and Watrous.

II JULY 1953

'UNBEATEN' HOGAN WINS OPEN BY FOUR STROKES

NEW CHAMPION HAS NO EQUAL

Leonard Crawley

Carnoustie, Friday

Ben Hogan, of the United States, won the Open golf championship here this evening with the wonderful total of 282. Peter

Thomson, of Australia; Frank Stranahan, the American Walker Cup player; D.J. Rees; and A. Cerda, of the Argentine, tied for second place with 286, and R. de Vicenzo came next, one stroke further behind.

Hogan had rounds of 70 and 68 today and I think we are all agreed that if he did not bring this great course quite to its knees his marvellous golf has at least humbled it and his winning score will be unbeaten here for generations. Hogan, who won his fourth American Open earlier this year, thus becomes the third American ever to have held the two major championships of the world at the same time. The others were the immortal Bobby Jones (1926) and Gene Sarazen (1932). It will be seen from Hogan's four rounds of 73, 71, 70 and 68 that he gradually warmed up in preparation for his final triumph. He is undoubtedly the best golfer in the world today and who shall say he is not the best of all time?

He seems to have the indefinable quality of being able to bring himself to his supreme peak when the pressure is greatest. His great predecessor Walter Hagen was much the same, but whereas he was a genius at improvisation and would play a number of bad shots, Hogan is the nearest thing we have seen to the perfect golfing machine. Today he made two mistakes, which included a disaster this morning at the 17th and this afternoon he did not quite hit his second shot to the 14th right out of the middle of the club. Mercifully he has not putted well or anything like his best this week, and his chipping might also have been better. Otherwise his winning score would have been fantastic.

It was a wet, dull morning when play began at eight, and the smoke was going straight up to the clouds from the hideous factory stacks about the district. Of those in the hunt, Stranahan was out first and went very well, though at a deplorably slow step for 13 holes. At the 14th he hit a shocking tee shot into a copse and took six, which made a heavy load on his back. A grand 3 at the 18th put him round in 73 for 217, but he had obviously lost ground.

Vicenzo came next. He was out in 37, which did not seem quite good enough, and 5s at the 12th and 14th, where he took three gratuitous putts, looked serious. But he came back like a wounded tiger and, bleeding but still sensible that the wound was only in the flesh, he finished gloriously in 4, 3, 3, 4, for 71 and a total of 214.

Thomson's golf was well nigh faultless, and apart from the 15th, where he took five, he did every hole in par. His 71 was a lovely exhibition and brought him into second place with Rees at 215.

Hogan, followed by a crowd the like of which I have never seen on any golf course, began 4, 3, 4. Then two 5s at the fourth and fifth made it essential for him to get a 4 at the long sixth to put himself back again on an even keel. Two glorious wooden club shots finished just short of the green, and though his chip was not a good one he holed out from eight feet. A fine spell of 3, 3, 4, 3, 4 followed, but the nightmare of three putts reappeared at the 12th. A superb 2 at the short 13th, where he holed from eight feet, put him three under fours. When he got his 3 for the first time in the championship at the one-shot 16th with just about the finest spoon I ever saw, he seemed to have the course record at his mercy.

One imagines he hit his long iron to the 17th a little thin, for he was bunkered in front of the green and with the customary splash from sand going wrong he had still to get down in two putts from eight yards. He took three and that frightful 6 spoiled the morning for thousands. His putt for a 3 at the home hole slipped past the tin by the diameter of a gnat's eyelash and 70 it was for 214, bracketed with Vicenzo in the lead.

After lunch the sun came out, and as Hogan was finishing his morning round Rees went off on the last lap. He was in tremendous form, attacking all the way. A 6 at the sixth was washed out by a 2 at the eighth and he reached the turn in 35. Vicenzo lost his chance by taking 38 to the turn, and 73 was the best he could do for 287. Thomson, playing almost flawless golf, joined Rees and Stranahan, and now everything depended on Hogan and Cerda behind.

Hogan's fourth round, strangely enough, requires little comment. He went off with four perfectly played 4s and then at the fifth had a break. His tee shot finished in a vile spot. He played a grand second but his ball spun back to the lip of the bunker. After infinite study he decided to chip with a straight-faced club, and holed out.

That made and inspired him once again. His 4 at the long sixth made one want to shout. An enormous tee shot, a gorgeous brassie, a chip and a four-foot putt. At the 13th he holed from 15 feet for a two and was now four under fours. His second to the 14th was short and he took his only 5 of the round. The rest, superlatively good, meant a 68 and a record, and though Cerda finished gallantly in 71, nothing else really mattered.

---

11 JULY 1960

FINE PUTTING AND RHYTHM BRING NAGLE TITLE

PALMER JUST FAILS IN THRILLING FINISH: HUNT'S EFFORT TOO LATE

Leonard Crawley

St Andrews

Kel Nagle, the 39-year-old Australian professional, won the Centenary Open golf championship over the Old Course at St Andrews on Saturday with a record 278 on this course, his four rounds being 69, 67, 71, 71.

A. Palmer, of America, finished second with 279 with four rounds of 70, 71, 70, 68, and there was a tie for third place between

R. de Vicenzo (Mexico), H.R. Henning (South Africa) and B.J. Hunt. G.B. Wolstenholme came next with 283 and won the gold watch for the best amateur. J.B. Carr and Maj. D.A. Blair, also amateurs, finished in 286.

The excitement at the end was intense, since Nagle, the leader, was out last paired with de Vicenzo, and Palmer, who has made a profound impression on this his first visit to this country, was just ahead of him; naturally each knew what the others were doing throughout the last round. The crowds were again enormous and, but for a shower late in the morning, the weather was fine and warm and there was no wind worth speaking of all day.

The more one sees of Nagle's play, the better one likes it. He has a charming rhythm which makes the game look an essentially easy one. His putting all through the Championship was magnificent and, even though it was not generally considered that he had more than an outside chance of winning, he is a most worthy champion. Palmer once again proved himself a lion-hearted finisher, and all who watched him hope that he will be back here again and become one of our best customers for the Open. One could not help feeling sorry for de Vicenzo after his superb exhibition all week. He virtually lost the Championship when going out of bounds at the 14th in the third round. Nor did his putter have quite the inspiration necessary to pull him through. We salute Hunt for his glorious last round of 66 and, as at Muirfield a year ago, the performances of the amateurs were quite outstanding.

The loop from the seventh to the 12th holes played a decisive part in the last round, for Nagle had lost two strokes to Palmer and one to Vicenzo after six holes. Nagle put his second to the seventh four feet past the pin and holed his putt after Vicenzo had stroked one in from four yards downhill and across the slope. The champion also holed a putt for a 2 at the eighth and all three were out in 34.

Palmer had very possible birdies at the tenth and eleventh holes, but failed with both putts. Vicenzo drove within two yards of the tenth green, but could not hole out in two more and, moreover, took three putts at the next. Nagle had therefore maintained his overnight lead of four strokes over Palmer and increased by one his two-shot lead over Vicenzo with seven holes to play. By then it was known that Henning had finished in 282, but on such an easy day this score could not stand up.

Palmer began playing like a tiger, walking between shots in his own dynamic way. Taking the left-hand line, he got a magnificent 3 at the 13th, though he failed to get his 4 at the long 14th, which was just out of range. But he did get his 4 at the 17th after a marvellous scuffle off the road. From a huge tee shot to the home hole he played one of the grandest pitches, four feet from the hole and, as he had done at the first and second, had his 3 for a round of 68 and a total of 279.

Nagle, full of smiles and playing so confidently behind him, had a number of critical strokes to play, the first being at the 13th, where he put a putt of some 30 yards within four feet of the hole. Again he might have gone into the Beardies from the tee at the 14th, but he did not and had no difficulty in getting his 5. He slipped a precious shot at the 15th where he under-clubbed with his second. And this hole was virtually the end of Vicenzo who, with an opportunity for a 3, took three putts.

Nagle's real crisis came at the 17th when he knew he had two 4s to win. His third from the edge of the green finished eight feet short of the hole. As he was lining up the next, a roar from the 18th informed him of Palmer's 3. It must have been a hideous moment but he struck his putt manfully into the middle of the hole.

With 20,000 pairs of eyes on him at the 18th he hit an even better pitch than Palmer had done before him and now had to go through the formality of getting down in two from a yard. He took due care after adjusting his cap and getting the line but never got a touch. What matter? He had won the Centenary Open.

II JULY 1966

NICKLAUS MASTERS 18TH WHEN IT COUNTS

THOMAS GIVES NOTICE OF CHALLENGES TO COME

Leonard Crawley

Muirfield

Everyone knew he would do it one day and over the historic links of the Honourable Company of Edinburgh Golfers at Muirfield on Saturday Jack Nicklaus, of the United States, at last came out Open champion with an aggregate of 282 (70, 67, 75, 70).

The finish was a splendid and exciting occasion with the handsome 26-year-old Nicklaus standing on the 18th tee requiring a par 4 to edge ahead of his fellow countryman Doug Sanders and our own David Thomas. Both had finished with the utmost bravery to post challenging totals of 283 on the huge scoreboard.

The narrow strip fairway, flanked by intimidating rough and pock-marked with bunkers where they are least wanted by a player under severe pressure, bends gently to the left at comfortable range from the tee so that the well-struck shot can overrun it into the knee-high hay on the far side. The pear-shaped lightning-fast green is defined by bunkers either side, and the pin 429 yards away was, of course, at the stalk end with the north-westerly breeze blowing firmly across the line of flight. The stands on either side were filled to capacity and 15,000 people lined the fairway and massed round the green at the back.

Nicklaus placed a powerfully struck number one iron dead centre and there was a hush as he studied the shot. He chose a number three iron and there was a rising cheer as it made for the flag always on the right side of the wind. His progress to the green was like a royal procession and even the great man himself, accustomed as he may be to such ovations, must have been almost overcome by the spontaneous warmth of his reception. Phil

Rodgers, who had led by two strokes going into the final round and had fought so hard for so long, had been overpowered and now played his role of second fiddle as one would expect of a great sportsman and hard trier in the moment of final defeat. Nicklaus putted safely down and tapped the ball home for a triumph he had twice all but thrown away and had finally secured with two superb iron shots to the nerve-testing 17th hole (528 yards) for the one birdie he required for victory.

I walked every step of the way with him on his final round, and to my eternal regret missed the fierce challenging thrusts of Dave Thomas, of whom I could only catch glimpses as the protagonists passed close enough to each other to allow one to scurry across and back. The roar that went up as he holed for 2 at the 13th shook all Muirfield and I am sure everyone on it. It was followed by a great shout as he holed out fast down the slope of the slippery 14th green for a fighting 4 and then came pandemonium as his tee shot to the 16th (188 yards) struck the pin and rebounded eight feet away. Even the sigh that went up as he missed the putt could be heard half a mile away.

Thomas had started with a 3 and with a little luck he would have finished with 1 for a tie, but it was not to be. That he used his mighty driver ten times from the tees against no more than half that number by his main adversaries is sufficient commentary on the all-out effort he made, and he will win one day if he keeps trying like this, Nicklaus or no Nicklaus.

The winner also started with a 3 and immediately wiped out the two-stroke advantage held by his partner Rodgers. His outward half of 33 was quite superb, marred only by missing a short putt on the ninth after he had brought the 495-yard stretch of terror to its knees with a number one iron followed by a number four iron and then a pitching wedge to one yard from the hole. His full-blooded belt to the eighth which carried over 300 yards and stopped within three feet of its pitch on the 23-yard wide fairway is one I shall not forget in a hurry, nor the brilliance of his second shot which got inside Rodgers, who lay only five feet from the hole.

Nicklaus almost lost the championship when he took three putts from seven feet on the 11th and committed a series of errors thereafter until he learned at the 14th green that he 'had blown his lead again' and settled down to finish like a champion.

———

21 JUNE 1970

BRILLIANT JACKLIN TAKES US TITLE BY SEVEN STROKES

Leonard Crawley

Minneapolis

Tony Jacklin, the British Open champion, made history at the Hazeltine course yesterday when he celebrated the 50th anniversary of Ted Ray's victory in 1920, the last Englishman to win the United States Open championship, by taking the American title by seven strokes. Jacklin beat a tremendous field, containing the might of America, and now ranks with the immortal Bobby Jones and Ben Hogan, both of whom held the Open championships of the United States and Britain in the same 12 months. No praise can be too high for Jacklin's performance, which earned him £12,500. As I followed this lonely little figure in the great heat among the swarming crowds, he seemed to be marching in a trance: a man of destiny.

With all humility, I would like to remind readers that at least I tipped Jacklin as one of three possible winners. I was with him after he had taken a fateful 6 at the seventh hole. He spoke quietly and one didn't know what to say. I did not know whether he felt what I felt, that, for the next half hour, the championship hung in the balance. I had earlier expressed my doubts as to whether Jacklin could stand up under the strain of the final round, with a determined man like Hill chasing him.

For four holes Jacklin did not put a foot wrong, save that he missed for a 2 at the short fifth after a superb tee-shot six feet past the hole. However, he promptly holed from eight feet at the sixth after Hill had bogeyed the short fifth ten minutes in front of him.

A tremendous shout went up when Jacklin's second to the seventh finished five feet from the hole; but, after an agonising silence, one heard muffled groans of sympathetic applause when he missed the putt. Then came that 6 at the long seventh, where he missed the green to the right, and at this stage he seemed to want steadying. At the short hole across the water, Jacklin hit a gorgeous long iron 15 feet behind the pin, but it was Gay Brewer, his partner, who got his par 3. Jacklin, short with his putt down the hill, took two more strokes to get in.

This was a stunning blow and one wondered whether Jacklin was going to slip. Indeed, he drove into the rough at the ninth, but found the green with a long iron and proceeded to hole the putt for a birdie 3 from 25 feet. This gave him a par 36 to the turn, the same score as Hill in front of him. Much more important, Jacklin was still four strokes ahead of his dangerous rival.

There was even better to come, for Jacklin, hitting a splendid pitch down the hill to the difficult tenth green, holed his putt from eight feet to become six under par and five ahead of Hill. Jacklin took pars of the 11th, 12th and 13th, but Hill matched him at each hole. Then the British champion drew away for a famous victory. He finished like a man relieved of all pressure and played the difficult last few holes relaxed and confident; happy with the ovation he received all down the line.

He holed from 10 feet at the 18th for a birdie 3 to finish with a 70, thus beating par in each of his four rounds on one of the most controversial courses ever selected for a championship. His winning score was 281, seven in front of Dave Hill, who, after a very brave performance, finished on 288, and eight ahead of Bob Charles who had a 289.

––––––––

12 JULY 1970

SANDERS, NICKLAUS MUST FIGHT IT OUT AGAIN

DRAMA ON LAST GREEN

Donald Steel

St Andrews

St Andrews' 18th hole, with a fairway 150 yards wide, no bunkers and a green that is impossible to miss, is probably the most straightforward finishing hole in the world of golf; except that is, when a player needs a 4 to win the Open championship. That was the setting and the prospect facing American Ryder Cup player Doug Sanders on the verge of a life's ambition but, with millions watching on television and every stand and window bulging beside the green, Sanders suffered the agony that is the basis of nightmares.

Off a good drive, he pitched too strongly when he might have been better attempting a scuffle and then with two for the championship from about twelve yards, Sanders putted four feet short down the fearsome slope. Anyone who has ever played golf at any level can imagine his feelings as he stood over the putt, and a few moments later as it slid tantalisingly past the right-hand side of the hole.

Instead of outright victory, universal acclaim and a fortune, there follows a night of remorse and a play-off for first prize of £5,250 at 12.30 today with Jack Nicklaus who, a few moments earlier, had taken three putts from the front edge of the same green for a total of 283. Two shots further behind came Lee Trevino and Harold Henning from South Africa, a shot in front of the defending champion Tony Jacklin who defended his crown most gallantly throughout a difficult week.

Last Sunday, in quiet mood before the championship began, Nicklaus expressed the sentiment that there was nowhere he would rather win than at St Andrews. As he took three putts on the 16th green, missed from six yards on the 17th after a superb second in the cross wind and failed to make his 3 at the last, it seemed as if his wish had been blown away on the wind, but now he makes a formidable opponent for Sanders in the play-off and I cannot see that he will be beaten.

It would have been sad if Nicklaus had been denied victory, for he played with massive calm and great control. Though over a stone lighter than he was during the Ryder Cup last year, he looked immovable in a wind that battered the best of swings and if he had managed to hole a number of holeable putts – his failing all week – Sanders would not have had his chance. Altogether Nicklaus had 39 putts. Twenty-one of those came at the last nine holes and though that is not unlikely at St Andrews, it must have been a sad disappointment to him. He spoke last weekend of his poor putting in the recent US Open and clearly does not enjoy the confidence of old on the greens. But he is still a wonderful player and competitor and it will be no surprise in the years ahead if he builds on his remarkable record in the British Open in which his placings since 1963 have been third, second, equal 12th, first, second, equal second and equal sixth.

Had Sanders won, on the other hand – and nobody would have chosen for anyone the climax he endured – his victory would have been most popular. He has not won a tournament in the United States since 1967 and there have been rumours of a decline. This resulted in his having to prequalify at Panmure but it also showed how loyal he has been to the British Open.

He was second equal to Nicklaus in 1966 and apart from the first hole on Wednesday when he started, as so many long handicap visitors do on the Old course, with a shot into the Swilcan Burn and taking 6, he has scored most consistently, going 39 holes before he took three putts. Typically he summed up his first hole by saying: 'I guess my game isn't built round an early morning start.' But for all the abbreviated nature of a swing that lacks the grace of Snead, he is a great manoeuvrer of the ball and that in the long run is what counts.

Trevino, who talks endlessly, and Henning owed their third places to stout finishing on the last few holes, but by the time the leading players had turned for home out by the Eden Estuary the outcome rested upon a straight fight between Sanders, Nicklaus and Jacklin. The fact that Jacklin could summon the mental resources to contest another finish, after his tremendous victory in America and his tiring preparations for this tournament, is a great tribute to him, and the crowd obviously took pride in their double champion. If the storm had not broken dramatically on Wednesday evening it could easily be a different story now.

After his third round, in which he wore an outfit edged with tartan, Sanders would not reveal what he had in store for the last round, though typically he promised: 'It won't be jeans and tennis shoes.' As he stood on the first tee in front of the big window and the more traditionally dressed members, there was some argument as to whether his shade was magenta or an off-shoot of mauve, but what mattered was that he played the first three holes in a lower score than anyone all day except Nicklaus, in conditions which, in fairness to the others, had eased a fraction.

Trevino, during his third round with Jacklin, remained faithful to his original plan of trying to draw the ball in the left-hand wind going out. But for a man who hardly ever tried to hit the ball dead straight, he let his second at the second drift away sufficiently to the right to prevent him from getting down in 2.

Meanwhile, on a day when there must have been fewer birdies in the last round of an Open than for many a year, Nicklaus was consolidating an auspicious start with a marvellous display of controlled striking. He judged his second shot to the second perfectly under the eyes of the Old Course Hotel's full balconies, holing from four yards for a 3, and followed with the day's only 4 at the long fifth, which in the circumstances constituted an eagle.

All this was of course witnessed by his partner Jacklin, who made little headway without doing very much wrong. He left himself an impossible pitch from the left at the second and by the sixth had fallen three behind Nicklaus.

At the turn Nicklaus and Sanders were level two ahead of Jacklin, but Trevino, with a spate of three putts, slipped away. The 11th brought Sanders level again with Nicklaus who was out in 35, Sanders getting down in two from the bunker whereas Nicklaus, not quite holing his tee-shot in the wind, took three.

There was no change at the next two, though both missed a chance at the long 14th, particularly Sanders who missed from a yard after a beautifully judged pitch on to the plateau. He did well to get down in two from behind the 15th and with every stroke meaning so much the tension was terrific.

Nicklaus, not certain what club to take from the left of the green, left his ball on the front edge of the 16th from where he took three putts, but his five iron to the 17th was a memorable stroke. Meanwhile Sanders in the last match got his four at the 16th but needed a wood for his second at the 17th, which like so many before him caught the Road bunker. His recovery from a good lie to 18 inches was the stroke of a player with a strong nerve, but in a few minutes his nerve — or his stroke — deserted him, although he said afterwards that he didn't feel any great pressure. I cannot say that I altogether believe him.

As early starters set forth against the billowing wind in pursuit of the richest prizes in the history of the Open — the 55th player received £125 – another huge crowd began to assemble, although the Prime Minister and Home Secretary were not able to wait to see the championship Jug presented by the captain of the Royal and Ancient, William Whitelaw.

Perhaps the Prime Minister, from a point behind the ropes, viewed the windy conditions on Friday more with the envy of a sailor than a golfer but, in an age of television, it is reassuring that there are thousands enthusiastic enough to turn out and to share and contribute to the atmosphere of a unique occasion.

There is little doubt that the R&A's bankers owed a considerable debt to Tony Jacklin and he gave them another bonus by being one of the main challengers with a round to go. Some of the morning's play, admirable though it was, was therefore regarded with the same impatience as the supporting bouts before a world heavyweight boxing championship.

In the Big Room of the R&A clubhouse, and every bar in St Andrews, the topic of conversation was the same, and it was easy to sense the rising tension. It made one realise, too, just what Jacklin, who has been invited to join Bobby Jones as the only Honorary Member of the St Andrews Club, had to overcome in winning at Chaska, Minnesota; yesterday the feeling of unease and anxiety which golfers experience before an important round was not helped by the wind, which was stronger than at any time during the week.

It turned the first hole, with the Swilcan Burn to be carried in front of the green, into a drive and long iron and then gave help for the rest of the round only with the second shot to the seventh and up to the 18th.

[Nicklaus won the play-off to claim the title for the second time.]

———

10 JULY 1977

ONE STROKE OF GENIUS

LAST DAY DRAMA AT AILSA

Donald Steel

Turnberry

Turnberry's first Open championship will not be its last, but it will never see anything more eventful, more dramatic, more stimulating and – for Jack Nicklaus – more cruel than Tom Watson's glorious victory yesterday. Nothing more could have been added to a sequence of final events which ran the full range of emotion, skill and bravery, as arguably the two best players in the world's oldest championship fought a sustained battle of epic proportions.

They had been the dominating figures for two days, watched by a record crowd for an Open in Scotland, and both beat Arnold Palmer's record aggregate of 276 at Troon in 1962, Watson by eight strokes and Nicklaus by seven. Watson, down early, was still two strokes behind on the 13th and just possibly the only person who gave much for his chances of making good the difference against a man who has won more major championships than anyone in history.

At his best Nicklaus is invincible, but Watson's miracle began to unfold with a modest putt for a birdie on the 13th and really came alive with one of an altogether more indecent length from the left edge of the 15th green. At the 17th, his confidence fairly bristling, he went ahead for the first time with a long iron to the green which an understandably jolted Nicklaus could not match. After a deft little pitch and run, he missed from four feet, but even then the story was only beginning.

Whereas Watson hugged the corner of the dog-leg with an iron from the tee, Nicklaus reached for his driver for the first time on the hole in four rounds. In the words of Peter Thomson, five times Open champion, quoting an old Australian sheep-shearer in a game of poker, it was 'Sydney or the Bush'. It was doubly apt, because another roll or two and it would literally have been the bush.

As it was, Nicklaus manufactured some sort of shot from the edge of the whins with an eight iron. It carried the ball to the front of the green and, amid unbelievable scenes, he proceeded to hole it. But it availed him nothing. Watson, playing his second shot first, had already hit a seven iron to no more than two feet and, while perhaps not expecting to hole it, was composed enough to finish a memorable task.

Nicklaus, as generous in defeat as ever in victory, conceded afterwards that 'he played better than I did and didn't allow himself to make any mistakes'. With third and fourth rounds of 65, in itself another record, there is no denying the fact, and Watson, the Masters champion, accepted the old trophy with an obvious sense of pride at a job well done and almost certainly the feeling that he will never be involved in anything quite like that again.

As one of the few to have held the Masters and the British Open in the same year, he is an obvious contender for Nicklaus's crown whenever he chooses to abdicate. For Nicklaus, who often brings the best out in his partners, it was a painful championship to lose, but he has some consolation in knowing that no one in the future is likely to better his performance in our Open. It is 12 years since he finished outside the first six and this was the sixth occasion on which he has finished second. Since 1972 his sequence reads second, fourth, third, third, second and second.

On a day when superlatives and records flew, Watson confined his comments to an obvious expression of delight at meeting Nicklaus for the second time this year in a major tournament. A lot can happen in a short time, but it seems almost incredible that back in April, American golf writers had labelled him a man who couldn't win. From now on Tom Watson can lose a golf tournament any way he likes and nobody but a fool is going to suggest he choked.

The cast for the final act was the same as Augusta . . . only the setting was different. Instead of the magnolias, Rae's Creek and Southern Comfort, there were the dunes, the lighthouse and the sea. Turnberry would never make a fertile nursery but it enjoys one of the most resplendent settings for golf in the world, and it rightly revelled in its glory. With one or two refinements, notably to improve some holes even at the expense of the Arran course, its first championship was an undoubted success. British golf is in a different league, but the Open's international and golfing appeal is set wide.

In the interview room at Augusta in April when Nicklaus was being asked whether something which Crenshaw had said about him ('We're not as scared of him as we used to be') had had anything to do with his shooting his final 66, Watson, waiting his turn at the microphone, stepped forward.

'Let me say something about that,' he said. 'I am always afraid of this man.'

'No he's not,' said Nicklaus, smiling. 'He's not afraid of anybody. That's why he won.'

Watson certainly now plays like a man with no fears. Leading money winner in the States this year with more than $269,000, his swing is almost unrecognisable from that which emerged at Carnoustie two years ago. An insatiable appetite for practice and a helping technical hand from Byron Nelson have transformed him; and of course he loves a challenge, which is why, after graduating in psychology at Stanford University, he gave up the security of a steady life and a promising career as an amateur golfer for the rough and tumble of the tour, the motel rooms, the airport lounges and the eternal humping of heavy luggage. Rare talent can blossom only in the right environment, and the thought of Nicklaus breathing down your neck as he did in the Masters is the real test.

Crowds began assembling at Turnberry from early morning yesterday, but they waited impatiently for the supporting bouts to finish. For them the bell didn't ring until Nicklaus, Watson, Crenshaw and Horton answered their calls to the first tee, where the flags stretched out for the first time in a wind for the north. The spectacle was a return fight which was every bit as enthralling.

If anyone else was to get in on the act, it was vital to serve notice early. In such company there was no shortage of candidates. There was, for instance, Johnny Miller, the defending champion, who made a startling charge in the third round of a memorable Masters involving him, Nicklaus and Weiskopf. There was Crenshaw, whose first major title must come soon, and there was Roger Maltbie, whose unspectacular approach hides his efficiency.

Hubert Green showed the up and down nature of his game with five 3s in an outward half of 32, but Nicklaus is not the world's leading player for nothing and, as he did on Friday, he opened with two birdies in the first four holes, which this time Watson could not match. They took him three strokes ahead of Watson, five ahead of Crenshaw and, by the time he headed up the fifth, nobody else seemed to have a chance. It seemed the perfect shut-out.

On the second, however, it was Watson who was better placed to set up the chance of a birdie. Nicklaus, down the bank on the left of the fairway, needed to produce one of his best shots of the week in order to prompt Watson to miss the green with his second on the left. Watson failed to get down in two, Nicklaus holed from about 12 feet to the first of the enormous roars which punctuated his progress, and Watson was behind instead of in front.

Although the third hole was playing almost twice as short as it was last Saturday, Watson had to save his 4 from a bunker there, and it was significant that Nicklaus's other birdie in his opening barrage came against the wind at the fourth, the short hole on the edge of the shore. Here Nicklaus holed from 20 feet, but Watson, missing from a good deal closer and sensing that he could not slip any further, replied immediately with a beautiful 3 at the fifth at just about the same moment as Crenshaw got a 2 at the sixth.

Horton, Crenshaw's partner, was by now in seventh position having bunkered his opening drive and his second to the second, dropping shots at both. Elsewhere, just about the sole item of note by British players was Martin Foster's hole in one with a five iron at the 15th. It rivalled that by Hubert Green at the fourth on the second day, and helped Foster to a respectable finish. But there can seldom have been less sign of a British champion.

Watson's 3 at the fifth heralded a definite revival and it was the turn of Nicklaus, who holed an awkward putt on the same green to save his 4, to hang on. Watson gained another stroke on the par-five seventh, where he was well home in two, but he drew level with another birdie at the eighth. By the turn, which Nicklaus reached in 33 to edge one ahead again, they were to all intents and purposes playing a match, for the ninth hole beside the lighthouse cost Crenshaw a 6 just when he could afford to yield nothing.

A few holes later, Nicklaus was nine strokes clear of everyone except his partner, and on the early homeward hole had a decided advantage in his personal duel with Watson, who was short of the 10th and 12th greens, and bunkered at the short 11th, doing very well not to drop a stroke to par.

Nicklaus, however, having missed birdie putts on the 10th and 11th, finally holed one of six yards on the 12th, where he drove into the right-hand rough. The question then became simply whether Watson could give him two strokes and catch him over six holes.

The answer, and the manner in which it was achieved, will be recalled as long as the game is played.

15 APRIL 1986

'ALL WASHED UP' JIBES SPURRED ON NICKLAUS

Michael Williams

Augusta

It was an article the previous weekend in the *Atlanta Constitution* that riled Jack Nicklaus. It said that he was 'done, through, washed up and finished' and that he had little business playing in the US Masters at all. Nicklaus had not seen it but a close friend, John Montgomery, out of devilment had stuck it on the refrigerator in the Augusta house where Nicklaus was staying for the week.

'It made me stew for a while,' reflected Nicklaus after his indomitable last round of 65 that was one too few for Tom Kite and Greg Norman, of Australia, 'but in the end I thought that maybe the writer, Tom McAllister, has a point. I'll show him.' What ultimately followed was what Nicklaus unhesitatingly accepts must be one of the greatest rounds of golf even he has played. He completed the final ten holes in 33 strokes – seven under par. Only Gary Player, with a 64 in 1978, has won the Masters with a lower final round and Nicklaus, at 46 years and four months, now surpasses him as the oldest winner of the Masters.

He is not, however, the oldest winner of a major championship. That distinction is still held by Julius Boros, who was 48 when he took the PGA in 1968. Nicklaus, nevertheless, is in a league of his own. This was his 18th major championship as a professional, and his 20th counting two US Amateur Championships, and it has come six years after his last, the PGA in 1980 when he also took the US Open. Nicklaus's tally is now three British Opens, four US Opens, five PGAs and six Masters. It is an astounding record and America was on its feet in salute, as, no doubt, was the whole of the sporting world.

Certainly this was the most riveting Masters that I have seen since 1975 when Nicklaus beat Tom Weiskopf and Johnny Miller by a stroke. 'Yet even that,' said Nicklaus, 'did not come up to this.' The utter bedlam that grew over those last ten holes during which Nicklaus accumulated six birdies and an eagle had not so much to be seen as also heard. 'I could hardly hear myself think let alone talk,' he said, and it will remain for ever as one of his most emotional experiences in golf.

On Sunday morning, Nicklaus was asked on the phone by one of his younger sons, Steve: 'Well, Pops, what do you think?' The paternal parent responded: 'I think a 65 to win and a 66 to tie.' Gary immediately replied: 'That's how I figured it, too. Go ahead and do it.'

Between them they got it spot on, as Nicklaus, more than once wiping a tear from his eyes, found again a brilliance that has captivated the world since he won his first US Open in 1962, nearly a quarter of a century ago. He was he said 'tickled pink' and had not enjoyed himself so much for years. 'But I am just not smart enough,' he added, 'to call it a day now.'

'I am going to continue playing because I know now that I can still win. At the same time I am not the golfer I was 10 or 11 years ago, and I am not going to increase my schedule.' Greater attention to his physical fitness through daily visits to the PGA tour gymnasium which accompanies all tournaments, a return to his best fighting weight of around 13st (at 12st last year he now considers he was far too weak) and a new short game have combined to revitalise him.

It was his eldest son Jakie, who was also his caddie, who gave him the short game via Chi-Chi Rodriguez, to whom the younger Nicklaus had turned for lessons. 'Basically,' says Nicklaus, 'he recommends a harshness through the ball. Before I have tried to be soft but I don't think I have ever chipped the ball as well as I did this week.' His putting – with a club that has a large and almost ugly head – was inspired too, though even

Nicklaus cannot explain why. 'At my age I should have been incapable of even getting the putter back,' he muses, 'but the more nervous I got, the better I seemed to putt.'

For all that, it was still a Masters others lost. Seve Ballesteros had it by the throat when he had an eagle at the 13th and then split the fairway at the 15th for another potential birdie at least. The four-iron which at a vital stage he mishit into the water reflected his lack of competition this year.

Tom Kite, forever seemingly left to stand in the wings, just missed a putt on the last green for a tie, and so did Norman, whose wild four-iron into the gallery at the last was indication of his questionable nerve when it matters most. It cost him the play-off and perhaps even the title.

---

20 JULY 1987

FALDO'S STEADINESS IS KEY TO TRIUMPH

Michael Williams

Muirfield

Nick Faldo yesterday became only the sixth Briton since the war to win the Open golf championship when he beat Paul Azinger, of the United States, and Rodger Davis, of Australia, by a stroke at Muirfield.

On a day of mist and high excitement, Faldo, who had celebrated his 30th birthday on Saturday, had an unprecedented, in recent times anyway, 18 pars for a 71 and a five-under-par aggregate of 279. He wins a prize of £75,000, though according to his agent subsequent contracts should bring him a conservative £2 million over the next few years. His voice choking with emotion,

Faldo said it was 'just wonderful', but he could not bear to watch as Azinger came to the last hole needing a birdie 3 to win and a par to tie.

The young American, 26 and making his first appearance in the championship, took five after hitting his second shot into a bunker while Faldo sat in a nearby room with his wife, Gill, and baby daughter. Faldo had been a stroke behind him with two holes to play but Azinger, who had lead by three after nine, made crucial errors, first with his drive to the 17th and then with his second at the last.

'The most important factor,' said Faldo afterwards, 'is that it furthers my career. I have played in only one US Open so far, now I can play every major championship for several years. Sunday golf is always the most important and I'm proud of the way I played today. I just hope that next time I will get a birdie,' added Faldo, who took the major decision to change his swing three years ago.

His leg movement through the ball is less eccentric but the plane is less steep, more repetitive. His coach, David Leadbetter, was here with him this week, but most of all it is in Faldo's mind that he is more settled. A broken marriage had already added to his problems but now, remarried and with a baby daughter, Natalie, Faldo has at last achieved his dearest ambition.

'Today reminded me of Royal Birkdale when I won my first professional tournament, the PGA championship in 1978,' he said afterwards, his voice choking with emotion. It was a misty day then, he recalled, and somehow yesterday that heightened the drama as a sort of North Sea Haar hung over the links, one half expecting the players to hoot mournfully that they were approaching every green. In this almost half-light, the championship came to its climax, Faldo striving tooth and nail for that elusive birdie, Azinger hanging on grimly behind him.

It was the American who cracked. While Faldo was escaping with a par 5 down the 17th, Azinger behind him was about to drive into the 'Trevino bunker' from which he could only make short escape en route to a 6 and not chipping in, as Trevino had done when he won here in 1972.

Faldo, of course, knew none of this but he gathered himself for one more assault on the 18th, finding the green with a five iron through the swirling mist in two and then, to alarm from the packed stands, putting some four feet past the hole. It was the most crucial putt of Faldo's life but he holed like a man and the cheers were doubled as, at the same moment, the news went up on the big scoreboards that Azinger had dropped a shot at the 17th. They were level.

Now it was the slim American who was in a corner. He had regretted taking a driver off the 17th tee and now he must have regretted taking an iron off the 18th. It left him with a second shot of 200 yards to the green and as soon as he had hit it, he cursed audibly as his ball found desperately difficult lie in the left-hand bunker. Expert though he is at escaping profitably from them, even this one was beyond Azinger. He came out short and the putt to tie was never there.

Dejectedly Azinger hung his head but later he said that he had proved to himself that he was a contender and that he would be a 'better player next time.' But the three-stroke lead he held after nine holes will live with him for some time. Faldo could never remember having had 18 pars before and that spoke volumes not only for the quality of his play but also for his resolution as frustration at the lack of birdies must have mounted. Certainly there were some great saves, three times out of bunkers and one miraculously so at the eighth which, he thought, was the most crucial of all.

Nevertheless Azinger had made all the running at first, a fine 2 at the fourth, a long pitch to the fifth for another, a dropped shot at the sixth, where another bunker defeated him, but a long putt straight as a die at the eighth. Out in 34, Azinger seemed home and dry but suddenly shots were dropped at the tenth, bunkered again, and at the 11th, where he took three putts from some distance. His putter was never the same again but under mounting pressure it is the nerves that matter. It told with his ever longer deliberations over which club to use and in the end his time, and his lead, ebbed away.

Understandably the attendance for the week was not only down on last year but even on the last time the Open was played at Muirfield. The weather had a lot to do with it. Saturday was as bad as I can remember, particularly in the morning. The wind was gusting up to 40mph and the scoreboard carriers became ball spotters because they would not have been strong enough to hold the boards aloft. The avenues between the hospitality marquees became absolute quagmires.

It was a sad, even depressing spectacle and the severest of examinations for the golfers. Had it remained that way all day, Sandy Lyle's 71 might have brought him back into contention. As it was the leaders had a better time of it and in the end he made up no ground at all, much to his annoyance when I bumped into him later that evening. Lyle, in fact, thought Turnberry last year was just as bad and in one way worse, since the fairways there were narrower. 'At least at Muirfield you have somewhere to aim,' he said, before adding a 70 yesterday.

Norman was quick to point out that the average score by the time he came in was 75.29 while for the remaining third of the field it dropped to 72.91. His 74 then took him out of the hunt and a 75 yesterday left the defending champion out of the picture. But he took it all in good spirit, a disappointing year all part of what he calls the 'learning process'.

The surprise was, of course, Bernhard Langer's retreat. He had looked so well placed after two rounds, but the 7 he took at the eighth in the third round broke him completely and he was not seen again. Perhaps, like Ian Woosnam, he had peaked too soon, though it was Seve Ballesteros who probably went home with an ego most bruised. He was never in the picture all week and one begins to wonder when he will be again.

Jack Nicklaus has not yet been invited back to this year's Suntory World Matchplay championship at Wentworth – and said yesterday, after finishing with a 76 for an 18-over-par 302 in the Open: 'The way I'm playing at the moment, I wouldn't want to play in the Palm Beach Matchplay.' Gary Player, 51, whose long career is littered with records, has another in his sights – but it will take him until 1994 to achieve it. Yesterday he completed his 33rd successive Open championship with a 75 for an aggregate of 300, 16 over. Ben Sayers has the record of 39 Opens.

———

15 APRIL 1991

WOOSNAM'S COOL FINISH EARNS THAT GREEN JACKET

FINAL EXCITING DAY SEES A BRITON WIN THE MASTERS FOR THE FOURTH SUCCESSIVE YEAR

Michael Williams

Augusta

Ian Woosnam, all 5 feet 4 inches of him, stood taller than he has ever done before yesterday when, in another exciting finish, he took his first major championship by winning the Masters at Augusta National by a stroke from José María Olazábal. Woosnam had a final round of 72 for an 11-under-par aggregate of 277 to become the third British golfer to collect the coveted green jacket that goes with the honorary membership of the club. Sandy Lyle won in 1988 and Nick Faldo in 1989 and 1990.

As ever, it was a most riveting final nine holes. The central figures in the end were Woosnam, who had held a three-stroke lead at the turn, Olazábal and Tom Watson, who had a chance to win playing the last hole but, sadly, took six and finished in a tie for fourth place with Steve Pate, Ben Crenshaw and Lanny Wadkins. It was, in fact, Watson who had earlier set the afternoon alight when, after dropping a shot at the 11th and hitting into the water at the 12th, he came back with two stunning eagle 3s at the 13th and 15th. This made a critical difference, for Woosnam had driven into the creek at the 13th and took six, but he held his nerve as Olazábal too came storming back from a bad run around the turn with birdies at the 13th, 14th and 15th.

Consequently, all three of them were level playing the last hole but it was Woosnam, recording his 26th worldwide victory by an unlikely route when he drove miles over the bunkers to the left and came in to the green from the left of the sand traps. He left himself a nasty putt of five feet, which he safely holed after both Watson and Olazábal had been in the bunker short left of the green. Olazábal made a 5 for second place on his own, but Watson three-putted for a 6 and an obscurity he did not really deserve.

As always it was a fascinating final afternoon in hot sunshine, Olazábal making the first move with three birdies in his first seven holes, which at that point tied him with Woosnam. The young Spaniard had holed from off the green at the first, from some distance at the fifth and from much nearer at the seventh. Meanwhile, though Woosnam had made two birdies, chipping and single-putting at the second and sinking a curler at the fifth, he nevertheless dropped shots both at the fourth and sixth. Suddenly it all went wrong, albeit temporarily, for the Spaniard as he dropped three shots in three holes from the eighth and Woosnam's lead at the turn was three strokes from Watson, Olazábal and Wadkins.

However, a three-stroke lead, as we have seen many times before, is nothing at Augusta; the picture can change with bewildering frequency as the pressure builds. This was no exception. Watson was the crowd's favourite but those tell-tale signs with the putter were soon in evidence as he missed from a yard for his par at the first and then three-putted the fifth as well. But he had said beforehand that he was the older and wiser player and it was his eagle at the 13th, after a double bogey at the 12th, that brought him back into the thick of the fray.

The first target had been set by Steve Pate, who is incidentally no relation to Jerry, the former American Open champion. He had a glorious last round of 65 for a nine-under-par total of 279. With all the things that can happen on the inward half at Augusta, Woosnam must have regarded it with some unease, provided he had looked at the scoreboard.

Afterwards Pate said that he did not think the pressure would get to those behind him, his attitude being the fairly typical one of some of his generation when he said that, 'You never have anything to lose, only money.' He is one who seems to treat major championships as 'just another tournament' but he enjoyed his last round, nevertheless, with five birdies and an eagle at the eighth. At 535 yards uphill to a hidden green, his three-wood found the green only five feet from the flag. With birdies at the three other par fives, Pate was consequently five under par for the long holes and finished by sinking a 45-foot putt on the last green to save par.

After a third round of 67 there had seemed just a faint chance that Faldo might find the launching pad to a last-ditch counter attack. Certainly he got the impetus with a chip in for an eagle 3 at the second, but the fire that had been within him in the previous two years was no longer there and he was never in a realistic hunt. It would seem that the meagre seven tournament rounds he had had coming into the Masters was not enough, though that was not exactly Faldo's fault. As a man who plans his calendar to the last detail, he could never have suspected that the Houston Open would be washed out altogether and that the Bay Hill tournament would be reduced to 54 holes.

No matter how much practice Faldo had – and he said beforehand that he felt 'well golfed' – there is no substitute for the hard edge of competition. Consequently, in his first two rounds Faldo had 11 opportunities to get down in two from the green for either birdies or pars, and succeeded only twice. He took three nine times and four once. At least Faldo finished presentably with a 70 for a total of 282 and also in good humour, particularly at the 16th where he chased a long twisting breaking putt almost as if he were engaged in a game of curling.

Severiano Ballesteros also ultimately had, by his previous standards, a disappointing Masters, though a total of 284, four under par, some would accept as very presentable. Not the Spaniard, however. He believes the ball is not running for him these days, though it seldom does when form is elusive. It also seems that the Spaniard is developing a considerable fear of the short 16th hole. Three times in the last three years he has four-putted the 16th and yesterday he took five there by another means, hitting his tee-shot into the water close to which the pin is always set on the final day. It had seemed beforehand that this was a week in which Ballesteros had to prove he is still the player he used to be, for Augusta is his favourite course together with Pedrena, where he grew up. It may well, therefore, be that we have now seen the best of him.

Bernhard Langer, after being so well in the hunt for the first two rounds, disappeared sadly with two finishing 74s and only just squeezed under par, having a total of 287. Every time one sees him on the practice ground he seems to have a massive collection of clubs, always trying something different. If only he would just settle on the same set. Nor, some would say, does the arrival of Langer's coach, Willie Hoffmann, help. He is the sort of man who gets more excited outside the ropes than Langer does inside and it may rub off elsewhere. Meanwhile, the amateur prize went to the highly promising left hander Phil Mickelson, though his first round of 69 turned out to be his best and the only one that had the crowds on their feet. After that he had 73, 74, 74.

16 APRIL 1996

FALDO'S REMORSE FOR A WOUNDED FRIEND

NORMAN IN NEED OF REWIRING

Martin Johnson

On top of the small media stand next to the 12th tee, the cathedral hush was broken by an American radio commentator whispering into his microphone: 'Greg Norman . . .' (*pause for dramatic effect*) 'trying to stop the bleeding.' However, on occasions such as these Norman is in the habit of tying the tourniquet around his own neck, and the condition golfers refer to as choking was turning into an audible death rattle.

The par three 12th is known as Golden Bell, and it was about to toll for Norman. The Australian had just surrendered the last stroke of his six-stroke lead, and two more were about to vanish as his seven iron struck the bank and toppled back into the water. If the turtles who live in the creek had all flipped themselves upside down, it could scarcely have been more symbolic.

Who said golf isn't a blood sport? The colour of Norman's face suggested that most of his eight pints had drained into his boots, and the fact that not all the spectators can be in the same place at the same time added to the drama. After each hole a new number went up on the leaderboard, and Norman's red 13 (which had already dwindled to a nine) was about to come down and be replaced by a seven. As the players walked to the 13th tee, the gasps from the other end of the par five dog-leg told Norman that his number, in every sense, was up.

This was sport at its most compelling, and yet you could scarcely bring yourself to watch. There were young children there with their families, who had doubtless been told about a gentle game which stood for great skills and Corinthian values, but this was something you felt they should not have been exposed to. It was a public flogging. The Shark had become the Great White Fish Finger. Battered.

There is something in golf known as muscle memory, when the swing repeats in the same way that, for players of this calibre, brings pars and birdies. However, when the pressure is on, Norman's muscles either suffer from amnesia or else they are remembering the muscles of some hacker he once got lumbered with in a pro-am. You can also see it in the eyes. When the Shark was gliding round in 63 on Thursday, they were sparkling. On Sunday they had all the glint of a dead mackerel on a fishmonger's slab.

It's hard to know what thoughts were going through Norman's head as his shoulders began their descent towards his kneecaps, but it would not have been along the lines of how nice the magnolias were looking this year. Maybe he was thinking of his countryman, Ian Baker-Finch, whose latest 12-handicap excursion prompted him to cancel his next American engagement, order a private jet to be filled up with Australian beer, and fly home to Queensland. Perhaps he was wondering what might have happened had he been paired with Phil Mickelson, as would have been the case had Faldo not holed a tricky putt at the 18th on Saturday.

There is no doubt that things happen to people when they end up in a Masters shoot-out with Faldo. Scott Hoch missed from two feet at the first play-off hole in 1989, and Ray Floyd hoicked into the water in 1990. This was also the equivalent of a shoot-out and, once again, Faldo's opponent shot himself. It makes you wonder, though, whether it is something to do with Faldo's unbelievable temperament under pressure: his opponent's knowledge that, when the heat becomes unbearable and you can smell burning flesh, Faldo is the man wearing the asbestos suit.

Norman said afterwards that he still believed in himself, and that his confidence in himself to do 'anything he wanted' remained unshakeable. 'If I wanted to be a brain surgeon, and take time to study it, I could,' he said. Leaving aside the fact that if it was your brain that Norman was operating on, you wouldn't much fancy your chances of being wheeled back out of the theatre if he was carrying out the operation on a Sunday afternoon, the brain surgery that would benefit him most is a transplant with Nick's. Faldo's circuitry is, like no other golfer's, perfectly wired for coming down to the wire.

It has also been said that it has been wired to bypass anything and everything that is happening around him on a golf course, but on Sunday not even Faldo could blank out Norman's suffering, and his open remorse for a wounded friend won him far more respect and admiration than did his murderously outstanding golf.

---

19 JULY 1999

VAN DE VELDE SO ELOQUENT IN HIS AGONY

A PERFORMANCE STRAIGHT OUT OF AN ANARCHIC FRENCH CIRCUS

Paul Hayward

Carnoustie

The reporter who asked Jean Van de Velde on Saturday night if he was 'a bit of a comedian' was closer to the truth than he could have known. When God created that breed of eccentrics to which this 33-year-old Frenchman unquestionably belongs, he combined a hero and something of a headcase in one incomparable package and sent him to Carnoustie to play golf. No wonder he is sponsored by Disney.

Van de Velde was a hero to be carrying a five shot lead into the final round of the Open championship after setting out four days earlier as an anonymous 150–1 shot. It was heroic also for him to be taking a three shot lead to the final hole after he had looked to be developing the constitution of melted brie over the first eight holes. But then came a performance that was straight out of an anarchic French circus. The abiding image of a tournament that seemed certain to be remembered as a dour sequence of bellyaching and bogeys was the champion elect removing his shoes, rolling up his trousers and leaping into the Barry Burn to examine his atrociously mishit ball.

As an impersonation of a British tourist on the beach in Benidorm it was priceless. Even Van de Velde's wife was in hysterics. Professional golfers have walked into water before to retrieve bad shots but nobody ever imagined he might be capable of playing himself out of the gorge-like Burn that functions as a moat in front of the 18th green. Van de Velde needed only to score a six at this 487-yard par four to get his hands on the old Claret Jug. By the time he had struck the grandstand with a wild second shot, taken a drop after deciding, wisely, not to play a sub-aqua hoik out of the Burn and then found a bunker with his fifth shot, this wretched former also-ran was left chasing a place in a three-man play-off, which he finally secured with a seven-foot putt which displayed, yet again, the heroic portion of his character.

But before we get too carried away with the idea of Van de Velde as chump not champ we ought to remember that this was one of the most savage humiliations in the history of sport. Only Devon Loch doing the splits when clear in the Grand National is even vaguely comparable to the trauma endured by Van de Velde around that 18th green. After the laughter stopped, a sense of profound sadness took hold. Van de Velde's wry reply to that question about his comic tendencies had been: 'Yeah, I have the red nose in my bag.' Talk about the tears of a clown.

'It just came out to be a nightmare,' he said cheerfully last night. At his press conference after dark he was a true star. 'There are worse things in life,' he said. 'I read the newspapers this morning and some terrible things are happening to other people. It's a golf tournament. Next time I'll use a wedge to get to the green. You must forgive me.'

Van de Velde is a clown only in the sense that he succumbed to impossible pressure with millions of folk watching and the most sacred lump of silverware in sport sitting on a table waiting to be grasped. There was also the small matter of a £320,000 first prize. No athlete, probably, has ever let so much go so quickly. We might have to travel to Munich to find people who have been struck by a comparable desolation. Bayern Munich's players will never forget the moment they punched the turf in despair after surrendering a 1–0 lead to Manchester United in added time in this summer's European Cup in Barcelona.

But Van de Velde was alone. The French supporter in the kilt had become, by now, a Shakespearean fool, observing helplessly the buckling of a man at the denouement of a play. 'Just wait a little longer. The tide's going out,' called Parry as our hero lowered his feet of clay into the brine. His intention, he said on Saturday night, was to promote the game and 'entertain people'. How magisterially he did both, though you would have a hard time convincing the traditionalists who watched his descent into the murky waters with bemusement and some disdain.

His explanation was lucid but hardly convincing. The talk led, inexorably, to that disastrous second shot into the stands. 'I took my two-iron, pushed it a little, and it hit the grandstand and bounced on the rocks. I had to hit it hard from where it landed but I couldn't hit it hard enough. So I went into the water, and, when I looked at the ball from the edge of the green, could see that three-quarters of it was sticking out of the water. But when I climbed down there I could see the ball sinking.'

It was not surprising that Van de Velde shanked his first shot of the play-off into a gorse bush. He would have needed to reinvent himself as some warrior god to forget his ordeal and beat Justin Leonard and Paul Lawrie in the final shoot-out. Inside he must have been on the edge of darkness. Yet it would be unjust to discard the memory of how ferociously he had fought up to that point. A lover of skiing and barbecues, of fine food and wine, it was a joy to see a man whose only previous triumph had been the Roma Masters in 1993 holding off a vastly more exalted field.

Van de Velde made a beautiful incision with his drive in the grey Carnoustie sky when a voice burst out beside him at the ninth tee: 'Keep your head up, Jean.' This engaging Frenchman, who had dropped three shots over the first eight holes, turned to deliver a reply that seemed to come from so far inside him that the word had a life-force of its own. 'Yes,' he said, nodding resolutely and almost shouting. Thanks to a friendly spectator he was back in the world of fantasy and possibility.

On he marched, sucking in air and hunching his shoulders. Here was a man gathering up his strength after a traumatic start to the biggest day of his professional life. A malign providence seemed to be swallowing him up. The raucous applause that had sent him up the magical vista of the first fairway was turning into the kind of sympathetic clapping that must haunt all the fallen of golf's final days.

It was a familiar and grim scenario. Those of us who marched with him thought then that we were watching a man reach the outer limits of his abilities. The outsider was imploding, reality was reasserting itself as Van de Velde's fourth and final round became a painful return to anonymity. But this time the narrative refused to develop along traditional lines. That stunning tee-shot at the ninth was converted with a 12-foot birdie putt. The vitality and purpose seemed to return to his stride. This Frenchman was here for a fight. And on they came, into the counting house of the last nine players. His rivals surged and then faltered, achieved brief mastery of this difficult game and then surrendered again to exasperation.

Van de Velde, pursued fiercely for a time by Parry, was as susceptible as any of the handful of contenders staggering home.

But the hero who had remained well hidden inside the overnight leader in seven years on the pro circuit was now bursting through his skin. He bogeyed the 11th to go three over and dropped another shot straight after as Leonard became the biggest threat. Again, though, Van de Velde's courage held. He made a mess of an eagle putt at the 14th but tidied up with a five-foot trembler to secure a birdie. From there he proceeded jerkily but steadfastly to that surreal denouement at the 18th, and finally that bitter play-off. Overnight fame had settled snugly.

As he prepared to tee off at the 18th with his three shot lead, I said to a colleague: 'He would have to have a nervous breakdown not to win it now.' And what, exactly, did we see, when Jean Van de Velde, the 6–5 favourite at dawn, hit the bleachers, the Burn and finally a bunker on a journey to monumental agony? Whatever it was, it was excruciatingly funny but above all sad.

---

23 JULY 2001

BAD CASE OF TWO-DRIVER BLUES

Martin Johnson

Royal Lytham & St Annes

When Ian Woosnam hurled his spare driver into the shrubbery by the side of the second tee, the sigh of relief from his caddie was audible. Medical science has come a long way since hickory shafts, but a successful operation for the surgical removal of a titanium-shafted, jumbo-headed Mizuno would by no means have been guaranteed.

The conversation might have gone something like this. 'What are you thinking of hitting here, Ian?' 'Er, you, actually.' At the start of this season Woosnam parted company with his regular caddie (to José María Olazábal) with a shake of the hand, figuring he had more chance of making some decent money on another bag. Yesterday, however, the handshake he had in mind was more like a demonstration of the Vardon grip around the jugular.

Woosnam, teeing off in the second last group as joint leader of the Open championship, struck a six iron to two inches for an opening birdie, and it would be fair to describe his mood as he stood on the second tee as chipper. This lasted all of 30 seconds, at which point, browsing through the bag for a club, Woosnam realised he had a choice of 15. This is one more than the R&A-approved allowance, and carried the instant penalty of two strokes. Miles Byrne, the caddie, looked pale when he began the round with sunblock plastered over his face, and what little colour he had to start with rapidly drained from his cheeks. Woosnam said (expletives deleted): 'I give you one job to do, and you can't even get that right.'

Remarkably, Woosnam said afterwards that his man would not be getting the sack – 'he's a good caddie and will be feeling sick enough' – while Byrne, understandably, was not in much of a conversational mood. 'The buck stops with me. It's my fault.' 'But how did it happen?' 'Fifteen clubs in the bag, end of story.' 'But how did 15 clubs get in there?' 'Are you effing deaf or what?' Exit caddie. Quickly.

And no wonder. He had just cost Woosnam the small matter of £218,334 (repeat £218,334) and an automatic Ryder Cup place. I wonder if he got his ten per cent prize money bonus. It will mystify many as to how Woosnam could make such an elementary mistake, but the fact is that professional golfers are not used to having to do things for themselves, and if you ever get marooned on a desert island with one, don't expect to be eating grilled swordfish for supper inside a waterproof bamboo hut. Woosnam would have expected his caddie to take care of the club counting on the same principle that a country squire with a butler doesn't expect to pour his own gin and tonic.

The error appears to have been the result of Woosnam taking two drivers on to the practice range, and intending to pick one of the two. As Woosnam does not even carry a three wood, the audible groan he made on that second tee was the result of seeing two head covers sticking up from the bag.

Preparation is not, in any event, Woosnam's strong point. Among his dislikes are travelling and hitting practice balls, and sometimes he is as brassed off about having to go to work as any Jubilee Line commuter. Only recently he said he would prefer to be in Australia watching the Lions, or just fishing.

As twilight was forming on Saturday, it came as no surprise to look out of the members' bar window and see Vijay Singh practising his putting. Woosnam, on the other hand, far from ploughing a lonely furrow, would have been in the Plough and Anchor, enjoying a relaxing pint and a fag.

Woosnam's way does not mean he is not giving it his best shot, though it is hard to imagine Singh misreading his tee-off time as Woosnam did yesterday, when he got to the tee with three minutes to spare. Had he been late it would have been another two shots, and anything over five minutes, disqualification.

Golf is not like Formula One, where equipment is subject to rigorous scrutiny, and if Woosnam had chosen not to mention the fact that he had 15 clubs in the bag, or surreptitiously jettisoned one on the way round, no one would have been any the wiser. However, golf is a game of honour, and in calling in the rules official as soon as he realised what happened, Woosnam made sure it remained so.

Woosnam did himself credit by refusing to throw in the towel (he didn't even light himself a calming cigarette until the third tee), and seemed to take heart from the extra support he got as word of the calamity spread across the links. However, any prospect of Byrne not finishing the round as Woosnam's excaddie seemed to have disappeared at the dog-leg 17th. 'What's the line?' Woosie said, preparing for his second shot. 'Over the bush,' his caddie said. 'Are you sure?' 'Yes.' Thwack. 'I hit it over the bush. Why aren't they clapping?' What his caddie could then have said, but thought it wise not to, was 'possibly because it's finished 30 yards wide of the green'.

---

12 APRIL 2004

MICKELSON THE 'NEARLY' MAN ENDS HIS LONG WAIT

Lewine Mair

Augusta

Phil Mickelson, having finished third three times in a row, finally won himself a green jacket here yesterday. Needing a birdie at the last to beat Ernie Els, he hit an inspired second to 15 feet and made the putt before leaping sky high.

Metaphorically at least, he will not come down to earth in a long time, so disbelieving was he that he had finally shrugged off the label of best player never to have won a major. 'I kept on believing that something good was going to happen, that this was going to be my day,' said the new champion, who had come home in 31 for a 69 and a four-round, nine-under-par aggregate of 279.

While Mickelson celebrated, so Els, who had been practising his putting in readiness for a play-off, scooped up his ball and walked slowly away. True, people would console him with the fact that he already had three majors to Mickelson's none but he, no less than the American, had set his heart on a green jacket.

For years there has been an element out there who have yearned for Mickelson to knock Tiger Woods from his pedestal. From what he said on Saturday night, Mickelson has sounded as one who is at last ready to start winning majors. As he saw it, he had finally reached the point where his shot-making was so secure that he was no less confident with a driver in hand than he was with an eight iron. 'In the past,' he expanded, 'my anxiety was down to my hit-or-miss style of play. How am I going to drive it today? How are my irons going to be?'

No one doubted his ability to hit the shots but there was still a question mark over whether or not he could make things work down the stretch. 'There are lots of grins and knowing smiles from Phil,' said the television commentator who watched him coming down the 18th in his third round. The commentator did not elaborate but there must have been countless folk who thought that Mickelson needed to be more obviously focused. Yesterday, as he took 38 to the turn, people were beginning to think that this would be one more near miss. Then, though he came to life with a trio of birdies from the 12th, there were just as many of the facial expressions, but the overall message was that he was enjoying the pressure.

Since 1991 the winner of the Masters had come from one or other of the players in the final group and yesterday it looked as if Els was going to ruin all that. He was a staggering six under par for the four par fives, while his short game was out of this world. Time after time, when it looked as if he might drop a shot, he would get down in a chip and a putt.

On Saturday night Els had been given a tough first question at his press conference. In a reference to how he had called for a further opinion when refused a drop from piled branches in the woods at the 11th, a writer had asked: 'Can you talk about your luck in drops in major championships?'

'What do you mean?' a shocked Els returned. The South African may well have had a fortuitous drop in the 1994 US Open and another on Saturday, but he has had his share of bad breaks across 46 major tournaments. Another issue concerned the fact that his ball had moved in the undergrowth. Overnight, people sent in their e-mails to the Golf Channel but, before too long, Augusta made it clear that there had been no question of a penalty shot. It did not apply because the player had taken a drop. If Els had been worried by the hostility of the media question, his wife, Liezl, made a pretty good fist of making him put it behind him. 'Ernie knew he was in the right and I was proud of the way he handled it,' she said.

Els, as always, was generous in defeat, conceding cheerfully that Mickelson deserved his major. As to how he was feeling himself, he asked to reserve judgment. 'I've got to take stock. It's very tough to explain what I feel right now.'

Paul Casey finished in a share of fifth place – disappointing for him, no doubt, but a great effort in his first Masters. On Friday evening, when Casey was asked what he thought of Justin Rose's position at the top of the leaderboard, he had said gleefully that it gave him 'someone to chase'.

Chase he did. Having started Saturday at even par to Rose's six under, he ended up seven ahead. Ken Comboy, Casey's caddie, had been telling him for weeks that he was looking forward to caddying for someone playing at Augusta for a first time and Casey had come to understand what he meant. He had heard others going on about how they were hitting three irons where they used to hit seven irons, and seven irons where they used to hit wedges. 'A few of the players,' Casey said, 'have definitely got that kind of thing lodged in their brains.' For his part, he was seeing the course as it was today and he loved it.

Yesterday, though, he clung on well at the start before tangling with trees as he slipped to a closing 74. He was not too disheartened. 'This gives me a real taste for it,' he said. 'It's been fantastic. I handled the nerves really well. It was mostly a question of the putts not dropping.' He added in a reference to his middle rounds of 69 and 68: 'Maybe it was tough to follow two good rounds with another.'

Bernhard Langer, who finished in a share of fourth place along-side Sergio Garcia and behind K.J. Choi, has saved himself from a more than minor dilemma. Had he won, there would have been pressure put on him to play in the Ryder Cup rather than be the captain. On Saturday night, he said he had definitely decided on the captaincy, but yesterday Ken Schofield, for one, was agreeing that it would be madness for Europe to go into battle against the Americans without the Masters champion in their midst.

Padraig Harrington, who had won the par three at the start of the week, closed with a hole in one at the 16th and a share of 13th place. Justin Rose, who finished in a share of 22nd place, followed Saturday's 81 with a 71. He liked the fact that people had admired the way he had handled himself after Saturday's disaster. 'It's embarrassing enough to shoot 81, let alone behave badly and make yourself look like a real idiot. The nice comments made the day more bearable.'

On Friday night, Colin Montgomerie, who was typically hot under the collar following the second-round 80 with which he missed the cut, had rushed from the course and lost his wife in the process. They were reunited later and are reportedly going ahead with their fortnight's holiday to the Bahamas. But with Montgomerie, you can never be entirely sure what will happen next. Only a fortnight ago, when members of the Wisley club were poring over the Scot's post-Players Championship quotes on how he was staying on in Florida to practise for the Masters, this incorrigible soul apparently joined them for breakfast.

———

23 JULY 2007

CRYING SHAME AS GARCIA FAILS TO MAKE SPLASH

Martin Johnson

Carnoustie

It was so wet yesterday that the groundstaff were using buckets to bail rainwater out of the bunkers, but, for the second consecutive time in a Carnoustie Open, the squeegees had an even more serious moisture disposal task to perform: drying out the shoulder pads on Consuela Garcia's jacket. Sergio fell sobbing into his mother's arms after a round of 89 here in 1999, and it would be a surprise if the Kleenex didn't come out again yesterday following the even more emotionally draining experience of blowing a three shot lead and eventually losing in a play-off to Padraig Harrington.

Harrington, leading by a stroke, looked to have it won in normal time before the ghost of Jean van de Velde came back to Carnoustie's 18th hole. The Irishman drove his tee-shot into the Barry Burn, and as he contemplated his penalty drop, he and Garcia actually met on the bridge as the Spaniard came up the 17th. Not a word was spoken, probably because both of them were too busy choking. Harrington then made another visit to the burn, but after the Irishman got up and down for a double bogey, Garcia was unable to make the par he needed to win. It was a bit like watching the Carnoustie monthly medal, although on this course, and under these circumstances, not even the best golfers in the world are safe from the game's capacity to bite you on the bottom.

Garcia probably realised the game was up at the first extra play-off hole when his golf ball, for just about the first time all week, declined to obey him. 'Get up!' he shouted. But his ball plunged disobediently into the front bunker, he again failed to make par, and Harrington made birdie to lead by two.

Somewhere among the hard-luck messages, Garcia might find one of congratulation from Colin Montgomerie after the Spaniard sconed a photographer on the 17th hole on Saturday. Monty has been wanting to do this for years, but it's been a bit like his 63 attempts to win a major. Close, but no cigar.

Garcia not only failed to become the first man to win a major using a belly putter, but also the player with the weakest bladder to win one. He was off to the Portaloo as early as the third hole yesterday, and by the time he burst into a sprint to find one at the 10th, the nerves were such that this one might have involved putting the seat down.

It was at the English Ladies' Championship in 1920 that Joyce Wethered, standing over a putt to win on the 17th at Sheringham, never even looked up when a train came whistling past. When asked whether she'd considered waiting until the train had passed, Joyce replied: 'What train?' This certainly wasn't the case for Garcia yesterday, as the 4.05 from Arbroath sounded its hooter when he stood on the tee. Garcia backed off with a smile, but it was a forced one, and somehow you felt that fate was taking a hand.

Just as last year the golfing gods were not going to allow someone to win the Open dressed like a canary, then this year they weren't going to allow the Claret Jug to be won by someone using a contraption as alien to the spirit of the game as a belly putter.

Tiger Woods couldn't make up an eight shot deficit, and the lasting legacy of his tilt at a third consecutive Open belonged to a 64-year-old Irish spectator who ended up with two stitches in her head, an autographed glove from Woods, and a souvenir golf ball with some of her blood still on it. Had it happened in America, she'd have ended up with a lot more: 'Don't send for a doctor — bring me a lawyer.'

Harrington came from six strokes back, but if we wanted a winner to come sprinting through the field, then it would have been the American Boo Weekley. When asked about the Scottish food, he said: 'It's rough. Ain't got no sweet tea, and ain't got no fried chicken.' And on why he refused to hire a car: 'Scary. On the wrong side of the road? Yes sir.' His acceptance speech would have been a collector's item, and if opinions of the greatest ever Open moment vary — Seve Ballesteros' win at St Andrews in 1984, perhaps, or the Watson–Nicklaus duel in the sun at Turnberry in 1977 — the sight of the tobacco-chewing Boo using the auld Claret Jug as a spittoon would surely have eclipsed them all.

———

CHAPTER 2
MAJOR MAESTROS

6 APRIL 1992

HALF-PINT OF BEST QUALITY

IAN WOOSNAM, THE DOWN-TO-EARTH WELSHMAN WHO
BEGINS HIS MASTERS' DEFENCE ON THURSDAY

Michael Williams

If the truth be known, Ian Woosnam would probably just as soon be down at the Golden Lion in Oswestry tomorrow night, having a pint or two with the lads. Instead he will, in best bib and tucker, be performing his last official act as the Masters champion. It is the tradition each year for the reigning champion to host a dinner at the Augusta National Grill Room for all the other champions, each in the green jacket they are entitled to wear as honorary members of the club.

Woosnam will not sit at the head of the table but, as the newest member, at the end of a sprig. A small presentation will be made to him. The only infiltrator will be Jackson Stephens, the club's new chairman in succession to Hord Hardin. Woosnam has chosen the sort of meal which he would probably plump for at the Golden Lion: leek and potato soup, Welsh lamb with mint sauce, Eve's (apple) pudding, cheese and biscuits, coffee. The choice of wine he is, wisely, leaving to the club, for its cellar carries the reputation of being no less impressive than its golf course, which is probably the most photographed in the world.

Woosnam enjoys his wine and is beginning to take an interest in it, but he will probably opt for a pint of ale before the night is out. Twelve months ago, when he arrived at the Courtyard Marriott on the night of his triumph, following the small dinner the club always gives the new champion, he was happy with a can or two of beer while everyone else drank champagne. By then Woosnam's tie was loosened and the top button of his shirt undone, as he underwent a late-night press conference just as Sandy Lyle and Nick Faldo had done in previous years. It has become part of the ritual in the American eclipse.

It was not really Woosnam's scene. He remains at heart a boy who grew up on a busy farm at St Martin's, 14 miles from Llanymynech, the course on which as a seven-year-old he first took a golf club in his hands. He had to be careful not to hit the sheep. The course is bisected by the border between England and Wales and though, technically, Woosnam was born in Shropshire, he is a Welshman down to the tips of the spikes on his golf shoes.

Not for him, then, the vogue of so many of today's tournament players who have moved into the fashionable Sunningdale area so they can be close to Heathrow. His roots are firmly in Oswestry – though he did last year buy a small aeroplane to make travelling easier. Naively he regarded it as 'no big deal' and at times he became quite testy at the attention it commanded. On occasions, when things are not going well for him, he is not appreciative of the attention he draws. His other concession to fame is that he has turned one room of his house in Oswestry into his office where his sister-in-law is his full-time secretary, though she also helps Woosnam's wife, Glyndreth, with their young family.

Being the world's number one in the Sony rankings did not sit easily on Woosnam's shoulders. He is more comfortable at knocking others off perches than being there to be knocked off himself.

In the nicest sense of the word, Woosnam is a fighter, perhaps because of his size. Together with Gene Sarazen, who was 90 in February, they are the smallest men ever to have won the Masters.

As a youngster Woosnam boxed, mostly against boys bigger than him, though he still beat them. He also had a love for soccer, but his father, Harold, steered him away from that as well, fearing that his son's competitiveness, allied to his lack of inches, might lead to him getting hurt. At golf he was a natural, though conversely his struggles to become a tournament player were such that he nearly gave up to take a club job. He played for Shropshire and Herefordshire boys and was in the same team as Sandy Lyle; many years later they met in the final of the 1987 Suntory World Matchplay Championship and Woosnam became the first British winner.

He has, with more than 30 victories worldwide, come a long way. Even so, he remains very loyal to his old friends. His closest companions on the European Tour are D.J. Russell and Martin Poxon, neither of whom could be called 'category one' players. Both, with their wives, were present last year at a dinner held in honour of Woosnam's Masters victory, as were the Lyles, the Jameses and the Torrances, senior and junior, since Bob Torrance is Woosnam's swing consultant. Eight of his friends from Oswestry are flying to Augusta this week to watch his defence. In the winter he plays with some of them most weeks, either at Oswestry or Aberdovey, where he has a mobile home close to the first tee. Woosnam has a high regard for Aberdovey, not only because of its peaceful setting beside the high dunes flanking the Dovey, but also because the greens there are always so good. His other relaxations include snooker, at which he has a highest break of 55, and occasionally he also goes pheasant shooting. In his cellar he has a workshop where he enjoys 'messing around' with clubs, mostly putters and drivers.

When at his best, which has been quite often in recent years, Woosnam is a wonderful player to watch, with the sort of swing that is a model for any youngster. He really launches himself into and through the ball. By any standards he is long, but he does have spasms when his putting becomes suspect, particularly from eight feet and closer. It is not obviously the twitch but he does admit to a 'fear of missing'.

It is on such black days that Woosnam's public relations front is clouded by a red mist. He was recently fined £500 by the European Tour when, after a first round of 74 in his defence of the Mediterranean Open, he refused to come in for the requested press interview. He said afterwards he had not read the newly-written rule in this year's tournament regulations. It had, nevertheless, happened before. Marginally quick-tempered, he sees little sense in having to field a barrage of questions when he might feel that his score tells its own story. On the other hand, when Woosnam was taken ill so badly during the Johnnie Walker tournament in Bangkok earlier this year that on completion of his round he had to be rushed to hospital suffering from dehydration, he did not leave until he had first dealt with the hovering group of reporters.

Following last year's Masters, I received a letter from a reader who suggested that 'no one in Britain before had been so generally popular through winning a sporting trophy than Woosnam'. It was further suggested that, in the fullness of time, Woosnam had it in him to be rated among the all-time greats. To achieve that status, a player needs – besides a natural talent – a burning inner ambition. There were those who doubted that he would win even one major title. They were wrong. But whether there are more in the locker, they may still wonder.

———

I MAY 1993

SINGLE MIND THAT CREATED THE CHAMPION OF MILLIONS

MISUNDERSTOOD, MAYBE, BUT THE WORLD'S GREATEST
GOLFER WON'T PLAY IT FOR LAUGHS

Michael Parkinson

The schoolboys were twittering with excitement at the arrival of the world's greatest golfer. Nick Faldo selected a wedge, loosened up with a few purposeful swings, and then said: 'If you boys will tell me your golfing problems, then I'll try and show you what to do.'

A small child raised his hand. 'What's your problem?' asked Nick. 'Please, sir, I only have one arm,' said the boy. The golfer didn't blink. 'I can hit a ball with one hand. Let's have a competition,' he said. The boy, frail and nervous as a chick, set up. His swing was rushed and excitable. Faldo realigned him, showed him how to turn, so he had a steeper swing. The boy swung again and hit the ball further than he had ever done before. Master and pupil beamed in satisfaction.

For more than an hour, in drenching rain, Faldo taught and demonstrated. It was the best golf lesson they will ever have. Moreover, it was free. Faldo showed great charm and patience with the children. In that respect he was like two other great athletes I have observed at close quarters – Boycott and Best – both of whom, like Faldo, have often been at conflict with the adult world. Their rapport with youngsters has something to do with the uncluttered enthusiasm of children, their genuine acceptance of heroes. Adults make preconceived judgments about people; children take as they find.

Nick Faldo drew the driver from his bag, unsheathing it in dramatic fashion as if revealing a magic sword. The children gibbered with excitement. He boomed a drive across the practice ground and over a hedge. 'That's in the swimming pool, sir,' said a boy hopping with delight. Another majestic drive disappeared from sight. 'That's the greenhouse,' the boys squealed. 'Any requests?' he said. 'Can you hit the clock on the pavilion, sir?' was one. 'Better not, but I'll hit a low one, just over it,' he said. The balls screamed a yard or so over the clock, as nominated. But this time the boys were wetting themselves with joy.

'Heroes are important, aren't they?' said Nick Faldo later. 'If you're lucky, they inspire you. Mine were Nicklaus and Palmer. When I was young, I'd play imaginary games against them. I'd take four balls out. There'd be Jack, Arnie, Tom Weiskopf and me. I'd play their shots, try to emulate their swings. I'd imagine features on the courses at Welwyn that weren't there, like lakes and extra bunkers. I'd start at eight o'clock in the morning and play until dark. Thirty-six holes and then I'd practise. Sometimes, I'd play a hole backwards. In other words, if it was a three wood, five iron to the green, I'd take a five iron off the tee and a three wood to the green.

'They sent me on a scholarship to college in America. It's the kind of situation young golfers dream about. But it wasn't for me. Studies got in the way of golf. Also, they reckoned they worked us hard, but I was working four times as hard on my own at Welwyn. I just walked away from it.

'I was good at most games but as soon as I picked up a golf club at 14 I knew this was the game for me. I didn't like team games, so I tried swimming but that bored me. Swimming up and down the baths all day long, until you were blue and wrinkled, wasn't for me. Then I got into cycling but that was boring, too. A good practice was if you fell off your bike, exhausted, and puked. Again, not for me. The difference with golf is imagination. That's the reason I'm never bored when I practise. It's such a complex and difficult game but it's also artistic.

'I remember the first time I heard someone say: "He played a shot punched low under the wind." It stirred my imagination. I couldn't wait to get out on the practice range and interpret what I thought it meant. It's the reason I prefer fly fishing to ordinary fishing. The idea of chucking a line into murky water, and sitting and hoping, doesn't appeal. But the joy of casting in clear waters, where you can see the trout and the bugger can see you, is wonderful because it's a great skill and a marvellous contest.'

At 35 and at the top of the heap, Nick Faldo would appear to have it all. His wife, Gill, is strong-minded and encouraging, the children bounce happily around the house, and he has just been declared one of the wealthiest 500 men in Britain. He is the archetypal working class hero, the man who demonstrated that by hard work and dedication you could take on the world and be the best. He is tall, fit and strong, with boyish good looks, size 11 feet and beautiful hands.

He knows he is the best golfer in the world but he is no braggart; he has more money than he can spend but he is not flash about it. So why is it that he is not beloved like Frank Bruno, or Gary Lineker, or Sandy Lyle, even? Is it that we are uncomfortable with true greatness? Are we, perhaps, misinformed by mischievous elements in the media who, for one reason or another, have it in for the likes of Nick Faldo?

'I don't know what they say. First, I'm a loner. Well, if that means that I don't go into a bar at the end of the day and have a few drinks, then I suppose I am. But I don't see that makes me a bad person. I've always preferred to concentrate on my game. When I'm at a tournament, I'm at work. I don't drink at work. It's as simple as that.

'Then they say I'm a miserable bugger. I like to be focused, to concentrate. I find it difficult to smile and joke like some do. Let's imagine I've just shot six birdies on the trot and, at the seventh hole, I laugh and joke with the gallery and then make a bogey. I wouldn't know if it was because I'd mucked about with the spectators. So I try to eliminate all the risks. Also, I'm shy. I do find it difficult to relate to the spectators sometimes, because if I start chatting them up some might think I'm a big-headed sod who's showing off.

'They say I'm not like Seve. But, then, who is, and why should I be? He hits the ball into the trees on three consecutive holes and keeps on scoring, but that's the way he is. If I hit three balls into the trees, I'd give the game up. He has this happy-go-lucky reputation. But I'll tell you what, he doesn't look that happy coming down the 18th when he's scored 74. Who would?

'Then they accuse me of being "Mechanical Man". This really gets my goat. Makes me sound like a battery toy. What my game is about is control. It's the ability to shape the ball at will, to make it behave just as I want it to. What's mechanical about that? The conclusion is that these people don't really want to know me. If they can't be bothered to take one step closer, to see the real person, then sod 'em.'

This is really what he was saying in that speech at Muirfield after winning his third Open. He remains unrepentant, pointing out he was merely trying to be funny, which is more than can be said for some of the media who appear unhappy that we have a genuine world champion among us. To expect Faldo to take a more measured, philosophical approach to his detractors would be to misunderstand the man and what makes him tick.

He works harder than anyone he knows at getting things right. He leaves little to chance and genuinely cannot understand people who appear not to comprehend what he is striving for. It's not just mere mortals, either. He has been known to walk down a fairway, head tipped to heaven, addressing the Almighty: 'Dear God, how much harder do you want me to work to get it right?' is what he says.

Only a zealot could have decided, as Faldo did in 1985, to change his swing. It was as if Geoffrey Boycott decided in mid-career to bat left-handed, or Lester Piggott to make his come-back riding side saddle. Faldo was already recognised as a world-class player, but it obviously was not good enough. The demons inside him urged him to try for something else. What was it?

'Perfection,' I suggested.

'No such thing,' said Faldo. 'What I was after, and still am, is control. I want to be in total charge of my game, hit, fade or draw, just as I visualise the shot. It was the right ambition, but it nearly brought me down. Those were the black days. I was very depressed. The mistake I made was in trying to play tournament golf while restructuring the swing. I didn't play well and they started writing me off. "We've seen the best of him," seemed to be the general tone. I'd arrive at an airport and I'd see some of the other pros waiting for their baggage and they'd be demonstrating my new swing or the exercises I had to do. They'd shake their heads as if they thought I'd gone mad.

'Everyone assumes that when I went to Lead (David Leadbetter, Faldo's coach) in search of a new swing, we had already designed one. Not true. It was an uncharted journey for both of us. I was a guinea pig. I'd hit 1500 golf balls a day. I'd have to go for a swim halfway through in an attempt to relax my body. My fingers were so sore that they swelled up and I couldn't grip the club properly. I'd come home and Gill would have dinner ready, and I'd sneak out because I would have a thought about what I was doing wrong. When I got back, dinner was ruined.'

Some sponsors lost faith and cancelled contracts. Faldo knows where they live. The company providing his sweaters gave him a new contract; Faldo will not forget the gesture. It was an unpleasant but important part of his young life. 'At least, at the end of it, I knew who my friends were,' he said. Apart from the expert help he received, there was friendly advice from the public. One letter, for example, read: 'Dear Mr Faldo, I am a 16-handicap golfer but I am regarded as the best putter in my club and maybe I could give you a few tips.' Faldo laughs at the recollection and says: 'Mind you, you sometimes wonder if they might be right.'

One day in 1987 he went to Hattiesburg in America and shot four 67s. 'Everything fell into place,' he said. 'It was like sunshine.' It was a rebirth. In Britain the same year he won the first of his three Opens, and in '89 the US Masters for the first time. He wants two more American titles to complete the set. Then? 'I still have the desire to hit a golf ball and to win. I look forward to another ten years at the very top. After that, who knows? The family is important. The kids say they have two dads and one is "Nick Faldo the famous golfer." I try to balance out the two Nick Faldos. I suppose that in the end I would just like people to say, "I saw that Faldo play and, by God, he was a good golfer."' Whatever else they might say about Nick Faldo, that much is guaranteed.

———

14 DECEMBER 1992

HE MADE A BARREN LANDSCAPE FLOWER

TODAY'S PRO GOLFERS SHOULD ORGANISE A WHIP-ROUND
TO ERECT A SHRINE IN MEMORY OF WALTER HAGEN

Michael Parkinson

This has been another year when I failed to get my name on the honours board. On the other hand, the article I wrote about my round of golf with Michael Barratt and Laurie Holloway has been framed and now hangs on the clubhouse wall as a reminder to all golfers that the prerequisite is not a smooth swing but an unfailing sense of the absurd.

The bunker at the seventh where Mr Barratt took an 11 is now known as Barratt's Bunker. It must be recorded that he substantiated his proprietorial claims during the summer when he struck his drive from the sixth tee into the bunker on the seventh.

To give you some idea of the wayward nature of Mr Barratt's drive I should explain that had he been playing cricket the ball would have cleared the square leg boundary. In a foolish display of optimism, Mr Barratt had left his bag in the centre of the fairway on the sixth. Because he was now playing the seventh hole he found it more convenient, not to mention less tiring, to visit the bunker before his bag. Which is how he came to play his second shot, out of sand, with a three wood.

It says much for Mr Barratt's unique golfing skill that he hit an impossible shot over the steep wall of the bunker, thus achieving in one inspirational blow with a three wood what he had once taken seven shots with a sand iron to accomplish. I have a feeling that before long one wall of Temple Golf Club will be taken up with accounts of his exploits.

What is salutary about playing golf with Mr Barratt is his unfailing enthusiasm. I am reminded of his cheerful countenance whenever I contemplate the advice the great Walter Hagen gave to golfers. Mr Hagen said: 'Don't hurry. Don't worry. You're only here on a short visit, so don't forget to stop and smell the roses.' Not only did Mr Hagen practise what he preached, but he ordered that the words be inscribed on his coffin when he died.

Mr Hagen's philosophy has always struck me as being one of the most attractive, as well as profound, observations made about the game of golf. No doubt some of today's grit and grimace brigade would dismiss Hagen's doctrine as being totally unsuitable for the present time when the stakes are so high and the pressure (that awful word) so extreme. That being the case, they should understand that the present financial bonanza in golf is due almost entirely to Walter Hagen, that he was the man who established the humble golf pro as highly paid star and that when it comes to 'pressure' the modern golfer doesn't know what he is talking about. The real pressure was on men like Hagen who inhabited a barren landscape and made it flower. All the modern pro has to do is turn up.

A thought or two about Hagen is particularly worthwhile at a time when *Forbes* magazine publishes its list of the top earners in golf in 1992. Arnold Palmer tops the list having made $11.1 million, Jack Nicklaus $9.2 million, Greg Norman $7.2 million and Fred Couples $7 million. Surprisingly our own Nick Faldo, by common consent the world's best golfer, earned a meagre $6 million. Missing from the list is Jumbo Ozaki of Japan who, it is reckoned, earns $25 million each year from his off-course activities alone.

When Hagen started his career the possibility of earning a million dollars from the game was unthinkable. Hagen did it. It took him a lifetime's work during which he won 11 British and American major titles. However, his fortune did not come from prize money. The prize for winning the British Open in the 1920s was $300. Hagen used to give the money to his caddie. Hagen made real money from exhibition games, gambling and having the clever idea 60 years ago that there might be a future building golf courses in Florida.

Today's pro golfers should have a whip-round and erect a shrine to the memory of Walter Hagen. I have always found him one of the most fascinating figures in sport. He won the British Open four times, in 1922, 1924, 1928 and 1929; the US Open twice, in 1914 and 1919, and between 1921 and 1927 won the American PGA Championship five times. This is all the more remarkable when you consider it was achieved by a man who chain-smoked, drank a lot of whisky and was never known to refuse a party. After winning the Canadian Open he wired ahead to his hotel: 'Fill one bathtub of champagne.'

On the last day of the PGA Championship, when Hagen was due to play Leo Diegel for what was then the highest prize in professional golf, he arrived at the course wearing a dinner jacket after a night on the town. He was seen by a fan who said: 'Do you know that Diegel has been in bed since 10 o'clock last night?' 'He might have been in bed,' said Hagen. 'But he wasn't sleeping.' He beat Diegel 5 and 3.

Hagen's real importance to golf was that by the force of his own remarkable personality and his innate belief that Jack was as good as his master (if not a darned sight better) he changed attitudes towards professionals. He made them respectable and gave them esteem. Even today his disregard for convention would ruffle a few feathers.

For instance, it was rumoured that he said to the Duke of Windsor during a round of golf: 'Hold the pin, Eddie.' Hagen denied the story. 'What I said was, "Hold the pin, Caddie",' he said. He was once due to play a round of golf with a prince of Japan. He arrived late. 'The prince has waited two hours for you,' he was told. 'Well?' said Hagen, 'He wasn't going anywhere, was he?'

Hagen wore beautiful suits, drank champagne and drove fast cars. He employed a glamorous blonde secretary who played the ukulele. He lived in style and expected to be treated like a star. If he arrived at a venue and thought the amenities inadequate he would decline to play until they were improved. He refused to be treated like a second-class citizen and by doing so made things better for all his tribe. He was an intriguing mixture: a showman and a revolutionary, a dandy and a radical. It is always fruitless to speculate what the great players of yesteryear would be worth in the modern game, but there is little doubt that Hagen, with his genius for golf and for living, would be top of any list that *Forbes* magazine might care to make.

He would be delighted with the money in the game, but what, I wonder, would he make of the grim and remorseless grind that modern golf has become? Not much time to stop and smell the roses. Still, I know a couple of members at my golf club who would bring a smile to his face and give him a good time.

22 JULY 1995

FATHER OF THE MODERN GAME BIDS EMOTIONAL FAREWELL

GREAT SENSE OF LOSS AS PALMER TREADS HIS FINAL OPEN
FAIRWAY AFTER MISSING THE CUT WITH 75

Paul Hayward

St Andrews

It was not as painful as the US Open, where he buried his head in a towel and was unable to speak, but saying goodbye was still an ordeal for Arnold Palmer. At the end of his final Open championship round yesterday his voice broke and the tears gathered before he was allowed to leave with one consoling gulp of Scotch.

The emotional pull of Palmer's departure from St Andrews after missing the cut was evident even in the most toughened and taciturn of witnesses. 'I promised myself I wasn't going to get sentimental about all of this,' Palmer, 65, said. But it was a hopeless cause. Too many of golf's virtues have been concentrated in this thoughtful and affable man for his leaving to pass without ceremony.

After 23 Opens and 80 rounds stretching back to 1960, Palmer's final, hopeful, tramp across the undulations of St Andrews was bound to evoke a sense of loss among those who have valued his presence. One of his playing partners, Peter Baker, emerged from the scorer's hut clutching a ball signed by Palmer and studying it in wonder as if he had found a Fabergé egg in the sand. It was that kind of day, even for those of us who are compelled by age to regard Palmer as a luminary of the past, rather than a master of the present.

It is said that some sportsmen carry an aura of endeavour and dignity long after their powers have begun to wane. So it is with Palmer, who allowed his audience to share in every one of his final

75 strokes. Some would expect the longevity of Palmer's career to lessen his pain at leaving. Few professional sportsmen are prepared to endure the rigours of top-class competition at such an advanced age. Palmer required a small extension of the age limit to play at one last Open but was not at St Andrews on a victory lap. Even at his age, falling off the edge of golf, as it were, has inflicted deep hurt.

From a distance the Palmer, Baker, Ian Baker-Finch threesome – group nine on the scorecard – resembled a pleasant family party, with Palmer as the sagacious father guiding the youngsters through the perils of St Andrews. Even the sky cracked into an approving aquamarine, the puffy clouds of morning retreating to the horizon, as if to allow the scene its proper light.

Just before 1 p.m., Palmer caught the view that he has probably been dreading this past week. It was a final look – in anger, at least – up the 354 yards of the 18th hole, over the Swilcan Burn and the devilish bumps, to the Royal and Ancient clubhouse, with its twinkling lights. A scything, determined drive – a little stiffer these days, for sure – and Palmer was taking one last walk through the Valley of Sin, the fiendish hollow that hides beneath the 18th green.

Some thought the reception at the 18th green was 'muted'. It may have been that the true significance of Palmer's last putt simply failed to register. They acclaimed him all right – but politely rather than raucously, as if refusing to believe that Arnold Palmer would not be back. Baker-Finch clasped a hand round his wrinkled neck and Palmer was off to the scorer's hut, where he sat and signed his scorecard like an old teacher inscribing an essay.

Perhaps it is too early to be talking about Palmer's legacy. He has a lifetime invitation to play the Masters at Augusta and will return to St Andrews to play in a Royal and Ancient members' event this autumn. But each of the players drawing handsome salaries at St Andrews should reflect that it was Palmer, above anyone, who drew such vast fortunes into golf and Palmer who spanned the divide between hickory and slickery. As Nick Faldo said: 'But for Palmer, we might have been changing in a hut on the beach.' Palmer was the first golfer to become one of those reassuring, avuncular TV sportsmen who encourage Americans to buy cars and pensions. As he and Jack Nicklaus became American icons in the 1960s, the earnings and stature of golfers began their inexorable rise to today's dizzying levels.

It was not always thus. Yesterday Palmer recalled: 'When I came [to Britain] in 1960 I had just won the Masters and the US Open. And I had to qualify over 36 holes at the British Open. The younger players here this week don't believe it. They thought Arnold Palmer never had to qualify for anything. 'The very next year I came back after finishing second [in the 1960 Open], and having won a couple of other championships. I won the Open at Birkdale. Then I came back the next year and had to qualify again. The younger players just don't believe these things happened in those days.'

As golf's wealth has increased, Palmer's powers have followed their inevitable downward path. On the scoring lists after the first day, he was a detached figure at the foot of the table on 11 over par – the least successful of 159 Open contenders – and dropped three more strokes yesterday to finish on 14 over for the two days. It was a case of 'and the first shall be the last': 'The first two holes [on Thursday] destroyed me,' Palmer said. 'When I four-putted from the fringe at the second it burst my bubble. I was thinking of things that had nothing to do with my golf, and you can't do that.'

The walk up the final fairway yesterday stimulated other such extraneous memories. Palmer said: 'When I came up the 18th I kept thinking about 1960, and what that led to. A lot of great years and a lot of happy times for me, both golf-wise and socially. I was looking at all the people and all the buildings. It was a very warm and happy time.' The press conference ended in painful silence. Finally, Arnold Palmer had run out of words and time.

———

I NOVEMBER 1995

PLAYER REFUSES TO REST ON HIS LAURELS

SOUTH AFRICAN REACHES 70 EXPECTING TO BEAT HIS AGE
AT LEAST 20 TIMES ON TOUR NEXT YEAR

Lewine Mair

Gary Player, who is 70 today, could sit back and celebrate some glorious years in which he won nine majors. Instead, he is as interested in the future as the past, starting with developments at his stud farm in Bloemfontein. His nine hole course, designed for family and friends, will soon be ready for play, while he will continue to shin up and down the 400 steps he has carved into the mountainside. 'I climb them with my grandchildren,' he says, omitting to mention whether they share his enthusiasm for the task.

In terms of his career, Player expects to beat his age at least 20 times on the 2006 champions tour, while there is still a small voice inside telling him that one more win in the senior arena – he captured the Shell Senior Masters at Wentworth as recently as 2000 – is not beyond the bounds of possibility. 'I would need to have a great putting week,' he suggests.

Trent Jones, of golf course architecture fame, would have been more than a little startled at this latest update in the South African's golfing life and times. In 1961, when Player won his first Masters, Jones advised all and sundry that the South African's career would be sadly short-lived. 'You won't see Gary when he's 35. You can't do weight training and last.' Just as there is no triumphant malice in Player's voice as he recalls Jones' words, so he tells matter-of-factly of what his old friend Jack Nicklaus used to say to him. 'When Jack saw me going through my fitness regime, he would ask, "What on earth are you up to, Gary?" Today, when we meet, he says, "I wish I'd looked after myself like you have."'

Player does not blame those who were sceptical. 'Even baseball players and footballers weren't doing weights when I started,' he said. 'No one did.' His motive was to enlist some of the extra yards which came so naturally to Nicklaus and to Arnold Palmer. His fellow competitors were no less bemused when, as one of the first to link performance and diet, he started on the thousands of bananas he was destined to devour across the years. Fruit and vegetables continue to be the mainstay of his diet, while the advice he has for his fellow septuagenarians is that they should 'under-eat and over-exercise'. There followed a warning about the Atkins Diet: 'Stay away from it at all costs.'

Player's mental powers are honed by the many disciplines he inflicts on himself. If, say, he has been impatient on the course, he will force himself to do extra press-ups. Enough to make him think: 'That will teach you . . .' If he makes an appointment, he does not allow himself to be late 'regardless of whether I'm meeting a beggar or a head of state'.

His reaction to the death of Michael Williams, the *Daily Telegraph*'s former golf correspondent, was typical. It was in the week following the 1997 Masters that Williams collapsed on his home course, Chelmsford. The journalist entrusted with writing his obituary spoke to Player's management team about the possibility of getting some comments from Player about Williams' contribution to the game, only to be advised that Player was in America and shortly to set out on a tournament round. They would tell Player, and he would ring back when he had finished. Since Player realised that that would be too late for British deadlines, he stopped off on his way from the clubhouse to the course to put over a wonderfully evocative and measured tribute to a journalist whose enthusiasm he so admired.

Player's own enthusiasm is legendary. Michael Campbell was spellbound when he played under Player in the recent Presidents Cup. 'He told us about Ben Hogan and he told us about Jack Nicklaus and Arnold Palmer in their prime,' said the New

Zealander. 'The whole team was riveted to what he had to say. We were seeing the game through a different pair of eyes.'

At the 2002 Warburg Cup at Kiawah Island, a contest between America and the Rest of the World at senior level, Player and Palmer, both serving as playing captains, had to do battle in the singles. Player, then 67 to Palmer's 73, approached that game with his usual zeal and was out on the practice ground a good one and a half hours before their tee-off time. Palmer, when he arrived at the club, paused on his way to breakfast to look out of the window. 'Gary,' he said cheerfully, 'will wear himself out.' Palmer won that day by 2 & 1.

Player had his revenge the following year, but in his eyes it was anything but sweet in that Palmer was struggling to get the club back. 'Arnold,' said Player, long before they reached the turn, 'you're going to have to get down to some serious stretching.'

Player's reluctance to concede that anything is beyond him was best captured by Peter Walker, the former Glamorgan and England cricketer. Walker, who had been one of Player's contemporaries in schoolboy days in South Africa, told a journalistic colleague that if Player had chosen to stay in cricket, he would have played at provincial level. When the journalist in question mentioned as much to Player, he was more indignant than pleased. 'If I'd stayed in cricket,' said this fiercely competitive soul, 'I'd have played for South Africa. What's more, if I'd stayed in rugby, I'd have played for the Springboks.'

———

26 JULY 1997

OBITUARY: BEN HOGAN

THE GOLFER WHO OVERCAME THE SUICIDE OF HIS FATHER AS WELL AS A SERIOUS CAR CRASH

Ben Hogan, who died yesterday at the age of 84, was the champion who throughout much of his life kept everyone on tenterhooks concerning the secret of golf. Even after he had revealed it in an American magazine, *Life*, there were still sceptics who wondered whether there really had been a secret or whether it had simply been a Hogan ploy to add to his already formidable mystique.

Hogan had colon cancer surgery two years ago and was a sufferer of Alzheimer's disease. In truth, he was never free of pain again following a car accident in January 1949 in which he was involved in a head-on collision with a bus while driving away from a tournament. He threw himself across his wife's lap, by way of protecting her from the impact of the collision and, by so doing, was generally held to have saved both her life and his own. However, he suffered a double fracture of the pelvis and a broken collar bone. He was in hospital for weeks, his recovery hampered by a tendency for his blood to clot.

There were fears that he would never play golf again, but 12 months after the accident, he entered the Los Angeles Open. Though his legs had to be bandaged each morning and he walked with a noticeable limp, he had a 73 and three 69s to tie with Sam Snead, to whom he lost in a play-off. Three of Hogan's four US Opens were won after the crash, as were both his Masters and his Open championship, which he won at Carnoustie in 1953. After Carnoustie, he had only to win the PGA to complete the modern Grand Slam. As it was, the boat trip home was such a long affair that he was never going to attempt the fourth leg.

If that was a disappointment – and one which has grown for those who have seen the modern Grand Slam becoming a more and more remote possibility – Hogan's achievements that year will almost certainly remain unique. All told, he won five of the six tournaments in which he played. Over his career, Hogan won a total of nine majors. Born in Dublin, Texas, on 13 August 1912, William Ben Hogan was the son of a motor mechanic who committed suicide while the then nine-year-old Ben was in the same room.

Many felt that had much to do with the character of a man who preferred his own company and was never prepared to see the press in too kindly a light. He once observed to the golf writing fraternity that there would come a day when 'a deaf mute will win a tournament and no one will know what happened'. Having started out as a caddie, Hogan turned professional at the age of 19 but it was another eight years, after toil, tears and sweat, before he won his first tournament in 1939. Then came the war, but in 1946 he burst to the fore by winning 13 of the 32 tournaments in which he played.

Of light build and 5 feet 9 inches in height, Hogan had a swing which was at once full, flat, fast and furious, all of which encouraged a hook. Recognising the perils, he worked on perfecting a fade which was the basis of his ultimate success. Once, the late Dai Rees, who captained the British Ryder Cup side on a number of occasions, was watching Hogan on the practice ground and was bold enough to suggest he might be of some help as shot after shot drifted left to right. Hogan glared. 'Do you see the caddie move?' he asked, by way of getting the message across to Rees that he was hitting the ball precisely to his own specifications.

There was a touch of dry humour in his dealings with Arnold Palmer when he, Hogan, was the captain. Palmer, then at the peak of his career, had arrived by his own personal plane and heard that there was the possibility of the Americans using the smaller 1.62 British ball then in wide use outside the States. 'Say Ben,' called Palmer across the locker-room, 'What if I haven't got any small balls?'

'Who says you're playing, Palmer?' was Hogan's put-down.

His win at Carnoustie, for which he practised alone every day for a week, was his last major. In 1955 he tied for the US Open at Olympic, San Francisco, only to lose the play-off to Jack Fleck. One of the last glimpses of the player he had been came at the Masters in 1967 when, aged 54, he played the inward half in 30 for a round of 66. He rarely went to Augusta again, living out the rest of his days at Fort Worth where he would practise in solitude or play with his friends. His book, *The Modern Fundamentals of Golf*, is considered a classic, while the sets of clubs his Ben Hogan Company produced were, like the man himself, totally trustworthy.

To return to his secret, to which he laid claim in 1947, the details he gave to *Life* magazine in 1955, and for which he was paid $25,000, involved a roll of the hands which opened the club-face to a maximum on the backswing, together with a 'weakening' of his grip and a cupping of the left wrist at the top of the swing. He was the ultimate perfectionist who dreamt, once, that he had had seventeen 1s but finished, at the 18th, with a 2. When he woke up, he was flaming mad.

---

23 JULY 2001

SUFFERING LYLE CONTINUES HIS ELUSIVE SEARCH

'I LOVE THIS GAME SO MUCH I HAVE TO BELIEVE
SOMETHING GOOD HAS TO COME OF IT ALL'

Robert Philip

Royal Lytham & St Annes

Imagine you are one of the most sumptuously gifted concert violinists ever to stick a Stradivarius under your chin; now imagine waking up one accursed morning to discover you have been turned into Jack Benny at his ham-fisted worst. How would you feel? Confused, sad, tortured? Sandy Lyle is all of those things. Oh, he can still hit all the right notes, only not necessarily in the right order.

If you listen to the experts, there is just cause for believing our 1985 Open and 1988 US Masters champion to be Europe's most accomplished golfer, 'the greatest natural talent in the world', according to Nick Faldo; 'the greatest God-given talent in history', in the opinion of Seve Ballesteros (both critiques offered before the emergence of Tiger Woods, it should be stressed).

So how did it come to pass that, at the relatively young age of 43, a man who was once the best player on the planet was being lifted away from Royal Lytham in a helicopter (perhaps it should have been an air ambulance) a good two and a half hours before Alex Cejka began his final round as joint leader of the 130th Open championship? 'The talent never goes,' says a wistful Lyle, whose error-strewn fourth-round 81 left him on a 17-over-par aggregate of 301, 'it's still in there somewhere. But how do you get it out? Aye, that's the problem.'

The maestro can still perform the sweetest of interludes: for the first two rounds he matched Colin Montgomerie's total of nine birdies and one eagle, but whereas his fellow Scot stood at the very top of the leaderboard come the halfway stage, Lyle barely survived the cut after adding ten bogeys and one double bogey to his discordant score. Let us rewind to the par five sixth on day one, where Lyle hooked a humungous drive into the rough, slashed his approach into a voracious greenside pot bunker, caressed the ball to six feet and sank the putt for a birdie. From the ridiculous to the sublime – or championship golf the Sandy way.

When he won the Open at Sandwich those 16 summers ago, he did so, as Peter Alliss memorably described it, 'playing in a cloud of unconscious competence'. After his triumph at Augusta, however, he consciously began tinkering with every aspect of his swing, experimenting with each new-fangled item of golfing gimmickry and consulting a veritable tribe of witch doctors. His mischievous old cronie Bernard Gallacher even sent him a copy of a Nick Faldo coaching manual as a 38th birthday present. 'Have I listened to too many voices? No, I'm glad I started fiddling with my swing because I was always inconsistent. [Two weeks before winning the Open he shot 90 in a tournament in Ireland.] It's hard not to listen because you never know who's going to walk up carrying the last piece of the jigsaw.'

Cue entrance of Lyle's latest guru, 70-year-old Canadian Moe Norman, generously regarded as a 'flake' in America and inventor of a box of tricks known as 'Natural Golf' which advises 'uncluttering your mind of complicated elements of the swing'. 'It involves not thinking [a return to the "cloud of unconscious competence"?] about your golf but feeling it,' says Lyle by way of explanation, before adding, 'Och, it's hard to explain, but it's all about keeping your swing simple which requires less thought, so less should go wrong.'

A word here about Moe Norman, the purity of whose ball-striking abilities was compared to that of Ben Hogan when he was an object of curiosity on the US Tour in the 1960s. Revered for turning eccentricity into an art form, Norman was playing in a tournament in his native Canada when his caddie informed him that a par four on the final hole would set a course record. 'What length is it?' enquired our Moe airily. 'A driver and a nine iron,' he was told. And so, as any self-respecting professional would do, Norman hit a nine iron off the tee, used his driver from the fairway, then sank the putt for a birdie and course record. In another tournament Norman arrived on the 18th green holding a three-shot lead. Boring . . . To keep the spectators' interest alive, he deliberately knocked his ball off the green into a bunker, chipped on again, then nonchalantly rolled in the putt for victory.

Is this the man entrusted with carrying the last piece of Sandy's jigswaw? 'Yes,' insists Lyle, delivered so flatly it resembles a Monica

Seles double-fisted forehand without the grunt, 'and I'm now striking the ball better than I have been for ages. To be honest, I became too involved with the mechanics of my swing and some of the ideas just didn't work out.'

One of this nation's most loveable and least spoiled sporting heroes, 'good ol' Sandy' ambled his way into our affections with the bemused smile of Stan Laurel as anecdotes surrounding his absent-mindedness and lack of sophistry became legion in the locker-room. Asked 'What do you think of Tiger Woods?' by an American interviewer before the teenager's debut in the 1992 Los Angeles Open, Sandy scratched his head and searched his memory. 'You know, the amateur who's playing here this week,' prompted the reporter. 'Oh,' replied a still-baffled Lyle, 'I thought it was a new golf course.'

Remember, too, a famous thank you speech in Tokyo, where he told an uncomprehending Japanese gallery 'I really enjoy Chinese food', or his apology when forced to reject an invitation from Margaret Thatcher to dine with George Bush Snr at 10 Downing Street: 'I felt terrible turning them down because they're very busy people themselves.'

Sandy can still make you smile ('The jockey's alright but the horse is a bit knackered,' he said of the renewal of his partnership with former long-term caddie Dave Musgrove) but it is depressing to remember that the last time he featured in the European Ryder Cup side was a golfing lifetime ago in 1987.

'It doesn't matter whether Sandy retired tomorrow or in five years' time,' says his Dutch wife, Jolande. 'It would always hurt. It would always niggle him that if he had just kept going then he might have started beating the players he used to beat so easily all over again.' Thus will Sandy put his faith in Moe Norman to unlock the secret to the glories of old. 'I still think you can be competitive well into your forties; Jack Nicklaus proved that when he became the oldest player to win the Masters at the age of 46. After that, it becomes much more difficult. But I love this game so much and have put in such a lot of hard work, I have to believe something good has to come of it all. It's like a doctor trying to find the correct cure for a particular ailment: you might have to take 50 different kinds of medicine to find the one which works.

'To win championships like the Open and the Masters makes me very proud, but I'd like to think I can do it again, that's the thing. When I think back to the years between '85 and '88, I was flowing. I only wish I'd carried on like that, but it was so very short-lived.' But, perish the thought, if the virtuoso perform-ances are gone forever? 'I won't cry about it if I never win another major, but there will obviously come a time when I have to say "enough is enough".'

———

12 APRIL 2002

SNEAD'S TEE SHOT IS A HOOT (BUT NOT FOR HOOTIE)

Martin Johnson

Augusta

They all predicted that the new Augusta would be difficult this year, and Sam Snead proved it with the very first shot of the tour-nament. Quite why an 89-year-old was invited to hit off the back tee down a 150-yard line of spectators is a question that everyone wanted to know – not least a man whose dimpled forehead was not so much the product of Mother Nature as a flying Titleist.

The next casualty will be the Augusta chairman, Hootie Johnson, with an attack of writer's cramp. Having already dispatched three fossilised former champions, Hootie will shortly scribble: 'Dear Mr Snead, in view of your advancing years, not to mention the receipt of a $10 million lawsuit from a gentleman with two black eyes and a pair of broken spectacles, the committee . . .'

The most curious aspect was the crowd breaking out into such a thunderous roar when the ball left Sam's clubhead that anyone watching on television would have thought he'd hit it 300 yards down the middle. Ball leaving clubhead was, in fact, all they saw, as CBS have to tug the forelock in all manner of grovelling ways to keep their annual contract, and the men in green jackets would have taken a very dim view of the sight of blood on live TV.

Sam's tee-shot produced the most spectacular collapse at the Masters since Greg Norman surrendered a six-shot lead to Nick Faldo in 1996, and Faldo, too, was indirectly involved in medical matters yesterday when one of his two prospective playing partners, Hal Sutton, withdrew with a rib injury. This left Frank Lickliter II with no one to talk to, as Nick chats to no one when he's at the office.

Fanny Sunesson is not so much a caddie as a private secretary ('No calls, Miss Moneypenny . . .') and Faldo was once so obsessive on a golf course that if one of his shots ever crusted a spectator, he'd have been more concerned about where the ball ended up than his victim. These days, however, Faldo is a man who almost plays golf for enjoyment, and the old Faldo would never have interrupted his practice-ground routine – as he did yesterday – for a chat with Fuzzy Zoeller.

Greeted warmly on to the first tee, Faldo has always been popular with the crowds here, largely because he drops them the odd crumb. The fake stumble when a longish putt goes in, or the exaggerated knee tremble when he just misses a hazard. But he always flicks the switch back off when it's time to play, and he would have relished the challenge of a course so altered that when Jack Nicklaus was asked what he still recognised from the Augusta he played for the first time, he replied: 'Well, it's green.'

Nicklaus and Faldo are the only two men to have presented the green jacket to themselves, and Faldo's back-to-back victories in 1989 and 1990 both came in play-offs on the 11th green. It was also a good hole for him when he beat Norman, and so it was again yesterday when he managed to get up and down after a spectacularly poor second shot. Scrambling was very much the story of his opening-round 75, although Faldo played so many good irons that he could comfortably have turned that into 72 or better. His approaches to the fifth and ninth were both within a foot of being perfect, but perfection is what you often require on Augusta's sloping greens, and both times he ended up in the kind of spot from where you putt either once – or three times.

The suspicion now is that Faldo, who was in contention for the Tournament Players' Championship until blowing up with an 80 on the Sunday, is no longer capable of putting together four good rounds in a row, and his relative lack of combustion after a bad hole yesterday suggests that he may have realised this himself. There were many superb shots from him yesterday, but every now and then he'd fire one so far wide that he'd shake his head in that way that people do when they're getting older, knowing that they've mislaid something, but can't quite remember what it was.

The bladder control is not quite what it was when he was younger – it took four visits to the trees to get round yesterday – but he will never play on past the age when he can no longer control his golf ball. If Nick takes out a spectator when he's an 89-year-old honorary starter, it will only be because Fanny's given him the wrong yardage.

———

16 JULY 2002

THE MAN WHO STOPPED THE SLAM

Art Spander

American viewpoint

The establishment was as much his adversary as the golf course. Lee Trevino might have a wisecrack on his tongue, but he also had a chip on his shoulder. When your childhood is one of torn jeans and ethnic insults, there is reason for suspicion. Time and money soften the pain, but they don't eliminate it. Lee Trevino will always have something to prove, to the big shots who never thought he had a shot, and, just as importantly, to himself.

In his mind, Trevino was always the ragamuffin playing in the Dallas cemetery where his grandfather dug graves, still working a dozen hours a day at a driving range in west Texas. He could never relax. Or concede. Humour was his way of keeping others off balance, but there wasn't anything funny about the way he competed. Trevino knew all the tricks, whether it was throwing a rubber snake at Jack Nicklaus before he beat him in an 18 hole play-off for the 1971 US Open or keeping the ball in play with that consistent fade off the tee.

In golf Trevino found security, wealth, fame, purpose. Pressure, he told us, is playing for $10 when you have a dollar in your pocket. Tiger Woods, in the past couple of years, has intimidated some of his rivals, but nobody in the 1970s intimidated Lee Buck Trevino, including Nicklaus. As we were to learn.

Thirty years ago Nicklaus had won the first two majors of the year and had come to Muirfield to play in what the headlines were calling the 'Grand Slam Open'. In January 1972 Nicklaus had initiated talk about the slam, about winning the Masters, US Open, Open championship and US PGA championship in a calendar year. And then he went out and won the first two. Nicklaus was headed for history. Except it was history to be made by Lee Trevino. Maybe a Phil Mickelson or Ernie Els or David Duval would be too diplomatic to make the comment about Tiger Woods's parallel quest this summer, but Trevino never worried about diplomacy, only success. 'I want to go down as the man who stopped the slam,' he said. And that is exactly what he did.

The weather was too kind along the firth in the last three rounds of the 1972 Open. Nicklaus was too conservative. He wanted wind. He got a heatwave so memorable that he sent his wife, Barbara, into the Greywalls Hotel next to the Muirfield links to cut the neck off a cashmere turtleneck. Nicklaus, as was his style, practised for a week at Muirfield. Trevino, who had won the Open in 1971 at Birkdale, arrived late, wearing a planter's hat and insisting: 'I brought this trophy back, but I shouldn't have. It's going back with me to El Paso.'

Nicklaus was even par 213 through three rounds and trailed Trevino by six shots. Tony Jacklin, the 1969 Open winner, was considerably closer, only one behind. Jack had been playing irons off the tee, a method that worked when he won the 1966 Open on the same course, but now, with the sun shining and wind still, it proved ineffective. Lee was playing good luck to the hilt, having holed three shots from off the green, two in the third round, including a skulled sand wedge from a bunker on the par three 16th that seemed headed for Edinburgh when it hit the flag and dropped into the cup for a birdie.

The Open ended on Saturday in those years and, on the final day, Nicklaus pulled the head cover off his driver and, miraculously, took the lead within nine holes. 'Look at this,' Trevino said to Jacklin, his partner in the final twosome. 'We're beating ourselves to death, and that son of a gun's gone crazy and passed us.' By the 71st hole, the par five 17th, Trevino and Jacklin were a shot ahead. Jacklin was on the green in two, 18 feet from a birdie. Trevino, distracted by a photographer, had botched up four shots and still wasn't putting. But he chipped in to save par, a shaken

Jacklin three-putted, and a bewildered Nicklaus came in second, one stroke behind Trevino's six-under 278.

'Golf can be a heartbreaking game,' Nicklaus said later, 'and that was my number one heartbreaker.' Trevino had the Claret Jug but little sympathy: 'I didn't come to Scotland to help Nicklaus win any Grand Slam,' he said. 'If I played golf with my wife, I'd beat the living daylights out of her.'

<hr />

2 OCTOBER 2004

MONTY STILL SMILING AFTER ONE TOUGH YEAR

RYDER CUP HERO ON HIS BROKEN MARRIAGE AND THE DRAMA OF OAKLAND HILLS

Lewine Mair

After Colin Montgomerie had holed from four feet on the 18th green at Oakland Hills to tie up the 35th Ryder Cup, he sent a text message to his 11-year-old daughter, Olivia. Nothing to do with the golf. It was a message to say that he would be back in time to do the school run on Tuesday morning.

He kept to his word, leaving his London flat at 6.30 a.m. to arrive at the old family home in Oxshott in good time. When he got there, Olivia, Venetia, eight, and Cameron, six, were speaking at once, vying with one another to tell the tale of how they had stayed up till 10.30 p.m. – long past their bedtimes – to watch the end of the match. 'They were thrilled,' said Montgomerie. 'They felt that bit taller as we walked into school together.'

For Montgomerie, whose marriage broke up earlier this year, it was a moment in keeping with what had happened when Bernhard Langer had called his 12 men to attention during the Sunday night celebrations at Oakland Hills.

'We have the flag from the 18th green and we, as a team, want to present it to Monty,' said the captain. It bore 12 signatures and 12 messages. 'It meant so much,' said Montgomerie, who is having it framed and hung alongside a Jean Donald five iron which his mother, who died from cancer in 1991, gave him by way of a first club.

In accepting the flag, Montgomerie took the opportunity to thank his team-mates for the understanding they had shown at every turn. Langer's handling of his situation had, he said, taught him a lesson he would not forget if and when he gets the Ryder Cup captaincy (the 'if' does not, in fact, apply). He says he would know precisely how to embrace someone in the same position as he was.

The presentation over, Montgomerie took time out for half an hour. Although he and Lee Westwood, whose wife had just given birth and was back in Nottingham, had been dubbed 'the odd couple' and duly played up to the title, he was suddenly feeling out of things. With the room full of players and their wives or partners, his thoughts were flitting through his six previous Ryder Cups when he had been in the same happy position as the rest.

When it comes to his children, Montgomerie is no less frustrated than any other single dad who is no longer living in the same home as his offspring. 'You don't get to tuck the kids up and you don't get to read to them. I don't know what they feel at night,' he said. He phones them when they are having breakfast, he phones them at bedtime and he takes them to school whenever he can. Yet, alongside the frustration, Montgomerie recognises that there is a new dimension to the father–child relationship. 'The time we spend together is more important than it was because there's less of it,' he ventures. Although he knows that the job of an itinerant professional is hardly the best for family life, he suggests that the fact that he has never been in constant attendance makes the present state of affairs easier for his children to comprehend.

Looking from the outside, he counts himself thrice blessed that he had a marriage which yielded three children whom he adores. 'That's what I take away from the relationship. A marriage contract can be ripped in two but the bond you have with your children endures, thank God.'

Montgomerie's fellow players, to a man, are intrigued by everything to do with this larger-than-life figure. During a cocktail party last week at Woburn Abbey, where Montgomerie was giving a vote of thanks to Ken Schofield, the outgoing chief executive of the European Tour, two former Ryder Cup men were musing on what questions they would like to put to him. 'Is he still ambitious?' wondered Ian Woosnam, whose name is among those to have been put forward for the Ryder Cup captaincy in 2006. 'How much longer will he be going on for?' asked Peter Baker. 'Does he want to get married again?' they continued, in unison.

Montgomerie remarked, lightly, that everyone seemed to want to know the same things, before seizing on the question about ambition. 'I'm as ambitious as I ever was,' he maintained. 'I want success. Success for me and for my kids.' For himself, he is desperate to add another European Tour event to the 28 he has under his belt.

Thomas Bjorn, who was one of Langer's assistants at Oakland Hills, hints that Montgomerie, at 41, could have not just one more Ryder Cup left in him but two or even three. The Dane, who was adamant that Montgomerie should not apply for the captaincy in 2006, said that the Scot was the best match-player he had ever known. 'It's a skill he's not going to lose in a hurry,' he added. Retief Goosen, in assessing Montgomerie's glorious contribution in Detroit, described Montgomerie as a player who is at his best with a team behind him, and Montgomerie, when he heard that, was not about to disagree.

Since Detroit, he has been grateful for the support he has been getting from his management company, his golf psychologist, his coach and his caddie. He suspects that he will not be feeling like his old self until 2005. 'This year,' he noted, 'has not been without its redeeming features but I'm going to have a big drink on New Year's Eve and start again.'

Though not prepared to say when he will call a halt to his career on the European Tour, Montgomerie has no intention of graduating to the senior circuit. Instead, he will throw himself into his course design and other business interests. 'The senior tour is not me,' he states. Apart from anything else, he believes that he will by then be burnt out on the travelling front.

His occasional on-course outburst is another thing which could by then be burnt out, though that would not necessarily work in his favour. There have been many instances of Montgomerie playing at his supreme best when heated, though this summer has been a quiet one.

On to the question of whether he would like to settle down with a new partner at some point. 'Who knows what the future holds?' he says. You never know when Montgomerie is going to lace his woes with a touch of humour and, all of a sudden, he was switching tack to recall the Woburn Abbey party and that moment when a lovely lady by name of Evelyn Wand had fainted at his feet. 'That was promising,' he said, before adding that the lady in question – she turned out to be 63 – was maybe a little old for him.

Montgomerie did not qualify for this week's Amex tournament in Ireland. A pity, because he had been looking forward to meeting up with the members of the vanquished US team who made the trip. 'Everyone will be noticing the difference,' he said. 'In the Ryder Cup there wasn't too much interaction between the two teams but this week they will all be discussing the event as old friends.' Montgomerie got on well with David Toms in their Ryder Cup single and does not mind saying that it was one of the best matches he ever played.

Although conscious of the Ryder Cup as a team event, Montgomerie was hell-bent on keeping intact his record of never having been beaten in a Ryder Cup single. 'My 15-footer at the

16th was a big one,' he recalls. 'It put me one up and I knew that if only I could stay one up through 17 I couldn't lose.'

His six iron at the short 17th was, to use his own words, 'a bit scratchy', finishing short and left and in a patch of rough to which Langer had drawn his players' attention on the practice days. Typically, Langer had worked out that a lot of balls would end up in that spot and asked Montgomerie and the rest to experiment with a variety of little pitches. Confident in the knowledge that he had done his homework, Montgomerie used his eight-iron for a species of pitch-and-run which finished three feet from the hole. He made the putt to keep his lead intact and walked to the 18th tee thinking along the lines, 'OK, I can't lose, now.'

After catching the home green with a relaxed three wood and five iron, he eased his long and curving putt from the top of the green to four feet. That done, he stood back along with everyone else and watched Toms. While European fans, to a man, were hoping that Toms would miss the 20-footer he had for his par and give Montgomerie the match, Montgomerie, would you believe, was hoping that the American would make it.

'In the theatrical sense,' he explained, 'I didn't want things to end with me being conceded a four-footer. I wanted to be in the position where I had to hole it. Even though there were no scoreboards around the green, a small voice inside was telling me that this was the putt which could win us the Ryder Cup.'

It was to Langer that he turned first in the immediate wake of his match. He wanted to thank him for everything. 'I've always respected Bernhard for his great faith in God but, at Oakland Hills, you had to marvel at everything to do with the man. We were honoured to have him as captain and, in my case, he did a bit of coaching, too. Would you believe that he was able to spot that I was doing something a little differently on the back swing?' Montgomerie was rejoicing with the other Europeans when Toms's father came across. 'OK, you've beaten my son,' began Toms Snr, 'but I want to say, "Well done!" and to wish you the best of luck in the rest of your life.' Montgomerie felt that he could learn from Toms Snr, just as he had learnt from Langer. 'I would like to think that I could say something like that if any of my kids lost a hard-fought match of any description,' he said.

Our Ryder Cup hero has nearly reached his ideal weight. All told, he has lost 40 lbs in the last six months. 'Twenty lbs from watching what I'm eating and 20 lbs from one tough year,' he said, sounding as certain of his figures as any caddie spelling out a yardage. Would that same 50–50 division apply to his relative happiness and sadness at the present time?

This time, Montgomerie was struggling. All he knew was that life was on the mend. 'I've got three wonderful, wonderful kids,' he began, 'and two Sundays ago, I holed the winning putt in the Ryder Cup. When you look at it like that, I have to be a little bit happy.'

---

16 JULY 2005

JACK SIGNS OFF WITH OLD CLARET HUG

Martin Johnson

St Andrews

The scene in front of the Royal & Ancient clubhouse just before one o'clock yesterday afternoon was so full of emotion it was reminiscent of Don Bradman's last innings in Test cricket. Legend has it that the great man, bowled for a second ball duck, could barely see for the tears in his eyes, so it was fingers crossed for Jack Nicklaus that he wouldn't start blubbing and shank his drive into the starter's hut.

Happily, the ball sailed off down the fairway, and a great avalanche of people surged away to accompany him around his final 18 holes of major championship golf. Mind you, very few of them were actually able to see any of it. In the historical sense, St Andrews was the most appropriate venue to wave goodbye, but from a spectator's point of view the Old Course — with its flat landscape and double fairways — hasn't provided a decent view since the days of Willie Park and Old Tom Morris.

Nicklaus didn't quite walk round to the strains of violins (or even more horribly, bagpipe music) but it is almost impossible to overstate his popularity, and when he left the first tee yesterday, the threesome on the adjacent 18th, Nick Price, Chris DiMarco and Henrik Stenson, stopped what they were doing to applaud and shake his hand. Hard to believe, watching all this, that Big Jack was once the most unpopular man in golf.

The first real golfing hero was Arnold Palmer, a man whose hitch of the trousers first made people wonder whether he'd got a bad tailor, but who soon realised that it was a prelude for some outrageously aggressive shot. Nicklaus, on the other hand, was meticulous and mechanical, and the more rowdy American spectators would gather besides water hazards holding up placards which read: 'Hit It In Here Fat Boy.' However, his popularity grew when he lost some weight and changed his hairstyle, and he's spent the better part of his career being fêted from tee to green. His economical wave, which is a bit like watching someone unscrewing a lightbulb, is something he's had to develop to save himself from tendonitis, and, in the same way as the Queen greeting her subjects from the royal carriage, the wave is usually delivered with a white glove.

Nicklaus first became famous at St Andrews for peeling off his long-sleeved sweater as a prelude to driving (an unheard of feat in those days) the 18th green, but we now live in more commercial times, and when he removed it yesterday, it was a reminder that a Nicklaus commemorative cashmere sweater — a replica of the one he wore for his 1978 Open victory here — is currently on sale for £600. If Jack's final round wasn't enough to make your eyes water, then the price tag on his jumper should have done the trick.

It also takes a special kind of sportsman to retire from the Open twice, and for those who may have forgotten, the Saturday morning newspapers in 2000 were also full of pictures of Nicklaus waving his farewells from the Swilcan Bridge. Bobby Jones once said of him, 'He plays a game with which I am not familiar,' but when Jack dragged his ageing body onto the practice ground and found that he was also starting to play a game with which he was not familiar, he said it was time to go. However, as various bits of plastic replaced some of the parts he was born with, there was still enough of a game there for the R&A to tempt him back by moving the St Andrews Open from 2006 to 2005 to keep him inside the age exclusion limit of 65. So this is it. At least it is unless he qualifies – maybe by renouncing his professional status and winning the US Amateur.

As the round drew to a close, people were hanging from the windows of the Old Course Hotel down the 17th, though at this point Jack was in danger of spoiling his own party. Two birdies would have had him back again for the weekend, but a bogey at the Road Hole put paid to that.

And so Nicklaus mounted the Swilcan Bridge for the final time, waved to the cheering crowd, and then beckoned his son and caddie Steve to come and join him. Steve cried, Jack didn't. Then he invited his playing partners, Tom Watson and Luke Donald, onto the bridge, followed by their caddies. It got so crowded on there that Jack was in danger of falling into the burn.

Finally, before the rules official could move in to whisper 'Sorry, Jack, I'm afraid that's a two stroke penalty for unduly delaying play', they moved on up the last fairway. And it all ended in the most appropriate way, with Jack holing his final major championship putt for a birdie and falling into his wife's arms in his dark red sleeveless jersey. He said hello with the old Claret Jug, and he said goodbye with the old claret hug.

CHAPTER 3
ENTER ELDRICK 'TIGER' WOODS
LIVING IN THE TIME OF TIGER

––––––––––

3 MARCH 1992

SNARES AHEAD FOR 'TIGER' AS HE STALKS THE BIG TIME

BENEATH ALL THE HYPE, AMERICA'S LATEST GOLFING PRODIGY IS SURPRISINGLY LEVEL-HEADED

Alex Lancaster

Eldrick 'Tiger' Woods, at 16 years and two months the youngest golfer ever to participate in a US PGA tour event, failed by six shots to qualify for the final rounds of the Los Angeles Open on the Riviera course last weekend. Yet it was clear to the thousands who watched him acquit himself with skill, charm and confidence that here was a great player in the making.

'It was a learning experience,' said Woods, a lean, handsome six-footer with a wide smile, who comes from a middle-class black family in Cypress, a town about 35 miles south-east of Los Angeles. Mischievously, he told the assembled media: 'I learnt I wasn't that good. I didn't really think I was ready to play among the pros; out there I discovered that I wasn't. I just have to grow up, that's all.' There was genuine humility in the way he spoke and you felt that all the hype and the excessive praise from his naturally proud father, Earl, had been put into perspective. Here was a surprisingly level-headed young man.

With American golf in need of bright new stars and the black minority anxious to see someone take over from Kelvin Peete, Jim Thorpe and Jim Dent, Woods looks as though he fits the bill. His father, a fast-talking extrovert who served as a commando and now works as an administrator in an aircraft plant, claims he used to hit shots into a practice net in his garage while babysitting for his six-month-old son. Mr Woods, who had been bitten by the game a year earlier, recalls: 'Little Tiger seemed mesmerised by what he saw and never cried. Before he was 12 months old I cut down one of my old putters and let him try a few shots. 'He started left-handed, but inside a couple of weeks, in the middle of one session, he just turned right around and has been a right-hander ever since.'

Mr Woods, like any proud father, tends to get carried away. He claims, for instance, that at the age of two Tiger studied some video pictures and decided he needed to shorten his backswing. He also reckons that at the same age the toddler won a local pitch-and-putt competition for boys of ten and under.

Making due allowance for exaggeration, there is no doubt that Woods Jnr is one of the best newcomers here since the 14-year-old Bobby Jones made his debut in the 1916 US Amateur Championship and prodigies such as Jack Nicklaus and Phil Mickelson emerged. At 14, Woods won the California High School Championship and the US Junior National title. In a special competition three years ago Woods' 72 beat 20 professionals. 'He had all the shots and was very disciplined,' recalls John Daly, the PGA champion.

Watching Woods on the tight Riviera course, it was hard to believe that he only turned 16 on 30 December. With an elegant, powerful swing, he drove well over 250 yards and appeared to have no real weakness in his game. Inevitably, he missed greens, but on most occasions he then produced clever little pitches and chips to save his par.

The big question is whether, given the adulation of his family and the unforgiving American public, and the high hopes of the US Golf Association, whose cap he proudly wears, he can graduate from boy wonder to Walker Cup player and then leading professional. When asked his chief ambition he replies: 'To be the best golfer ever.' He is unlikely to become that and one hopes he heard the story of how Sandy Lyle, when asked, as an ex-boy wonder himself, what he thought of Tiger Woods, replied: 'Never heard of it. Is it a golf course?' Even Tiger probably laughed at that one.

———

16 JUNE 1995

WOODS GREEN AND COLOURED BUT QUICK TO PUT MEDIA IN THEIR PLACE

Paul Hayward

It was on land still tended by the Shinnecock Indian tribe that Eldrick 'Tiger' Woods yesterday fired his first formidable strike in a US Open. The gasps of admiration that followed this gifted 19-year-old's tee-shot were for the quality of the drive. But they also marked an important breakthrough in American sport.

Woods, the American amateur champion, has already complained of being 'hounded' by the media, has stopped giving 'one-on-one' interviews, and felt compelled earlier this week to issue a statement on the question of his race. In a less fractured world it would seem a triviality, but here it counts for much: Tiger Woods, in short, is not white.

There are those in the golfing hierarchy who would prefer this issue to go away. That is an optimistic wish in one of the few sports yet to be penetrated by African-Americans and on a course which sprawls across the ancestral land of the Shinnecock Indians, who call themselves 'the People of the Shore' and have tended these fairways and greens for over a century.

The most heartening feature of Woods' breezy emergence from a mixed Asian and black background is that a gust of goodwill as strong as the Long Island wind appears to be blowing him on into history. It seemed a suitable reflection of the obstacles placed in the way of black golfers that he had trouble yesterday finding his way onto the first tee.

What followed was an unforgettable cameo of youthful zest. After a long, friendly talking-to from the defending champion, Ernie Els, Woods might have been expected to defer to his peers (Nick Price completed the threesome) and follow their every act. Instead, he watched his eminent companions tee off with woods and then dropped his ball casually to the turf before whacking it almost to Manhattan with an iron.

This is the way to make an impact in your first US Open. A selection of the shouts that greeted this brazen challenge to the elite would have to include: 'You're da man', 'Go geddem Tiger', and, most excitedly of all, 'I think we godda champion on our hands.' It was not the most helpful send-off for a teenager playing only his second major and with career earnings (he is still an amateur) of precisely zero.

As with the Shinnecocks, who are unable to take out mortgages (it is illegal to repossess a house on a reservation, and thus an unattractive proposition for banks), the subject of ethnic origins complicates Woods' every move. It is impossible to believe that an interest in amateur golf rankings prompted the producers of *Good Morning America* and *Prime Time Live* to invite him on their shows, and his declaration before this tournament commenced read like a *cri de coeur*. With the stress of exams at Stanford University recently he lost 13 lbs in weight.

'The purpose of this statement is to explain my heritage,' Woods wrote. 'The various media have portrayed me as African-American, sometimes Asian. In fact, I am both [his father is black, his mother Thai]. The critical point is that ethnic background and/or composition should not make a difference. The bottom line is that I'm an American . . . and proud of it! That is who I am and what I am. Now, with your cooperation, I hope I can just be a golfer and a human being.'

In 50 years social historians may consider this pronouncement a minor landmark in American sport. If he continues to progress so rapidly, he will be regarded as the player who broke down the door for black players in golf. Despite his wobbly start yesterday after the flourish at the first hole, it is almost unthinkable that Woods will fail to make the grade. At 6 feet 2 inches and 11st 6 lbs, he has the suppleness and ease of the natural athlete and is a big-hitter who is not constructed like a behemoth.

With his statement etched into official record, and his first round in a US Open behind him, Woods can leave others to assess the social implications of his rise. ('If he makes it, it would help the democratisation process greatly,' said Richard Coard Snr, a black caddie.) His main tasks are to keep hitting the ball as power-fully and joyously as he did on occasions yesterday and try to enjoy the attentions of a growing and noisy fan club.

To direct eager spectators to where Tiger Woods was playing, security officials were saying simply: 'Just follow the crowds.' History's train was a long one.

———

15 APRIL 1997

WOODS BREAKS THE MOULD TO THREATEN WORLD DOMINATION

YOUNG AMERICAN'S HISTORIC VICTORY AND GRACIOUS MANNER MAKE HIM THE SPORT'S IDEAL ROLE MODEL

Michael Williams

Augusta

It may only be coincidence but the day after Nick Faldo and Colin Montgomerie played with Tiger Woods, who won the Masters by a record 12 strokes at Augusta National on Sunday, each of them took 81: Faldo in the second round to miss the cut; Montgomerie in the last to tie for 30th place. Put whatever interpretation you like on that but it was as if both these best of the British – Faldo, three times Masters champion, three times Open champion; Montgomerie, four times in the last four years the leading money winner in Europe – realised that the game was about to be taken to a level they could never attain.

Not that they were alone. The whole of the American Tour must also have been shell-shocked as Woods proceeded to do what no other man had done before, break the 17-under-par record of 271, set first by Jack Nicklaus in 1965, later equalled by Raymond Floyd in 1976. He did it by one stroke, and that despite the first nine holes of his opening round having taken him 40. Even par then and Woods would have smashed the record by five strokes, not one, and while it would be ludicrous to suggest that he is going to win everything in which he plays, there is no doubt that if he sets his mind to it, the rest are going to have one hell of a job stopping him.

Woods himself cited Nicklaus, who had the gift and strength of mind to peak at the right time in winning 18 major championships as a professional and two US Amateurs, as a significant influence. Woods, 20 when he turned professional last August, had three US Amateurs under his belt. Since then he has won four US Tour events, two last year and now two this and has exceeded $1 million in prize money quicker than anyone.

He broke all manner of records in the Masters. He was the youngest winner by nearly two years, compared with Severiano Ballesteros, who was 23 when he won for the first time in 1980, while his winning margin of 12 strokes from Tom Kite had never been achieved in any of the four major championships this century.

Most significant of all, however, is that Woods is black and triumphed at a golf club which elected its first non-white member only six years ago. Now there are three, the third being Woods, who as champion becomes an honorary member with the privilege that, when within the grounds of Augusta National, though not elsewhere, he can wear the club's distinctive green jacket.

Lee Elder was the first black golfer to play in the Masters, in 1975, and it is only in the last 20 years that players have been allowed to bring their own caddies, regardless of colour. Before that it was the tradition for the club to allocate its own caddies, all of them then black. 'I'm so proud,' said Elder, who had driven up especially from Fort Lauderdale in Florida and picked up a speeding ticket on the way, of Woods' victory. 'We have a black champion and that's going to be of major significance. It will open doors for more blacks to become members of clubs and it will inspire more minority kids to get involved in golf.'

As Woods walked triumphantly up the 18th fairway, he admitted that one of his thoughts had been of Elder and also Charlie Sifford, another of the first blacks to have played in the tournament. The importance of what he has achieved compares with that of Arthur Ashe when he won Wimbledon. Today is also the 50th anniversary of Jackie Robinson becoming America's first black baseball player.

Quickly on the line with a congratulatory telephone call was President Clinton, who told Woods that 'the best shot I saw all week was the shot of you hugging your dad'. Throughout Woods' life it has been his father, Earl (who recently underwent heart surgery), who has been the force behind him, though his mother, Kultida, a Thai, is also close. The young man they have raised between them is not only an exceptional golfer – one Tom Watson says 'can emerge only once in a millennium' – but also one who promises to be an excellent ambassador.

He is well educated, studied at Stanford, speaks with modesty and good sense and has the looks and athleticism that will make him a role model for the young. Phil Knight, chairman of Nike, the sportswear company who gave Woods a $40 million contract when he turned professional, said: 'You run out of superlatives. He's off the charts. We expected great things but he's gone way beyond.'

No golf tournament in the world will now be complete unless Woods is in the field. The demand for him will be unprecedented which leaves Hughes Norton, of Mark McCormack's International Management Group, with a mammoth portfolio. So far a balance has been kept. This was, after all, only Woods' ninth tournament of the year, one of which was in Asia (and he won that by 10 strokes).

Such is the length that Woods hits the ball he hardly needs 14 clubs in his bag, though he refuted one suggestion that he could have won the Masters with only four. In four rounds he did just about go through the bag but it was the driver, the wedges and the putter that did most of the work. It is this which is so frightening to every other tournament player. In four historic days they have been left feeling weak and inadequate, asking themselves, as the great Walter Hagen once put it many years ago, 'Who's going to be second?'

13 SEPTEMBER 1997

WHAT WE ALL OWE TO TIGER

W.F. Deedes

It is time to reflect on the inestimable services that Tiger Woods has rendered to golf this year – not because of what he has done, but because of what he has failed to do.

Soon after his victory in the Masters at Augusta, there was much loose talk about a man about to dominate the game. 'Who's gonna be second?' they cried, echoing Walter Hagen's old quip. There was confident talk of a Grand Slam for him, which meant going on to win both the US and British Opens and America's PGA. Nobody had done anything like that since Bobby Jones, in a less fiercely competitive world, took the Amateur and the Open on both sides of the Atlantic in 1930. As it turned out, Tiger Woods' best place was 19th in the US Open. He finished in 24th place in our Open and 29th in their PGA. Once you have been built up as unbeatable by the modern news media, the let-down comes hard. For someone of only 21 in his first year as a professional, Woods met it heroically.

But what disappointment for Woods conveys to every golfer is the maddening elusiveness of the game, from which none is exempt, not Woods, nor Faldo, nor Montgomerie nor Ballesteros.

There comes a moment in all our lives when we reckon we have mastered it. It never lasts long. It brings to my mind the closing lines of Scott Fitzgerald's *The Great Gatsby*, where he writes of Gatsby's green light, 'the orgiastic future that year by year recedes before us . . . It eluded us then, but no matter – tomorrow we will run faster, stretch out our arms further . . . And one fine morning . . .'

We never lose hope of that green light. Knocking balls into the golf net I use most mornings, I have just stumbled upon a small adjustment associated with the right elbow which I am convinced will make the world of difference to my game. I am more optimistic than I have been for a long time, wishing only that I had uncovered this secret at the start of the summer rather than at the end of it. In such respects golf runs parallel with life, with its alternating moods of optimism and despair. But it helps as we grow older to feel that everyone else in the business, no matter how eminent, experiences the same moods.

Which brings us back to Tiger Woods. If he had proved supreme this year, if he had won everything in sight, that would have been a bad blow for this philosophy we golfers cultivate. For that philosophy depends on its universality. I may suffer, as I often do these days, a disappointing round. But, irrationally, I draw comfort from the fact that in that same week Faldo has missed the cut.

It produces a sense of brotherhood. Yes, of course his worst score is still better than anything I could achieve, but my golfing philosophy bridges that gap. Golf is his profession, I reason, just as journalism is mine. Supposing we reversed roles. Would my round of golf score fewer points than his editorial on, say, the way ahead in Ireland?

What is indispensable to this philosophy, which keeps us perpetually hopeful and binds us together, is the inevitability at times of broken dreams. It follows that, in the wider interests of golf, I watched closely the misadventures of Tiger Woods on the famous eighth hole at Troon during our Open. Known as the Postage Stamp, it measures just 126 yards, which makes it one of the shortest holes in golf. Woods was five under when he came to that hole. Badly bunkered, he finished up with a ruinous six, went from five under to two under and destroyed a dream.

No matter that at 21 he has everything in front of him, and according to recent assessments has enormously enriched commercial golf. Folk who never thought of watching a tournament go to see him. But in my book he has enriched the game for a different reason. He has proved that no golfer, not even the best, is immune from heartbreak. Welcome, Tiger, to the brotherhood.

––––

7 FEBRUARY 1998

GOLFING PHENOMENON ON THE PROWL AGAIN

TIGER PICKS HIS WAY THROUGH JUNGLE DESPITE DISTRACTIONS THAT WOULD BUNKER A LESSER PLAYER

Martin Johnson

It is the kind of medical condition that used to afflict teenage girls at Beatles concerts, except in this case the virus is so potent that elderly grandmothers and dribbly-bibbed infants have been known to keel over at the same time. He has more security guards than the President of the United States, and while he too would play off scratch if he decided to take up serial womanising, he'd have considerably less chance of keeping it quiet.

As his courtesy car sweeps him through the gates, adoring cries of 'Way to go!' and 'You the man!' echo around the golf course – and that's just from his fellow players. The US PGA Tour has no shortage of millionaires at the top end of the scale, but thanks to Tiger Woods every Tom, Dick, and Harry Gump III Junior will soon be making room for another Cadillac in the garage.

The latest strain of Tigermania, for which there is no apparent cure, is currently sweeping through San Diego, where symptoms among his fellow professionals include a particularly nasty swelling around the back pocket/wallet area. The Buick Invitational is a standard US Tour event, but offers no less than $2.1 million in prize money. Next year, however, thanks to the fact that Woods has raised the game's profile way beyond the levels that Palmer and Nicklaus ever achieved, this sort of purse will be relegated to peanut status on the back of soaring TV ratings, and more than double the current annual level of prize money. Tiger himself is just about managing to keep the wolf from the door with endorsements worth around $70 million, not to mention the occasional raid on the prize money himself. Add to all this the vast difference in facilities on this side of the Atlantic, where the tee-beds are better manicured than a lot of European greens, it is little wonder that the European Tour's finger in the dyke of haemorrhaging players is beginning to turn purple under the strain.

Richard Coughlan, a highly promising 23-year-old Irish golfer, has just won his card on both tours, but is in no doubt which one offers him the better chance of making a lucrative career from the game. Coughlan, who is playing at Torrey Pines this week, said: 'This is definitely the place to be. The conditions, money, weather, they're all superior. And in terms of being pampered, there's no comparison either.' You don't need a crystal ball to work out that the European Tour's system for Ryder Cup selection (namely, stick with us or you won't get in) will provoke even more bickering next time than it did before Valderrama.

There are, however, a number of reasons for thinking twice about going to America, in that certain aspects of golf here can seriously damage your brain. Leaving aside all those plane trips, motels, TV dinners and invitations to prayer meetings, the sheer banality of American golf galleries is enough to give any golfer not in receipt of at least two whoops and one holler per hole grave doubts as to whether he can play the game at all.

Mind you, this is nothing to the banality involved at the press conferences, during one of which this week Justin Leonard was asked whether he would join the list of refuseniks in returning for last week's rain-postponed event in Pebble Beach. 'Of course I'm going back,' said Leonard. 'What if you guys had a couple of important questions left to ask in an interview with Monica

Lewinsky. Wouldn't you go back?' Cue puzzled looks all round, until it became clear that he meant a skater by the name of Tara Lipinski rather than someone whose name crops up rather more often at White House press conferences. Justin, incidentally, still lives at home with his parents, which naturally enough prompted the question on everyone's lips — namely, whether he packed his own suitcase when leaving for tournaments, or had some help from his mom. A bit of both, apparently.

Leonard is also one of many otherwise high profile American golfers who has reason to be grateful to Woods for allowing him to get around golf courses without being unduly pestered. Holder of what qualifies on this side of the water as a relatively insignificant tournament known as the Open, Leonard teed off on the North Course on Thursday — along with Tom Kite — at the same time as Woods was starting 30 yards away to his left on the more difficult South Course. Leonard took 17 people with him up the first hole, while Woods had something close to 2000.

Mark O'Meara, Woods' Florida neighbour and golfing father figure, was talking the other day about how the one thing he did not envy the young Tiger was his lack of privacy. Before his first round, Woods was putting on the practice green, much to the amazement of two teenage girls. 'Look, he's right there in front of us,' said one. 'Amaaaaazing,' gasped the other. 'I thought he would have had a cage around him or something.' The analogy was poignant. Most of the tigers these days are in captivity, and this one, to all intents and purposes, is no exception.

In the match behind Woods was the former pied piper of American galleries, John Daly, and though his pairing with Phil Mickelson and Jesper Parnevik drew a healthy enough audience, it was nothing like the gallery tracking Woods, Duffy Waldorf and Chip Beck. With all due respect to the other two, Waldorf is best known for painting things like butterflies on his golf balls, while Beck drew the kind of morbid interest that goes with having missed your previous 26 cuts.

Poor old Chip is not too far away from the Ian Baker-Finch school of hacking, and while he was nominally playing the South Course, he also got a good look at the North in preparation for the second round. It was like watching a yacht tacking, and he did not really need the avalanche of TV cameras that gets attached to any round with Woods. Beck's lowest moment in a round of 82 was when it took him three shots to get on to the par three 16th, and three more putts from three feet to get his ball into the hole.

Woods, however, did not play particularly well either for his one-under-par 71, but scrambled through on the back of some phenomenal putting. Augusta might be just a pitch and putt course for him (he could become the first man ever to start the Masters odds-on) but by far the most remarkable statistic from last year's triumph was not a single three-putt in 72 holes. In fact, in 180 holes on Augusta's frightening greens, Woods has three-putted only four times.

The battle that Tiger was having with the course was nothing, however, compared to the battle the spectators were having trying to get a glimpse of him. The marshals all wore red jackets, and while a couple sufficed for most matches, Woods had more redcoats than Butlins during the entire summer season. Not only that, he had security guards as well, which led to one or two fraught moments.

One of these guards had an appearance that would have been rejected as too provocative by the Hitler Youth, though the sinister effect of his dark glasses was somewhat spoiled by a haircut – two-thirds totally shaven, with a kind of Brillo pad on top – which actually made him resemble a crème caramel pudding. At one hole he barked at an elderly man who had smuggled himself the wrong side of the rope. 'But I work for NBC,' said the man, who, by way of evidence, was wearing a hat emblazoned with 'NBC Sports'.

'Look, I'm Tiger Woods' personal security,' growled the Hitler Youth, 'and that hat don't mean nuthin'.' With the aerial end of a walkie-talkie up his nostrils, the George Burns lookalike (the entertainer, not the golfer) duly withdrew. As if to emphasise that a Woods gallery spans all ages, a man whose tree-climbing days ought to have been at least 40 years behind him got stuck up a pine overlooking the seventh green and had to be rescued. If Tiger started fast, with a birdie at the first, the gallery started a little more slowly and we had to wait until the sixth until the first cry of 'You the man!' The ice now broken, this was swiftly followed by 'Get in the hole!' and 'Go get 'em, Tiger!' Tiger mostly cocks a deaf 'un to this sort of thing, though his wizened caddie did appear to be slightly startled by one yell of 'Go get 'em, Fluff!'

There were the usual efforts to secure an autograph, the most optimistic try coming from a garbage can collector in a Buick boilersuit thrusting a biro and what appeared to be a piece of kitchen roll at him, but the Tiger kept his head down, having done most of his signing at the previous day's pro-am.

Such is the media clamour for Tiger titbits here that the pro-am turned one of his amateur playing partners into an overnight celebrity. No sooner had Bryan Schock, of team Coca-Cola, completed his round with Woods, than he was surrounded by TV cameras and reporters' notebooks. 'Were you nervous, Bryan?' 'Was I nervous?' 'What was it like?' 'Oh, like, awesome, I mean, he's just so down to earth, a great human being, a real honest guy, you know . . .' One of the woman marshals rushed over to a friend, and waved a notebook. 'You know what, I wrote down everything he said. I mean everything.' 'You don't say?' said her friend, but she did say. 'I think he musta gotten aware of it, 'cos he kinda clammed up.'

Tigermania. Coming soon to a golf course near you.

———

24 JULY 2000

UNIQUE GENIUS IN MAGIC CIRCLE

Paul Hayward

Golf has been terrorising people for five centuries or more. Now the game itself is on the receiving end. The most technically demanding sport known to man was supposed to be as unconquerable as the sea that lapped obediently on the St Andrews shore. Then along came Tiger Woods.

People moaned that the 129th Open championship had become a procession, 'fallen a little flat', as one TV commentator complained. Nobody rolled his trousers up and jumped into a canal or dragged us into a play-off with nerve endings ablaze. Some people thought that Muhammad Ali's conquest of Sonny Liston meant the death of boxing. Others still argue that the unfailingly brilliant Pete Sampras is a robot built of the same material as his racket. Impossible to understand.

The genius that Woods has brought to a Grand Slam of major titles is not dependent on extraneous dramas or anyone else out there on the rolling course. It works just as well on its own, as it did for Ali or Pelé. Golf was designed never to be conquered. It is the history of broken spirits. The pack trudges round. One player pokes ahead to win by a stroke or two. This is how it works. Nature itself and human frailty decreed that it would always be so.

Five hundred years later, in the first summer of golf's second millennium, the game made an evolutionary leap. The Claret Jug is now filled with a whole new vintage. It is a sin to mention any emerging sportsman in the same sentence as Ali or Pelé unless the case for inclusion is inarguable. This time it is. At 24, and with the peak of his powers still obscured by the cloud of time, Woods has completed the Grand Slam faster than the departing Jack

Nicklaus. So young is Woods, by normal golfing standards, that his emblem remains a striped cuddly toy.

Gene Sarazen, Ben Hogan, Gary Player, Nicklaus, Woods: this is golf's magic circle. Yet none of the game's previous greats could wake with a surer conviction that they were the finest player on earth. Imagine the power that comes with that knowledge. Woods exudes it, and the opposition smell it each time he walks to the tee. David Duval flung himself against that aura yesterday and was repelled. Resistance was futile.

The white flag was already rising ominously in some players' minds. They will have to fight hard to force it back down. Some will be tempted to find a Tiger-less tour, tracking his movements with pins on a map and then heading the other way.

This is a long sentence, with no remission in sight. Nothing about Woods' background or demeanour implies that he will tire of victory or cascading wealth. Jay Brunza, his sports psychologist, promised: 'He's not going to burn out because he plays for his own joy and passion.' Fancy that: a modern sportsman who has won everything worth winning and is hit by a daily avalanche of money playing for 'joy and passion'. Normally we might suspect this statement of having been spewed out by the Nike PR manual. Not this time. Woods defies the theory that people who are thrust into sport before they can even speak end up on a bonfire of emotional damage.

His hotel rooms will never be trashed. Bottles of Jack Daniels will never be found strewn around his bed. This makes some people faintly uncomfortable. The absence of obvious weaknesses or flaws is a throwback to the time before sport was a form of soap. Doting parents, beautiful girlfriend, flashing white grin, youth, and above all talent: in this age of auto-scepticism, it may take us a while to accept that an uncomplicated tale of historic importance is forming in front of our eyes.

'For him to be able to do all the things he's done, with all those distractions, is just amazing to me,' says his former Stanford

University room-mate, Notah Begay, a Navajo Indian and fellow standard-bearer for ethnic minorities in American golf. Nobody in the sports 'industry' can quite comprehend how Woods has stopped commercial 'distractions' from retarding the development of his game.

Michael Jordan's position as the pre-eminent earner in world sport is now under threat. And so it ought to be. The thread that unites these two American legends is that a hermit could have seen that they were the best in the world within two minutes of coming out of his cave. The difference is that Woods has crushed the rest of the globe in a sport that is stubbornly resistant to world domination. Jordan crushed only the rest of America. A better contemporary comparison is with Sampras, who possesses the same capacity to slide through the gears of his own ability and to impart the sense, when it really counts, that the other man is doomed.

On the final day of these tournaments, the immaculate amphitheatre of the 18th green seems to suck the players towards it with irresistible force. Watching Woods walk that way yesterday, it was tempting to think of the final cup as a plug-hole sucking a whole generation down the tube. Duval did his best. The world's two highest ranked (and physically fittest?) players laid on what drama they could. St Andrews, though, played host not to a contest but a coronation.

Five years from now, golf could be praying to a pagan god to send a fresh face up the fairways. Nick Faldo thinks that 15 year olds will study the Woods master-plan and come up with a way to surpass even his exemplary example. Faldo should have been on the fifth tee, where Woods drove his first shot 428 yards to leave him 140 yards from the green on a par-five. The gasp was of the sort you hear in a circus after a death-defying act. If a boy with the ability to match such power and accuracy has been born then we will see the star hovering overhead.

'I love the game to death. It's like a drug I have to have,' Woods said once. It's valium all round for his contemporaries. Great final day crescendos are fine, but give me genius every time.

————

14 NOVEMBER 2000

BORING? NO, I'M JUST VERY MELLOW

Jan Moir

Tiger Woods sits on a spindly chair in a pale hotel suite, a study in controlled stillness. Now and then, an unsettled look flits across his face, as if he would like to flee this hot room, filled with sponsors and agents and can-do business bustle. Instead, he just sits there, as calm as a Buddha, with those almond-shaped eyes forever watchful under a lowered Nike cap. In his quiet, cultured voice, he tells me that while other sportsmen need adrenalin surges to survive – 'otherwise they get hurt' – professional golfers like him have to learn to suppress emotion or excitement if they want to succeed. I don't doubt it for a second. If I leant over to take his pulse, I suspect it would be as slow and sombre as a funeral drum.

'You can't be fired up in golf. You have to be a little bit mellow and I am very mellow,' he says. Is that the same thing as boring? 'Uh, I guess it can be at times,' he replies, after some thought.

Underneath a black polo neck, his powerful shoulders spread out like wings and his torso looks as flat and strong as a pile of bricks. He is slighter than you might imagine and has those weird golfer's forearms, where one looks as pumped up and muscled as Popeye's and the other one looks just muscled. As singular testament to his mixed heritage – he calls himself Caublinasian, in reference to his black father, Thai mother and American Indian and Caucasian strains in the family tree – he has a rather beautiful face, with a glowing complexion that looks as though it has recently been drenched in Mr Sheen, then given a vigorous polish. And, just as on the golf course, his expression veers between two distinct extremes: although his smile is joyful and exuberant, in repose he always looks as though he is going to burst into tears. Please don't cry, Tiger!

'This is not really my environment,' he confesses. 'When I get out of here and do the things I like to do, my life is, uh, much more fun.' And what Tiger Woods likes to do more than anything else is win. Since turning professional in 1996, he has become a golfing phenomenon, one of those rare athletes who have somehow moved their chosen sport into a different dimension, a whole new ball game. As records are smashed and titles and awards thump down around his feet, the rest of the pack can only look on in awe or grumble about the 24 year old from California who has been sent from golfing galaxies unknown to torment them.

After having corrective eye surgery last year, Woods – who is not above psyching out his adversaries – teasingly remarked that now the holes on the greens looked even bigger. As if the others weren't frightened enough already. After triumphs at the British and US Open championships this year, he has propelled his projected career earnings above £4 billion, making him the richest sportsman on earth. His sponsorship deal from sportswear manufacturers Nike alone is worth £58 million a year and he is in London on a lucrative mission to help American Express launch its new green credit card.

The corporate dudes circling the room are very keen that I should ask Woods a question about this, so I do. What colour is his own American Express card? 'Platinum,' he says, which is a shock. You would think that someone with Woods' monstrous bank balance and earning power – not to mention the fact that he is the company's current pet celebrity – would be upgraded to their fabled black card status, to say the least. But Woods likes to keep his finances to himself, claiming that, despite the billions, he is still a regular guy who even lugs his own clubs around the courses at home – 'I did exactly that last year, playing with my buddies, carrying my bag just like amateur days, having a great time.'

There are others, however, who can think of Tiger Woods only in more celestial or reverential terms. Recently, Jack Nicklaus complained that Woods made all other golfers look 'puny' in comparison, while fellow veteran Tom Watson described Woods as 'something supernatural'. 'But I am human,' insists Woods. 'I can't win every time – and I don't. Losing is part of the game. You just have to go out there and try your best, and that is what I do.'

Indeed, at the American Express World Championships held in Spain over the weekend, Woods seemed hell-bent on proving just how human he could be. At the tricky 17th hole, he hit shots into the water on three separate occasions and had a tantrummy moment when – like any weekend hacker – he threw one of his clubs away in disgust. 'I looked at the footage of myself doing that and I thought it was pretty funny, kinda comical. I mean, it didn't look too good on my part and it is frustrating not to accomplish your goal, but you've got to have a sense of humour about it.' Even with all that money at stake? 'Maybe especially so,' he says.

'The best way to look at it is that golf is just like life, you have got to be able to enjoy what you do. My father has always told me that golf is a microcosm of life and the more I play, the more I understand what he means. Golf is frustrating and exciting: you run through the whole gamut of emotions when you are out there playing – every golfer understands that.' But I thought you said you had to keep emotion out of it? 'I play with emotion. I play as hard as I can and I play my best when I release my emotion – frustration, whatever.'

His father, Earl, put a golf club in his son's hands as soon as he could toddle, and baby Tiger first appeared on television at the age of two, chipping marshmallows into Bob Hope's mouth. Prodigiously talented, he took every junior title going in America and settled himself down to learn the ways of the golf world. 'It taught me a lot about discipline and rules, etiquette and honesty. I remember as a kid moving a twig on the ground and my ball moved. I was off in the trees by myself, no one saw it but I owned up. So it helped me learn about honour and how to behave properly.'

Certainly, he seems – in comparison with many professional sportsmen of similar age – to have something of an interior life and a full existence away from the cloistered world of golf. There is a knowingness and a quiet intelligence about him, although he is guarded about his personal life to a degree that borders on paranoia. Perhaps it is understandable that he does not wish to discuss his girlfriend of two years, Joanna Jagoda, but it seems bizarre that even simple questions about his fitness regime are off limits.

His intriguingly limber and supple frame seems to hint at someone who spends more time on a yoga mat than on a driving range, yet this attempt to keep his workouts a secret is revealing in itself. Does it mean that, unlike his admirers, most of whom seem to think he came to the game a fully formed miracle, Tiger Woods believes that it is what he does in training that makes him so special? When he stands up to leave, he shakes my hand gently – golf professionals usually like to give you a bone crusher, just to show how strong their drive is – and unleashes another of those radiant smiles.

By the time you read this, he will have flown by hired private jet – 'I don't have my own yet, I just rent some hours' – from London to Thailand and begun to take part in yet another tournament. At the moment, he knows that when he is on form, he is the greatest golfer in the world, yet he claims that he is also ready for the day when that is no longer the case.

'I am prepared for the lessening of my powers, that is part of reality,' he says. 'It is going to happen, the only question is not if, but when. There will be players who will be stronger than me, who will be able to do things to a golf ball that I will never be able to do. It's just part of the evolution of the game. All I can hope is that it will be later rather than sooner.'

———

9 APRIL 2001

WOODS CLINCHES SLAM WITH FINAL FLOURISH

CHAMPION HOLDS ALL FOUR MAJORS AFTER PRODUCING ONE OF BEST PERFORMANCES IN GOLF HISTORY

Lewine Mair

Augusta

There was a 20-foot putt and a triumphant punch of the air as Tiger Woods completed his Slam of four consecutive majors. If not the Grand Slam, it was entirely grand enough to go down as arguably *the* performance in the history of golf.

Instead of romping to victory as he did in 1997, Woods had to fight all the way before adding that flourish of a finishing putt. With a 16-under-par total of 272, he was two ahead of David Duval and three clear of Phil Mickelson. As his putt went down, his parents, separated but together for this moment of moments, watched as Tiger cried tears of emotion into his cap.

Everything had conspired to make Woods' last round of the 2001 Masters the most telling test the game has known. Bobby Jones was only up against one opponent on the last day of the final leg of his Grand Slam in 1930, in that the event was the US Amateur. Woods, on the other hand, had a blaze of the hottest players in the world on his tail.

There was every sign that he was shaping to escape them at the 10th. At the time he was level with Duval, who had notched a noisy haul of seven birdies ahead of him, and one clear of Mickelson, his playing companion. He could have been frustrated when Mickelson's ball kicked out of the trees at the 10th and his picked up a lump of mud. Instead, he holed for his par from 10 feet, a steely putt if ever there was one. Then, he hit from 149 yards to a foot at the 11th for the birdie which gave him the lead at 15 under.

At that, most had the feeling that he had the tournament won, but there was still a flurry of scoreboard activity to come. When he caught the green of the 15th in two as Duval dropped a shot at the short 16th, he was set to move two ahead. As it was, he three-putted and, before too long, Duval had a six-footer on the 18th green to draw level with him on 15 under. Duval failed, his error contributing as much to Woods' triumph as almost anything Woods did for himself.

Even when all the overnight leaders had been at their most closely packed, Woods had worn the look of one who was light years removed from the rest of them in the mental sense. The extent to which he was in a world of his own was perfectly captured by Nick Faldo on Saturday. The former Open and Masters champion had gone to the practice ground to film the Woods swing, the reason being that he felt he could learn from his stability and the efficiency of his turn. He filmed the player from both sides and then he crouched behind.

Had he felt obliged to ask Woods before he started? 'Heavens, no,' Faldo said. 'He wouldn't even have noticed I was there. He was in the zone.'

The local Sunday papers were talking of Mickelson's 'courage', not least with regard to his birdie–birdie finish in his third round. But, well though he stayed with Woods for much of the way yesterday, the big question was always one of whether he had enough of that commodity to break through and win his first major.

How things have changed from the day when a man would play down his chances. Today's golf psychologists are not merely telling their players to believe in themselves but to see everything that happens to them in a positive light. It has become such a habit with Mickelson that, had he slipped in the shower and broken a leg yesterday morning, he would almost certainly have been assuring people that it was for the best. On Saturday evening he was swearing, blithely, that there was nothing he wanted more than to play in the last round alongside Woods. Did he really think that or did he, in his heart of hearts, suspect that he would have been better off playing in the penultimate group where he could operate away from the gaze of the Tiger? Would he for instance have missed fewer of the short putts, such as the one which got away at the sixth?

You would like to think that Darren Clarke, who defeated Woods in the final of last year's Andersen Consulting World Golf Championships, would have thrived on playing alongside Woods yesterday. He was shaping to do as much until he fell from nine under to five under as he finished 5, 4, 6 against the par of 3, 4, 4 for his third-round 72. 'If I'd parred the last three I'd have been in position to make a charge,' he said ruefully, as his wife put a consolatory arm about his shoulders.

Going into yesterday, Clarke was lying alongside Miguel Ángel Jiménez, the quiet man of Spanish golf, and one behind Bernhard Langer. He had a closing 73 to finish at four under while Jiménez had a 69 to finish at eight under and one ahead of a tiring José María Olazábal. Langer, after a run of four birdies in five holes, mounted the 18th tee at nine under for the tournament and stayed at that mark.

What with his third place in the recent Players' Championship, Langer will assuredly have caught the eye of the European Ryder Cup captain, Sam Torrance. Two years ago, the German suffered the indignity of being called to a press conference at the BMW International Open at which he was expected to be told that he had been given the last wild card in Mark James' team for Brookline. Instead, he had to do a vanishing act as James named Andrew Coltart.

Of the rest of the European contingent, Harrington made the cut, if only by the proverbial whisker. He was looking for more from this Masters, yet it is not just a Mickelson who would be able to put a positive spin on his performance. His attitude was once again first-class as he came out on the winning side of his fight to make the cut. Where he struggled was in judgement of distance. A good player who is reaching for the next level, he seemed to be hitting the ball further than he could believe. His caddie was inclined to put it down to a new purity in his striking allied to the adrenalin that goes with playing at Augusta.

Regardless of the result at this 2001 Masters, Augusta did what it had to do in terms of identifying the best players. In the weeks ahead, the club will start lengthening the course by way of combating the latest in modern technology. Their announcement was one which had an exasperated Jack Nicklaus saying that if they carried on allowing the golf ball to do what it is doing, 'we'll soon be teeing off downtown somewhere'.

Tom Lehman seemed to feel that the destruction of the game's traditional courses was not imminent. He said they could carry on 'tweaking' them. And if and when they ran out of room to adjust tees, they should concentrate on the bunkering. To him, the bunkering they put in for Carnoustie two years ago was the best example of a traditional course keeping in step with the modern game.

Though Faldo does not like what they are planning to do to Augusta, he believes that things are turning the corner. 'There are boffins who understand what they are doing and everything points to the fact that the length which a man can hit a golf ball is reaching its maximum. I believe that there cannot be another leap such as there has been recently.' Was Faldo not among those who were saying as much two years ago? Apparently not.

Meanwhile, there was a teenager at Augusta at the weekend who, had he committed armed robbery, could not have done more to fall foul of his family. The family have had two tickets for the Masters going back 70 years but on Saturday all that came to an end when the young man and his friend took to the course with a bottle of liquor. The pair were sent packing, but only after the badges had been cut in half and the numbers logged.

---

17 JULY 2003

PLAYERS' STANDARDS ENJOY A KNOCK ON FROM WOODS

OPPONENTS HAVE BEEN QUICK TO LEARN FROM THE MAN AT THE TOP

Butch Harmon

Tiger Woods may not hold any of the four majors at the moment, but he has a lot to do with the lofty levels at which the game is being played. With the exception of Phil Mickelson, who remains far too aggressive for his own good, the rest have been quick to learn from Tiger, and they've learnt well

They have noted how he has worked on every aspect of his game, including his fitness, and they have seen his power and the way he manages it. Even when he is enjoying a spell when swing and body are perfectly synchronised, he seldom hits more than the occasional shot flat out. Mostly he is trying to play well within himself, weighing up each shot with the next in mind.

That, of course, was why he was so mad with himself in the last round of the Masters, when he hit into the trees from the third tee and had the double bogey which ruined his chances. He used his driver when he knew that he should have turned that club down in favour of a three iron. As he said afterwards, it was a mental mistake and he doesn't make mental errors.

Jim Furyk, who played so determinedly and so well to win the US Open at Olympia Fields, is just one who would seem to have picked up some of Tiger's best traits. He stopped trying to do the impossible and concentrated on consistency above aggression. Nick Price is another. Players like Price and Furyk know that if they do not do everything to the best of their ability, they are going to lose out every time to the longer, stronger brigade who, thanks to the Tiger influence, are themselves more canny rather than less.

Royal St George's, with its mammoth bunkers and occasional blind shots, could come as something of a shock to the latest generation. Tiger has been preparing by looking at videos of old Opens over the course – as, I hope, has Adam Scott, who I also coach. Greg Norman's win in 1993 provides just about as good a crash course in how to play the links as you can get. Greg and I had been working together since 1991. We had steadied his right foot and shortened his backswing and, going into that Open, he was controlling the ball as well as he had ever done. He ended up with four rounds in the 60s, with his last round a 64 in which he hit everything as intended.

The kind of thing Tiger and Adam will have been studying is the route Norman took that day and how the ball reacted in a given area. Theory apart, Tiger has been working on his repertoire of links shots, with his determination sharpened by what happened last year at Muirfield when, as the winds and rain took hold on the Saturday, he was blown to an 81.

Everyone has been harping on about Tiger not having a major at the moment and, yes, it is unusual for him. But he has not had a bad year. You can hardly accuse him of that when he has won four times in ten outings. What his current situation tells me, above all else, is that Tiger is mortal and that golf is golf. Everyone experiences problems at certain stages of their career. Just look at Jack

Nicklaus. He had two three-year breaks in which he made no additions to his eventual haul of 18 majors. Even if we have not seen Tiger the golfer at his most commanding over the last four majors, we have had some interesting insights into Tiger the sportsman.

Great champions – and he truly is one of them – know how to handle defeat as well as victory.

-----

23 JULY 2003

WOODS LEFT BECALMED AFTER STORM OF HIS OWN SUCCESS

Paul Hayward

In the rush to anoint Tiger Woods as one of sport's all-time greats, one word was missed out. Longevity. Pelé, Muhammad Ali, Michael Jordan, Jack Nicklaus and Donald Bradman all had it. So did Pete Sampras. Michael Schumacher has it now. The greats go on driving the nail of their own talent into history until their opponents can bleed no more.

Woods has won none of the last five major championships. No hysteria should be read into that statement. It is a factual observation, and here's another: golf's four most coveted titles are now held by Jim Furyk (US Open), Mike Weir (Masters), Rich Beem (PGA) and Ben Curtis (Open), who on his first visit to these shores last week was shocked to find cars being driven on the left.

These are not lucky fools – especially Furyk, who was regarded by many Americans as the best player besides Phil Mickelson not to have won a major. But imagine how this looks to Woods, who began last season by winning the Masters and US Open before the mass share-out of silverware. For the world number one, each of those unexpected triumphs had a dark resonance. At the PGA,

Beem held him off to win by a single stroke. At Augusta, Woods had the dubious pleasure of handing the green jacket to Weir. When Furyk finally made his breakthrough he equalled the US Open scoring record – previously set by Woods. Cut to Royal St George's on Sunday: Woods creeps to two under par after seven holes but then stumbles through the last 11 three over par. Result, as Mr Micawber would have said: misery.

If next month's US PGA Championship falls to another Curtis or Weir, Woods will have completed his first fallow season in the majors since 1998. For consolation he can cling to the knowledge that he has won eight of the 27 majors he has contested, and has harvested $37 million (£23 million) in prize money alone since his pro debut in the 1996 Greater Milwaukee Open (earnings $2544).

The machine of his soul has its sights on Nicklaus's record of 18 major championships. If the pattern of the first seven years holds firm, Nicklaus will hand over the gong around 10 years from now, when Woods is 37. But will it hold? Are the future's flags already planted, or is Woods becoming a victim of his own precocity? At the majors, they give you a magnificent booklet headed *Tiger Woods – How He Did It*, the only problem with which is that it leaves you wondering how on earth he can keep doing it.

Here is a man who shot 48 for nine holes at age three, who appeared on the *Today Show* and *Good Morning America* at six, who was a scratch golfer by 13, who won three junior and three senior amateur championships between the ages of 15 and 20, and who won his first Masters – on his debut in the majors – by 12 strokes. So much has happened to him since then that you can forget what people were saying at Augusta back in 1997. They were proclaiming the end of golf as a competitive spectacle. The end of Augusta, too (Tiger-proofing solved that).

The idea that golf is too hard a game to be annexed by individual genius was running around with its slacks on fire. A terrible shadow of terminal disappointment and pessimism fell across the rest of the US Tour. Life, now, was the pursuit of silver;

evading humiliation became a full-time job. This was the mood, the tone, when Woods was attacking the old image of golf as a game that was resistant to conquest. Here we fall back on intuition. What can be said for sure about his final round at Sandwich is that it lacked aggression, dynamism, self-assurance, *joie de vivre*. Something was wrong. Something felt wrong. Maybe, inside, he is becalmed. There is a theory that he is playing far more conservatively these days, and that caution has become his enemy.

Those of us who walked round with him at the weekend would have emptied our wallets on him extending the momentum of those first seven holes. The back nine, with its humps, bumps and lumps, confounded him all week. Still within striking range of a play-off, he bogeyed 15 and 17. Ben Curtis, a debutant, too strong for Woods to catch? It jars in the head, even three days on. From this particular hillock it looks as if Woods has temporarily lost faith in his own pre-eminence.

The complaint about a rival player allegedly using 'illegal equipment' may just reflect anxiety about the speed with which his contemporaries are catching him. At Furyk's US Open, there were 83 rounds in the 60s – a tournament record, surpassing Baltusrol in 1993, where there were 76. Ernie Els was saying the other day that he was cured of 'Tiger-itis' by his victory at last year's Open at Muirfield. Four Sundays a year, the field set out with the knowledge that Woods has yet to come from behind on the final day to win a major championship.

The quickest way to get reclassified as an idiot (assuming it isn't too late) is to predict terminal decline for a mighty 27 year old on the flimsy basis of a single quiet year. Woods, remember, has won four of his 12 tournaments this season. In 2002 he won two majors, was second to Beem in the PGA and seized five other titles. On Sunday he was two strokes from hauling Curtis into the maelstrom of a play-off. Maybe that's the point. The 'first serious mental lapse in a final round' that some American commentators diagnosed in the Weir–Woods struggle for this year's Masters has been followed by a second: this one in an event where Woods is increasingly disconcerted. 'I think sometimes the media loses perspective on how tough it is to win a major,' he argued last year. But it was his own precocious talent that first refracted the light. On Sunday, it just felt as if he had entered the next great phase of his career: the age of struggle. Watch now, while he goes out and wins the PGA.

———

18 JULY 2005

MASTER LEAVES HIS RIVALS IN THE DARK

COURSE SUBMITTED TO HIM WITH EACH SWING AND EVERY
STEP: RESISTANCE WAS FUTILE

Paul Hayward

A twinkle of electric bulbs in the old clubhouse greeted Tiger Woods at the end of his long walk back to dominance, but for all the world's other leading golfers the lights are going out. The pause in his reign as the nonpareil of golf is over. This year in major tournaments, the conqueror of St Andrews has won the Masters, finished runner-up in the US Open and repeated his triumph of five years ago over the Old Course. Men who were emboldened by the lull in the storm, in 2003–04, will now be looking for a new rock to crawl under. Sensing the return of his trophy-hogging tyranny here yesterday, most of his major rivals went down without a fight.

Though his winning margin of five strokes was three fewer than five years ago, Woods has his boot back on the head of this most intricate and sadistic of sports. Walking with him on the back nine holes, it was as if time had launched us back to the summer of 2000, when his victory in the US Open heralded a clean sweep of major titles, completed, the following season, at Augusta, where he was able to plant all four trophies on his coffee table.

As he drove the ball some 330 yards to birdie the 12th and take a three-stroke lead over Colin Montgomerie, the crushed local hero who ended as he began (nine under par), you could feel the old power retaking a generation by the throat. The old hegemony. On the game's most evocative stage, golf was again condensing itself into Woods against the rest.

Only if you resent domineering skill and devotion to the task will your spirits sag at what Woods did to his profession here. Sure, the average television viewer was entitled to hope for a more protracted battle on these Scottish links. But what made yesterday's pageant so interesting was the sense that Woods is now entering the second great phase of his career.

As he coasted into double figures – two Opens, four Masters titles, two US Opens and two PGA Championships – immaculate choreography took Woods into the void left by Jack Nicklaus, who departed the stage on Friday clinging to his record of 18 major crowns. At 29, the greatest golfer of the last eight years is now more than halfway there. Ten down, nine to go, if he is to put Nicklaus in history's shade.

Not that the Tiger is showing his fangs when faced by the Golden Bear's legacy to the game. In his acceptance speech, by the 18th green, Woods reminded his audience that 'the greatest champion that ever lived walked down that fairway on Friday – Mr Jack Nicklaus'. It's hard to remember an era in sport passing so obviously into a new one. The same patch of grass, the same appreciative crowd, the same traditions of dignity and respect protecting the game from the endless encroachments of greed and money.

Really, it was obvious on Thursday evening that Woods knew he would win this tournament. It was apparent in his eyes. Interestingly, he got worse (or at least, less good) as the days wore on, shooting 66, 67 and 71 before resuming normal service with a two-under-par 70 on his final round.

Any remaining doubts were dispelled on the tenth, a 380-yard par four hole he had reached from the tee on a previous round. This time, he dropped his first shot of the day, not with a grimace but with a comedy routine. As he stepped forward to tap in, he pretended his knees were knocking and pulled a dazzling grin. Since when, one wondered, did Eldrick Tiger Woods turn a bogey into slapstick? By the time he teed off at the 11th, Monty was only a shot behind, but Woods strode on with unshakable authority, riding the wind at the 12th and attacking the green with ruthless conviction.

This was the hole where he had broken David Duval five years before, and now it was Montgomerie's turn to be destroyed from afar. The balloon of public expectation deflated. Electricity no longer coursed along the fairway ropes. From here in, we would be observing a master at work. By the time he reached the 14th green, Woods was leaning on his putter like a club golfer. The course was submitting to him with each swing and every step. Resistance was futile. Spectators bustled along to embellish the tale they would tell their families: 'I saw Tiger Woods win the Open, St Andrews, while golf was still packing away its memories of Jack.'

The 18th green was a scene of veneration, not excitement, because Woods was striding into an already conquered city. His penultimate putt rolled through the 'Valley of Sin', an appropriate metaphor for the recent course of his career: down, and then up, to an impregnable position at the summit of his trade. His celebration was modest: two arms raised, a smile, and an especially grateful hug for his caddie, Steve Williams, who then made off with the flag. Even Woods, perhaps, felt the inevitability of victory so keenly that the emotions were slow to flow.

Unless some malign fate knocks the new Open champion off course, it seems inconceivable that Nicklaus's record will survive. The Bear was 46 when he caught his last big fish. If we adopt that age criterion, Woods has 17 years in which to seize nine titles. By reconstructing his game in 2003–04, he surrendered his hold on power, losing his spot as world number one to Vijay Singh. Even the greatest champions can succumb to an urge to regroup. If anything, Woods was a victim of his own restlessness.

The last three Open winners have been Ben Curtis, Todd Hamilton and Tiger Woods – and most of us know which triumph we enjoyed most. To see genius at work is not always a pleasure but it's invariably a privilege. The trick is to lock the gaze on the majesty – even when it lacks the context of a real test. While the opposition sinks into darkness, our internal lights go on.

———

24 JULY 2006

RELENTLESS TIGER GIVES HOYLAKE HIS MIND, BODY AND SOUL

Mark Nicholas

Hoylake

Seventy-one years ago, Gene Sarazen sensationally forced his way into the play-off that led to his only US Masters title when he holed his four wood second shot at the ultimate risk-and-reward hole in golf, the 15th at Augusta National. It became known as 'the shot that was heard round the world' and a plaque celebrating this moment of brilliance is there to this day.

Perhaps the exquisitely engineered four iron that gave Tiger Woods his eagle at the 14th hole at Hoylake on Friday will one day have such status but more likely, from his opponents' point of view, the eagle Woods constructed with such chilling certainty at the 18th early on Thursday evening will have been the play that sent shivers all around the Wirral.

Just a two iron, a four iron and a putt to render 560 yards of parched dog leg terrain utterly defenceless and a field of 149 other competitors utterly dumbstruck – good night everybody, and good luck. Tiger had played OK but not one-shot-off-the-lead OK. If you were Graeme McDowell, whose 66 led the field, you could rightly feel put out that your very best deserved better than a show-stealer from a bloke whose mind had been elsewhere for much of the year. But this was Tiger's way of telling us that his broken heart was mending. That the grieving for his father was now a motivation, that the journey to honour Earl's memory with the Claret Jug had begun. The inevitability of it was alarming – the precise iron from the tee, the towering iron from the burnt fairway, the pure 20-footer that hit the hole dead centre. Over the television replay, as the Nike swoosh fell from view, Peter Allis said: 'Not fair, is it?'

Unsurprisingly, huge snaking crowds had followed Woods from the off, a human caravan of worship living each moment as if it were their own. And there is so much to see. He is not as big as you think, not alongside Nick Faldo or Ernie Els, and not as long as you think, not with two irons and three woods anyway. His looks are startling, the merge of Asian mother and Afro-American father, and dominated by that strong, gleaming smile which emerges just enough to remind us it is there. When he scowls, boy turns to man, and the sense of a world against him prevails.

You wonder what he thinks as he stands apart, waiting for the others to play. Does he really think Nick is a pain? Is Ernie a genuine threat or, truly, too gentle a giant? Is Sergio Garcia an upstart, an irritant, or can he inherit the earth? Or could Tiger not care less? Does he live alone on the course, in a world without reference?

Then you watch him swing. The ideal, orthodox set-up at address and the way in which the club rests in his hands to appear an extension of his arms. Then the stillness as it is taken away in a wide and beautiful arc before returning to the ball so dramatically, so thrillingly that gasps are drawn from those close enough to appreciate the combination of power and precision at impact. In the execution of long shots, there is the tiniest dip of the head in that downswing, before the long right arm takes over in the follow-through and the hands are thrown at the target and on to their high finish where perfect balance presides over all else. This is the most athletic golf of all. Not so fluent or downright dashing as Seve Ballesteros, 20, 30 years ago, and certainly not as easy as Els, definitely the Big Easy, but modern, exciting and irresistible.

With it all comes the mind, the bit that matters most. Without quite leaving his heart on our sleeves, Woods lets us into his emotion, encouraging us to share those smiles and scowls and join in the roars and remonstrations. Thus he turns us, unwittingly, against his challengers, for we feel that trip upon which he takes us is like no other. It is a kind of bullying and, as it dawns on us that we have become addicted, we begin to understand why the power of his personality overcomes so many of his opponents.

Woods eagled the 18th late on that first day with his mind every bit as much as with his talent. It was his marker; his first move in the long psychological struggle that was to follow and it scared the life out of the lot of them. He was back and wasn't going anywhere, certainly not down the road of self-pity and loss that overwhelmed him at Winged Foot.

Now all he had to do was find that wretched A game they all hate so much, and the serenity that comes from it, which, of course, he did on Friday, before putting so ordinarily on Saturday that Els really should have forged past him. Three three-putts on Saturday! We couldn't believe our hay-fevered eyes as we jostled for position on knobbled humps and in bare hollows, peering through the last vestiges of wisped grass that was once rough and had turned to tinder. Oh Ernie, you had your chance.

Was the fact that Tiger had played so little golf these past months starting to roost or was there a crack in the ice after a decade of nailing the sort of three, four and five-footers that wear most men down? Would the long irons that come from the shorter tee shots lead to the long putts that are so hard to judge on the inconsistently patched greens? For sure he loves the links in this, their purest form, but his plan to conquer them depended on that putter.

And depend on it he could.

Has their ever been such single-mindedness with a putter? The zone into which he takes himself is rarely achieved by the masses who play sport all over the planet. When they find it, they, too, become special but only for a day, an hour, a minute. For Woods it is routine, an extraordinary height of senses and touch that respond to the ferocity of his concentration. He will not be moved, turned or distracted. Witness that amazing business when he stops the making of a shot in the downswing. That tells us all. Yesterday afternoon he merely confirmed his greatness and endorsed the warning he gave on Thursday evening.

Magnificently as the course itself responded to the challenge of hosting the Open, Hoylake's mainly flat terrain made it darned difficult to see as much as one would hope for the ticket price. Fifty thousand people per day may be a trophy but it is not a practicality in this environment and from outside the ropes. You had to really know your Ordnance Survey to get a glimpse or two of Woods, and even Ballesteros, David Duval and Adam Scott were hard to make out in their various matches. The Open is very big business and should be staged at a very big venue. If not, the numbers have to be tailored for the space, otherwise the suspicion of a fleecing persists with many of the fans, old and new, who make the pilgrimage.

———

CHAPTER 4
MAJOR MUSINGS

---

7 AUGUST 1993

'WRINKLY' STILL DETERMINED TO CALL SHOTS ON LIFE'S BACK NINE

AGE PROVES NO BARRIER FOR GOLF'S ELDER STATESMEN

Michael Parkinson

Sunningdale

Standing on the first tee at Sunningdale, Tommy Horton acknowledged the polite applause with a typical touch of his white hat and said: 'I brought the wife along to clap just in case no one turned up.' This was the first day of the Forte PGA Seniors' Championship. The three-ball teeing off at 9:30 a.m. had sunk a few putts in their time.

There was Horton, a rookie senior, clearly enjoying his new lease of life; Neil Coles, inscrutable of countenance, elegant of swing; and Peter Thomson, a man who won the Open five times and therefore carries with him that special aura of a sporting legend. I had come to interview Mr Thomson, who was making one of his rare appearances on an English golf course. When was he last at Sunningdale?

'Well, it's so long ago that this was a heathland course,' he said. What is it now, I inquired? 'A forest,' he said. I should explain that Mr Thomson had just shot 76 and was not best pleased.

But let's go back to the beginning of the day. We assembled in the morning sun. A love of golf apart, both competitors and spectators had one other common denominator: we were all aged fifty-plus. Even one or two of the caddies were using battery-operated trolleys. It was like a convention of wrinklies or a golf trip organised by Saga Holidays. The genius of golf is that it thumbs its nose at age. It allows men like Horton, Thomson and Coles to compete with real skill and purpose, far beyond the time when participants in every other sport are past their sell-by date.

Moreover it encourages those not blessed with their skill to pursue a dream of breaking 80 before they die. In any other sport the purchase of a new set of equipment after the age of 50 would be classified as a vainglorious gesture; in the case of golf it represents a sensible investment in the future.

So for those of us who now see that the back nine of life might have more to offer than we had at first been led to believe, Sunningdale was a good place to be. The Old Course at Sunningdale is my idea of perfection. Every hole poses a different problem and reveals another breathtaking vista. A mature setting suited to our mellow entourage.

It was the first course Peter Thomson played when he arrived in England from Australia in 1951. It has remained a favourite ever since. Thomson was one of the players who provided the foundation of the modern multi-million dollar industry called golf. He won a hat-trick of Opens in '54, '55 and '56. The following year he finished runner-up to Bobby Locke. In 1958 he won it again.

The critics said these victories didn't count for much because the great Americans were not competing at the time. In 1963 he answered them by winning at Royal Birkdale in a field containing all the top Americans, including Tony Lema, the holder, Arnold Palmer and Jack Nicklaus. When he joined the American senior tour as he turned 50, he won 11 tournaments in 13 months. He was a pioneer of the Asian tour, a pithy commentator, a journalist and erstwhile politician. He is one of those nuggety Australians who only speak when they have something useful to say and who observe the world through crinkled and shrewd eyes. Nowadays he builds golf courses, with 20 projects on the go including a new course at St Andrews. 'A great honour,' he says.

He was and is a maverick, a man set apart by his ruthless ambition to succeed. It made him successful but it didn't win him many charm contests. Gary Player wrote of him: '. . . he was aloof and could be very sarcastic at times. It always seemed to me that he wanted to reveal his superiority and knowledge to people.'

One incident particularly narked Player. The South African took 29 hours of air travel to get from France to Melbourne but in spite of the delays got off the plane, went on the course and won what he thought was the most amazing triumph of his career. Thomson remarked: 'What's so amazing about that? You were sitting down and resting all the time in the plane, weren't you?'

Judged by our talk, I wouldn't say that Peter Thomson has allowed old age to soften him. Physically he is much the same. Broad shoulders, narrow hips, slight fold at the belly but not too much to worry about. He's 63 and looks ten years younger. He has started writing his life story. He didn't bother during the years when he was a superstar golfer, the time when he might have cashed in on his life story. Why didn't he write it then? 'I've not grown up until recently,' he said. Similarly when, after winning his third Open title, he was asked to write a golf instruction book he declined.

Why? 'Because I didn't think I knew enough. Still don't.' Starting his autobiography has meant asking questions about himself and what happened. Cricket was his first love. He wanted to be a leg-spin bowler like Shane Warne. His mother went to an aunt who read the tea leaves. She saw the young Thomson standing triumphant in a green field. She said he would be famous throughout the world. Mrs Thomson took this to mean that her son would captain the Australia cricket team. She didn't tell him in case it turned his head. She finally told him about his aunt's prediction when he was 50.

He came to golf by chance. 'I had bandy legs. My mother was told by doctors to put my legs in irons. She thought this was pretty radical. She took me to a physiotherapist. In those days they were treated like witch doctors. He told her that what I needed was long walks. I used to go with my uncle and his dogs and walk the golf course. It started from that. I didn't have any heroes. The men were at war, there was no one to learn from. I just picked the game up myself. I've never had a lesson, no one taught me how. I have a suspicion about the coaching that goes on nowadays. I think it ruins young players. You have to be self-reliant to play golf well. That's the key to it; you have to do things for yourself.

'I went to America when I was 21 and saw Sam Snead and Ben Hogan play. I learned more by watching them and players like Bobby Locke than any coach could possibly have taught me. I wanted to be like Hogan. He played like a machine. He would go a whole round without hitting one bad shot. The rest were slapdash by comparison. I set my sights up there. When I came to England the difference between myself and people like Dai Rees and others was that they were club pros and relied on what they made at the clubs for a living. I had nothing. I had to win tournaments to pay the rent. It instils in you a powerful need to win.'

For winning an average tournament he was paid £300. Winning the Open earned him £750. When he totted up at the end of a successful season he would have made about £3000. Nonetheless, he doesn't moan about the money in modern golf.

'Let the golfers have it. Otherwise who takes it? The agents, those people on the edge of the game. They're not important. I don't think I was born too soon. I won enough to live comfortably, I've made enough to spend what I want and know there's more where that came from. Money isn't everything. When someone says that you can be sure they have plenty,' he said with a rare smile.

The changes in the game? 'Golf courses. Some designers have a terrible ego problem. They design courses for Open championships, courses that would be tough for the likes of Faldo and Norman. They think of themselves as being wimpish if someone goes round their course in 64 or so. The great art of designing is to make the course suitable to all kinds of golfer.

'Coaching has become big business. I count myself lucky that I received no coaching. Children should be left to their own devices. In Australia we have the Institute for Sport. There are 500 coaches, it costs AS$36 million a year. That money should go into grassroots sport providing facilities at schools. I'm against spending money to create a sporting elite.

'I think the biggest difference in golf in my time has been the change in the golf ball. The larger ball has made it much easier to play and taken some of the subtlety out of the game. It's bigger and heavier and it doesn't move in the wind like the small ball used to. My suggestion would be to make the ball a couple of pennyweights lighter and then we'll see a difference,' he said.

Gary Player called Peter Thomson 'the best I have ever seen with the small ball on a links course'. Thomson's record gives him an unchallenged place in the pantheon. He remains unconvinced about something as fanciful as his own legendary status. He is keen to get back to his book, finding the voyage of discovery 'very therapeutic'. What would he call it? 'Oh, I haven't really thought about that,' he said.

'Nothing fancy,' he added. What a good title.

———

12 SEPTEMBER 1997

BALLESTEROS GOES DOWN ON HIS KNEES FOR INSPIRATION

RYDER CUP CAPTAIN SHARES LEAD AFTER SHOWING FLASHES OF HIS FORMER BRILLIANCE

Martin Johnson

Just when we feared that the amnesia might be permanent, Severiano Ballesteros took us back down memory lane with yesterday's opening round in the Lancome Trophy. No one who has witnessed the Spaniard struggling to hit a barn door over the past couple of years will feel anything but relieved for him, though it's probably safe to predict that his six-under-par 65 was not followed by a message of congratulation from Miguel Martin.

If Europe's Ryder Cup captain is in any way bothered by the palaver surrounding Martin's exclusion from Valderrama, he kept it well hidden yesterday — and the only thing that might be worrying him this morning is whether he's packed enough shirts for the weekend. It's a rare Friday night when Mrs Ballesteros does not have her ear cocked for the old man's car coming down the drive, and it would have been a touching act of faith to call up the Ceefax yesterday afternoon and not send for the TV repair man.

Ballesteros was playing with two of his Ryder Cup men in Jesper Parnevik and Darren Clarke, a getting-to-know-you process that is normally hindered by Seve wandering off to play most of his golf from places inhabited only by the local wildlife. Yesterday, though, Ballesteros rarely strayed from the short grass, and on the one occasion he did, produced the kind of sorcery that established his reputation as the best player out of car parks in golfing history.

Seve was still smouldering quietly after his first and only bogey at the par four fifth (his 14th) and a slow play warning, which he parried by pointing out that they were not holding up the group behind. As the group behind contained Bernhard Langer, he would have had to have been playing on his knees to hold them up, which is precisely what he did after hooking his drive underneath a pine tree at the par-five sixth.

Ballesteros pondered for a while on how best to play his ball . . . out of the rough, under the branches, with no backswing, a maximum elevation of two feet to prevent a sudden-death rebound, and a sharp right-to-left trajectory required to locate an invisible green 190 yards away. Why it took him so long to come to the same conclusion that any of us would have arrived at is hard to say, but he finally sank to his knees, addressed the ball with the heel of a four-wood, and thrashed a low, swinging hook to within ten yards of the putting surface. There are not many times when people have their breath literally taken away, but for those who saw the shot yesterday, this was one of them.

Seve being Seve, he then duffed his chip, and Seve being Seve, he then holed from 15 feet for a birdie. Had he ever played a shot on his knees before?, he was asked. 'Sure,' he said, 'I practise it all the time,' which is probably a wise move when you're 97 over par for the year, have a third-best finish of tied for 70th in 16 starts, and finished more than £300,000 short of the last automatic qualifying place for the Ryder Cup.

When he was at the height of his powers, Ballesteros once played an entire round of golf on his knees, against the owner of the course at La Manga. He also gave his opponent a stroke a hole, and won by a street. When you can do this sort of thing, and have a temperament capable of making Krakatoa sound like a car backfiring, suddenly being unable to play at all does not come easily. When someone asked him whether he ever went home and kicked the dog, he smiled and shook his head — though any dog of Seve's would quickly learn to make itself scarce when it heard the master putting his key in the door.

That improbable birdie was the first of four consecutive ones to finish with, and his golf at long last lit up the old Ballesteros smile. 'Very few times I have fun in the last two years, but today I felt very much like the old days.' The old days must be stacked with memories of amazing recovery shots, but even Seve could recall only two better than this in his entire career.

He was eight shots better than either of his playing partners, and though a little bit of Ballesteros rubbed off on Clarke, unfortunately for the Ulsterman it was a bit of the early season model. Clarke blocked his final drive into the trees bordering the tee and he had to hit out down the first fairway. He then had to wait so long for the fairway to clear that both Ballesteros and Parnevik had long since arrived on the green, and had no idea where he had got to until a marshall warned them that Clarke was still playing the hole. Finally, en route to a triple-bogey seven, Clarke clambered on to the green and apologised for holding everyone up. 'It's okay,' said Ballesteros. 'I've been there before.'

———

21 JULY 1998

THE WEEK THAT CHANGED MY LIFE

FROM THE PRACTICE ROUND OF MY DREAMS TO MY UNREAL
FINAL SHOT AS AN AMATEUR: MY OPEN DIARY

Justin Rose

Sunday

Eleven twenty-five tee-off time at Hillside for Open qualifying. For the first time in days I was feeling better following a bout of flu during the World Invitational at Loch Lomond. The wind seemed more robust, too. Much stronger than when I practised yesterday. Played with Ross Drummond, who encouraged me all the way; I returned a 74 in which I got my act together over the last three holes, finishing par, eagle, birdie. There were two shots good enough to get as far as the supper table at our Italian restaurant – my three wood at the 17th, all 380 yards of it, and my drive down the 18th, 400 yards.

After a slow dinner in which the waiters, had they been golfers, would have been put on the stopwatch, we returned to Avondale Road North where my dad and I had managed to get a room in the Edendale Hotel. My mum and my sister, Margs, ended up in an attic bedroom in the Victorian Hotel on the other side of the road. Apparently, it was just about the last room left in Southport. I went to bed at ten o'clock – my usual time when I'm playing in tournaments. Dozed off feeling pretty good about things.

Monday

A 7:55 starting time today. Bursting with health, at least until I started dropping shots. By the turn, I was as many as five over par and conscious of the fact that I might struggle to qualify. Luckily, things turned out all right and I was back in four under for a 72. It was good enough to have me leading for most of the day. Thomas Levet eventually came in with a 145 aggregate to my 146.

I was whacked but thrilled to have qualified. Knowing that I was going to be turning professional after the Open, I was keen to make the most of my last week as an amateur.

Tuesday

A great day. I felt a shade apprehensive as I arrived for my first practice round at Royal Birkdale but things got better all the time. Lots of people came up and congratulated me on getting through qualifying and I started to feel that I belonged.

I practised with David Carter, who is with Carnegie, who will be my management team. We had a relaxed round, one in which we both put in a lot of reconnaissance work without keeping score. Afterwards, we were on the practice ground when David Leadbetter, who is going to be keeping half an eye on me, turned up with Nick Faldo. He came across and asked if I'd like to practise with Nick, Ernie Els and Mark McNulty the next day. My jaw fell open but I managed a nod.

I happened to have seen my starting time for Thursday by this time and I was worrying about it being so late – 4:05 – when Dad came up and asked if I knew when I was out. I told him and, typically, he said: 'That's brilliant . . . the wind will all have blown through by then.' He's a bit of an amateur psychologist, my dad. What he said was positive. It was the right way to look at it.

David Leadbetter overheard and joined in the conversation. He told us how Nick plays it when he has a late starting time. He gets up at the normal time and has breakfast before going up to the golf club to do a bit of chipping and putting. He then returns to his accommodation and watches TV, or whatever, before returning to the course a couple of hours before his starting time. Then he goes through his usual practice routine.

Wednesday

The practice round of my dreams. Nick didn't chat but it was fascinating to watch him at work. He's like someone preparing for an exam and no one would want to interrupt his train of thought. Ernie, on the other hand, is laid back and seemed to want to talk. As for Mark McNulty, he was brilliant in sharing this, that and the next thing about how to play the course.

It was a thoroughly worthwhile day. At the end of it, Dad, Mum, Margs and I went to McDonald's for supper. Funnily enough, we weren't joined by the other members of my four . . .

Since the Edendale and Victorian hotels have had to give our rooms to people who booked long before we did, we had to move.

Phil and May Marron, a lovely retired couple who had heard of our plight, made us welcome in their home. We are going to stay there for the rest of the week.

Thursday

The Nick Faldo tips worked well. I followed the advice to the letter and felt great. I felt even better when, shortly before I headed for the practice ground, I put on a brand new set of waterproofs – straight out of the wrapping – and found a fiver in the pocket. I wasn't about to hand it over to the amateur status people.

When I got to the range, professionals from all over the world came up to wish me good luck. That meant a lot. I hadn't expected such kindness from everybody in the professional environment. Thanks to David Leadbetter, I didn't feel rushed when I finally got to the first tee and the starter called my name. What a moment. A bit of me was scared stiff and the rest of me was loving it.

As everyone knows, the wind was horrific, but I had lots of encouragement from family and friends and managed to grind out a 72. On such a day, it was more than satisfying.

Friday

A normal, 11:25 tee-off time. I dropped a shot at the third, where I hit a two iron and a sand-wedge to six feet, only to take three putts. However, I made up for it with a birdie at the next. At that, I was away. Things started to happen and, at the end, I finished eagle, birdie for a 66 which had me summoned to the press room.

Someone asked if I had ever thought I could be just one shot off the lead at this stage of the championship. 'Definitely not,' I told them. 'My aim was to come out here today, to have a good round and to make the cut.' I admitted that, in the circumstances, it was the best round I had played.

I was also asked if I could explain how I'd played so well in the conditions. My reply here was that I hadn't been worrying too much about them. I had thought clearly, hit the shots I wanted to hit and holed the putts at the end of it.

Then they wanted to know who were my heroes. Ernie Els and Nick Price, I told them. I said that I loved Els's easy swing and his attitude and that I'd always admired Price for his fighting spirit and for the fact that he gives everybody his time.

Went out for dinner with the Carnegie people. This time, it was Le Frog rather than McDonald's and I chose Steak Rossini. I would like to think I could afford a few more of those when I'm a professional. It was fantastic. Still in bed by ten.

Saturday

The feeling I woke up with was one of not knowing quite what had hit me. The morning papers arrived. I saw a few pictures of myself but decided not to look any further. Thought it better to block out the attention and to let my family look instead.

We embarked on the Leadbetter/Faldo routine but this time it didn't go quite according to plan in that there were thousands more people milling about the place. For instance, after I had finished practising and was trying to walk smartly towards the tee, I found myself ensnared in the Tiger Woods gallery.

I dropped a shot at the first through taking three putts from the front edge but settled down at the second when I made a seven-footer to escape with nothing worse than a bogey. The wind was hostile but the people were wonderful. I got an ovation up every hole. It was incredible. People were shouting my name and that pushed me on. Mind you, I think I became somewhat euphoric towards the end – so much so that I lost a bit of concentration. I finished with a five and a 75 but, bearing in mind the conditions, I think I hung on pretty well. Three shots off the lead.

Sunday

First thing in the morning, at a time when I was still asleep, my brother, Brandon, rang from South Africa. I rang back at ten and he told me that the general consensus of opinion out there was that I could win.

I allowed myself a little extra time today and it was on my 'second' arrival at the course that I bumped into Ernie Els on the putting green. He said: 'Justin, you can win. Go out and do it.' My twin aims, up until that point, had been to win the silver medal and to finish in the top 15 but, when Ernie said that, I began to look for rather more. Now, I had at least one eye on the impossible dream.

I dropped a shot at the first and was no better than 36 to the turn but, as I got into the round, so the crowd put me more and more at ease. I had birdies at the 12th and the 15th. Then, at the 18th, there was a touch of the unreal as I holed out from 50 yards or so for my three. That was my last shot in the amateur game and one I shall never forget until my dying day.

After that, everything, from the prize-giving to the press interview to all the television interviews, was a bit hazy, with one exception. As I walked from the recorder's hut to the press centre, I could hear some giggles behind me. Then, would you believe, someone pinched my backside.

The finger of suspicion would have to point to the girls of Greenbank High School who were working at the tournament. Hands up girls . . . I'd like to know who was to blame?

---

18 JULY 2000

HOW I LEARNT TO RELAX WITH SLAMMIN' SAM

Nick Faldo

The millennium Open at St Andrews: the year alone guarantees that whoever gets his name on the trophy this week is sure of a unique place in the history of golf's oldest championship. For Tiger Woods, barely a month after his 15 shot annihilation of the US Open field, the implications are even more significant. Victory over the Old Course would make him the youngest player, at 24, to clinch a career Grand Slam, a record held by Jack Nicklaus, who won all four majors by the time he was 26. Tiger will rightly start as the overwhelming favourite, though I doubt the Old Course will let him have things all his own way.

Traditional links golf conceals too many dangers and, no matter how well you strike the ball, good fortune plays a huge part. Blind tee-shots, huge double greens, extravagant slopes and terrifying bunkers – there are accidents just waiting to happen everywhere. When the wind blows – and I hope it will – St Andrews is not only a wonderful test of a player's strategy, but also a great leveller.

Tiger may have other ideas, but I don't see a runaway champion. It hardly seems plausible for me to admit to this, finishing some 20 shots adrift, but at Pebble Beach I began to sense that my game was getting back to something like the kind of form I can remember bringing to St Andrews in 1990, which remains probably the greatest ball-striking week of my life. That's why I have to believe that going into this Open, if everything clicks, I have a chance.

Confidence-wise, I know I still have a long way to go, but technically and physically I feel comfortable, and my putting is as good as it's been for a long time. Going into the US Open my goal was simply to get my name on the leaderboard, and to consolidate my position over the weekend. To finish seventh was a fantastic result. It was like the old days; I was working the ball into the green, seeing shots clearly and pulling them off without having to think about the mechanics of my swing. That's what I've missed. The last couple of years saw me get so bogged down with it all that mentally I have been unable just to go out there and play.

All that began to change in May, following an unforgettable weekend in the company of a man many believe possessed the most natural swing the game has ever seen. Personal curiosity aside, the official reason for my meeting with Sam Snead at the Greenbrier, in West Virginia, was to quiz him on how he managed to sustain his performance over six decades, for a proposed revision of my book, *A Swing for Life*. After all, if anyone on this planet can identify with the secrets of a golfer's longevity, surely it is him.

Slammin' Sam's career is littered with astonishing feats of scoring. He was the first to break 60 in an official tournament (a 59 at the Greenbrier, in 1959), he shot a round of 60 at the age of 71, and was the first man to beat his age on the US tour, shooting 66 when he was 67 at the Quad Cities Open. He has won more tournaments than anyone in history, his tally of 84 including eight majors – one of which, the 1946 Open, he won at St Andrews. Not bad when you consider that Snead's contemporaries included the likes of Gene Sarazen, Ben Hogan and Byron Nelson.

On the range, Sam pulled up a chair as I began to hit balls. I felt like a junior having his first lesson with the pro, strangely self-conscious about my swing. Starting with the basics, Snead's casual observations crystallised the fundamentals we (me included) habitually overcomplicate.

'I always said a player should grip the club the same way he would hold a bird in his hands – not so tight that you hurt it but just enough so it cannot fly away,' he said, and there was no stopping him. 'That keeps the arms loose, and means you can swing the club head. Get the butt-end of the club under the pad at the base of your left thumb – hold it firm with your pinkie.' I made that adjustment to my grip, and slightly narrowed my stance, as he had also suggested. As a result I found myself turning my body and swinging my arms more freely. 'You couldn't do that when your feet were wide,' Sam chimed, delighted at the simplicity of it all. 'When you get your feet too wide, your hips won't turn properly and that costs you speed and distance – little things like that are all you need to think about to play good golf.'

Theories I have spent a lifetime trying to understand were dealt short shrift. I asked him if he ever used to focus on the plane of his swing – something I have always been watchful of. 'Nope, never,' came his reply. 'A good swing is all about left-side control: you swing the left arm up, then pull it back down. That's all you need to think about. When the left side works properly, the right hand can hit it, and hit it hard.'

This was the advice of a born natural, a man who clearly played the game with a vision and feel that negated the need for specific thoughts or phrases to keep his mind and body in tune – a salutary lesson for all of us. There is no doubt in my mind that his words have helped me to rediscover the art of swinging the club. And when Snead tees it up in the Champions Parade tomorrow, which he will do as the oldest living Open champion, I'll wager he cracks one right down the middle.

———

2 APRIL 2001

OLD MASTERS IN PERFECTION

AUGUSTA NATIONAL REMINDS ME OF NOTHING LESS THAN
MOSES AND THE TEN COMMANDMENTS

Peter Alliss

Many years ago, even before Arnold Palmer was winning tournaments, a man called Moses came down from the mountains with a list of things called the 'Commandments' which would make us better people. However, do you think, when his work was done and he contemplated his magical list of ten, he wondered if he hadn't missed something out? Had he covered every eventuality?

The answer, obviously, was yes. He had. Although some of his ideals have fallen by the wayside, 'the boy did good'. I feel the same way about Augusta and I hope, without sounding too sacrilegious, my thoughts on the coming Masters run along similar lines. I can sense raised eyebrows. Let me explain.

Like Moses, I've covered everything. I've been visiting Augusta as a player, commentator, observer for years. Some people think my mode of transport for my first visit was a wagon train, but not so. Aeroplanes flew, even if they had things called propellers sticking out of the front, and had toilets inside.

You look at pictures from the late '50s of the golf course on 8mm film and it looks much the same – and yet everything is different. Now it's reminiscent of the Chelsea Flower Show: everything perfect. Then the grasses were coarse, but not now. Everything has been covered. It's extraordinary how Augusta, a private club with but a few hundred members, has become the scene of one of the world's great sporting events. There's no great back-up organisation other than a small committee and a golf course with a unique history. All this packed into less than 70 years, which perhaps typifies America, where there aren't many buildings over 70 years of age. It's just the way they are, you see.

To many people, the rules and regulations of Augusta are hard to follow. Pedantic, unbending, out of date, snobbish, elitist: it's been called all these and more. And yet, like the R&A, Augusta have made dramatic changes to how the event is run and the condition and, to a lesser degree, layout of the course. One of the club's greatest assets is that they are not, and never have been, afraid of change. That is not to say that all things that should be changed have – oh no, we must keep a little something up our sleeve. But I digress; back to Moses.

Once you've come down from your eyrie and made your A-list so complete you can't think of anything else, you're stuck, it's as simple as that. I confess, I'm stuck! What's new? Help! Augusta on occasions looks as if it's been in a time warp from the year before. The only differences? Sometimes the azaleas and wisteria, along with all the glorious bushes, shrubs and dogwoods, have come and gone, in which case a call to the local nursery is on the agenda. Colourful plants arrive and are placed in strategic positions round the course so no one would know that Mother Nature had passed this way several weeks before.

When Rae's Creek washed away a huge area in front of the 12th green and round the back of the 11th, not to mention the damage it did alongside the 13th, one wondered how they would be ready to play the event in just a handful of months. And yet they did, and – without altering the flow of water – they created different shapes, which has made it aesthetically better.

The number of changes made to the golf course over the last 40 years has been amazing and I think I know where most of them are – although I wouldn't bet on it. It is being constantly tweaked, a bunker enlarged here, one taken away there, a tee moved back 10 or 12 yards, an extension to a green, the removal of a hump, the placing of a hump, the smoothing out of a fairway, the sharpening of a bunker face, all things done with an idea of improvement, all done without visible signs.

I suppose the boldest step was when they changed the greens. They decided that the old grass wouldn't do and, even though the climate is not conducive to delicate grasses, they decided to give it a go. Out came the experts with their plastic covers; they pegged them over the greens and then fired in gas, which killed the grass in the twinkling of an eye. Off it came and new materials were put in and, although in the first season the greens were a little 'thin', they were puttable. Since then they have become even better and faster, some would argue to the point of being ridiculous, but that's all part of the examination paper.

The shot into the par five 15th green is cruel; it makes the 17th green at Valderrama look almost sensible. The green is narrow; there's a bit of room beyond but, if you're too strong, it's very easy to go into the lake in front of the 16th tee. I've seen many a ball pitch four, five, six yards onto the green, but favouring the right hand side; for some inexplicable reason the ball takes that little bit of extra spin, starts to go sideways and then turns left, backwards – and starts its slow, inevitable journey to the water.

And the 12th, a par three, looks the simplest thing in the world. About three and a half acres of beautifully mown grass, a little stream, a raised green, a bunker, a bank and a few bushes at the back, a mere bagatelle, and yet what dramas we have seen here, and will again. It's at the heart of Amen Corner, running from the 11th to the 13th, which has reduced many a strong man to tears.

It's worth noting that since 1940 the Masters has been won 19 times by only five players: Faldo, Jimmy Demaret and Player three times; Palmer four; Nicklaus six. A host of others have won twice. It has been dominated by just a few players. You could say that about a number of events, but I don't think they appear to be as obvious as the records of the Masters. Tiger Woods' score of 270 in 1997 is the lowest total, but in 1965, 32 years prior, Jack Nicklaus was only one shot worse. One year later Nicklaus posted 288, the highest winning score. Figures can tell you anything and you can have an awful lot of fun diagnosing all the scoring feats that have gone on at Augusta.

So many things to look forward to, so many memories from the past, some amazing scoring feats, like the homeward nines of Gary Player and Jack Nicklaus in their victory years. Nicklaus, especially, in 1986, and Seve's demise.

But, for me, Tiger Woods' second nine holes in his first visit as a professional in 1997 is still the most remarkable. He arrived in a torrent of ballyhoo, he'd won everything as an amateur and now he was going to take the world by storm. Forty for the first nine; the wiseacres nodded: 'Well, there you are, it's just too much for the lad, what can you expect, but he may in time get into it.' What happened? He came home in 30, a round of 70, two under par, and then went on to beat the all-time record, finishing with a four-round total of 270. Extraordinary, perhaps all in all the best nine he's ever played.

Augusta is still one of the most spectator-friendly events you could possibly go to, although they have to abide by very strict rules. You can't bring your own ladders, food or booze into the course, and running is strictly taboo, but the price of food and beverages for such a huge event is ridiculously low, draw sheets are free and they don't have anything as vulgar as a programme, which could generate many millions of dollars a year (although the programmes they have on a couple of occasions produced are now real collectors' items). And – would you believe? – there are no advertising signs. Just think of the possible income if they changed their tack.

The BBC will be there once again bringing you an extra 30 minutes viewing on a couple of days, more than goes out on CBS in the United States. The club, for their own reasons, do not wish to have wall-to-wall television coverage of their event. It's just another of their quirky traits. We salute the way they do things, which may not always be to our liking, but then not all of Moses' ideas were met with acclamation, though they should have been.

———

25 OCTOBER 2002

WHEN THE HECKLING BECAME WAY OUT OF ORDER

Colin Montgomerie

The heckling I have faced in the United States cannot be divorced from the fact that I find it hard to keep my emotions to myself. Any heckling element in a crowd has always seemed to me an easy target, and that is why they come back for more, or at least have done until now.

It started in earnest on the Friday of the 1997 US Open at Congressional. David Pepper, who has been chairman of the R&A's rules committee and is currently chairman of the championship committee, was officiating in the match behind mine. He has a clear memory of three well-groomed but clearly intoxicated women in their early thirties swaying out of a hospitality tent after the rain delay. They homed in on my match and started to regale me with wolf whistles. Before too long, a few men joined in the fun, only their contribution was to yell abuse.

'Go home,' said one. 'Piss off,' said another. They were looking for a reaction from me and, before too long, they got it. 'Why don't you save that for the Ryder Cup,' I said, stupidly. When the heckling failed to subside, I made the further mistake of calling one of them a 'pillock'. I returned a 76. I had started to feel jet-lagged and fractious even before the hecklers had come into the picture, but there is no question that they did not do anything to help my fitful concentration.

It does not take much for things to ignite on the eve of a Ryder Cup, and on the occasion of the 1997 match at Valderrama I found myself involved in a wholly unexpected furore following an interview with two Scottish journalists. The journalists in question were Gordon Simpson, who now works for the European Tour, and John Huggan, then with the *Glasgow Herald.*

In what was a pretty comprehensive interview about all aspects of the match, they had asked me to run through the list of Americans. What did I think of their individual games going into the match? I had plenty of respect for the US players, but when it came to Brad Faxon I noted that this might be a tough time for him since he was in the throes of a divorce. When it came to Phil Mickelson, who can still be wayward but who is straighter off the tee now than he was then, I said he might be hitting all over the place. And then there was Tiger Woods. My feeling there was that the course might not suit him as well as it might suit others. Someone with his length and strength could find it a little fiddly.

In context, the quotes were pretty harmless, but by the time they had been plucked from the *Scotsman*'s website I was in deep trouble. CBS flashed up each remark in turn and somehow managed to convey that I had been running down the opposition as a whole. In the end I had to write letters of apology to the players concerned. They said they understood that my comments had been taken out of context and were fine about it. But, as you would expect, CBS and some of the tabloid papers were not going to let bygones be bygones in a hurry.

There were no problems in Spain but things had taken a definite turn for the worse by the time the press had given my remarks a fresh airing before the following year's US Open at the Olympic Club in San Francisco. To give just one instance, a local radio station man called Jim Rome had encouraged his listeners to come to the course to bait me. 'Enjoy your day,' he told them. In the wake of Rome's recommendations, the Friday was particularly bad, as I played alongside David Duval and Jim Furyk. 'It wasn't like it was a lot of people,' said Duval afterwards, 'but some of them were brutal. I mean, it's a little embarrassing because as an American you don't like seeing someone from another country treated that way. It was way out of line.'

It was at the 1999 Ryder Cup at Brookline that the heckling became nothing less than vitriolic. Paul Lawrie, who was playing alongside me in the fourballs and foursomes, could not believe some of the insults he was hearing. Previously, he wondered if it was all more mischievous than anything else. Now, he realised that the hecklers' only aim was to put me off.

The Sunday singles at that Ryder Cup were even more extreme. The trouble had its origins on the first tee where some of the American players started whipping up the crowds before they drove off. Payne Stewart, my opponent, was not among them. He was the perfect gentleman from the start and could not have done more to try to protect me from the afternoon's events.

To the irritation of the mob, I was three up after six holes though back to two by the time we arrived on the ninth tee. After Payne had hit, I teed up my ball and, for once, though it was never going to last, there was complete silence as I shaped to the ball. I managed to get as far as the top of my backswing when a man standing a couple of rows behind the tee could contain himself no longer. 'You ****,' he cried, with the key word so coarse and so alien to anything I had ever heard before on a golf course as to be unrepeatable. I stopped and had to re-address the shot. Prince Andrew (a keen golfer with whom I've become friendly over the years), my brother Douglas and Eimear all swooped on the culprit, an overweight fellow in shorts who was apparently reeking of beer. As the marshals helped to subdue him and led him away, I turned to the crowd and said, 'First to go. If anyone else says that, they'll go as well.' My legs were now shaking.

Payne, who had just won the US Open at Pinehurst, was brilliant. He knew that there was more than one troublemaker out there and, from that moment, he kept going into the crowd himself and saying to the security men, 'Get rid of him, him and him.' It sickened Payne only slightly less than it sickened my father. In Dad's eyes, it was as if the very game had been defiled. I looked for him after the incident but he had walked back to the clubhouse, his lifelong love of the game having taken an irreparable blow.

Years ago, David Feherty did me no favours when he christened me Mrs Doubtfire. David is a friend and a gifted commentator, but I hated the name and could not disguise that fact. Everywhere I went there would be a couple of people who would yell, 'Hey, Mrs Doubtfire!' from behind the ropes, perpetuating the label and making my blood boil. I complained to David's face at the end of the Brookline match because the goings-on of that day had revived the feeling that many of my problems in the States were down to him. The match was not long over when he and I bumped into each other in the team room. Though a former Ryder Cup player, he should not have been in there in the first place and, though I am not usually one to bother about such things, I said that either he would need to leave or I would. When he took no notice, Eimear and I left. David followed and asked: 'What's the problem?'

'What's the problem?' I repeated incredulously. I suggested that he should sit down in order that I could spell it out.

Eimear and I both proceeded to give him a piece of our minds, with both of us wanting to know why he should have made so much trouble for someone who had been a team-mate at the 1991 Ryder Cup at Kiawah Island. He accepted what we were saying, but only up to a point.

The atmosphere between us remained less than cordial until we came face to face at the 2000 PGA Championship at Valhalla. In one of those circumstances where someone has to say something, I spoke first. 'You have got a job to do and I've got a job to do,' I began. 'You hurt me a lot at Brookline but the time has come to put this behind us.' We shook hands, though the indifferent grunt that came with the handshake suggested that he did not care overmuch either way.

Though most of the players are agreed I have had more than my share of heckling, Butch Harmon was not wrong when he said that I hear more of what goes on around me than most: 'Rabbit Ears' is what he has called me. He points to Tiger Woods as the player from whom I should take my lead. Tiger, he says, has had to put up with 'all sorts' from the crowd.

I envy Tiger his putting stroke and not a few other aspects of his play, but, above all, I envy him his ability to turn the other cheek when people make their remarks. I have tried to be Tiger-like and was making little progress until I managed to get through the whole of that 2002 Players Championship without reneging on my good intentions. That was a start.

---

8 APRIL 2004

GREEN MONSTERS

MEN BEHIND THE MASTERS GO UNDERGROUND IN TOUGHEST TEST OF NERVES

Ken Brown

In my travels I've putted on bumpy greens, true greens, island greens, elevated greens, slow greens; learnt how to read greens; even been told to eat my greens. But there is nothing quite like the Augusta greens.

The Augusta National golf course designers Bobby Jones and Dr Alister Mackenzie were both ardent admirers of the Old Course at St Andrews and its boldly contoured putting greens. Greens similar are a distinctive feature of Augusta but with one important difference . . . the speed.

In April 1988 I arrived at Augusta a little apprehensive on a warm but breezy Thursday morning for my midday tee-off time with the 1967 Masters champion, American Gay Brewer Jnr. In his mid-fifties, Gay didn't exactly seem a junior, nor after playing the first two holes in silence did he leave me with any feelings of gaiety. There's nothing quite like a little drama on the greens to break the ice with a frosty playing partner, and things began to thaw on the third green.

My first putt from 25 feet down a pronounced slope dribbled three feet past without even threatening the hole. Addressing the return putt, the line was left edge of the cup, it needed to be struck firmly so as not to break too much. I focused my mind. 'Trust your stroke, don't second-guess the line, keep your head still, and remember from three feet and under you hole 98.5 per cent.' I did all this, only to see the ball go in the left edge, disappear momentarily, then horseshoe round the back of the hole out the right side and start rolling slowly back towards my feet. Eventually the ball stopped when gravity came to the rescue and pulled it into an old pitch mark, leaving me the same putt to try again.

'Kiss mi grits! I ain't seen nothin' like that before,' mumbled Gay. And Gay had seen a thing or two before.

The Augusta officials are coy about just how fast the greens are and although they do vary from day to day, Augusta guarantee that all the green speeds are identical. Such a promise is made possible by heating and humidifying systems laid underneath each green that can help control their speed and texture. In recent years Augusta have developed new cultivars of grass that are more tolerant to very short cutting. Unlike most varieties of grass which, when cut close to the ground, go a sandy, fawn, quite frightening colour, the Augusta cultivars still look green, giving a psychological advantage.

Competitors arriving at Augusta, the first major, will be hoping that they are content with all their clubs, especially the putter. Putting is as much a mental as a physical skill and the right equipment is crucial to both. What suits one is often abhorrent to another. Big headed, face balanced, putters with two balls that help you line up, inserts that give different feels, heel-toe weighted with a bigger sweet spot and long shafted are just a few examples.

Confidence and belief in your choice is half the battle. Top professionals now have putters tailor-made with the lie, loft, weight, length and grip all just to their liking. Up until recently putters were adapted to suit by adding lead tape or bending the head; my old hickory shafted putter was treated like one of the family.

Choice of equipment is just the start. How are you going to arrange your hands on the grip? There's overlap, baseball, cross-handed, pencil, reverse overlap, split handed, claw or the saw grips. This week we will see many different styles. To putt well you need to have good nerves, confidence in your equipment, technique and in yourself. Without all these any weakness will be exposed. Mike Weir, last year's winner who hardly missed from inside 12 feet all week, looked as if he could have holed putts using a walking stick and an orange.

There is no place like the Augusta National in Masters week for showing that putting is an art and not a science. Whoever buttons up the Green Jacket this Sunday will be a Master of the Augusta greens.

---

18 JULY 2006

HEART OF A LION BEATS WITHIN TIGER

MY PERFECT GOLFER

Jack Nicklaus

Whatever you want to call it – mental strength, heart, competitive spirit – Tiger Woods has got it. In fact I think Tiger has got more of it than anyone else. He never gives up. When he has to get it done, he gets it done. It's obvious he is doing what he loves to do, which is competing against the best.

To be a winner you have to have heart. It's an individual sport – you are out there by yourself and you have everyone else coming at you. You really have to control your emotions and your golf game.

Billy Casper was wonderful at this. He won more than 50 times and does not get the credit he deserves. He didn't have all the shots that others had but he was able to will the ball into the hole. Perhaps his defining moment was beating Arnold Palmer at the 1966 US Open when he was seven behind with nine to play. Tony Jacklin, for a period of time, had a lot of competitive spirit. He won a British Open and then a US Open back to back and meant so much to the game in Europe.

You can't really play golf for someone else. It is all well and good saying you won a tournament for someone else later, but you have to be strong enough and tough enough and selfish enough to say: 'I've got to do this for myself. I've got to get this done for me.' One exception may be Ben Crenshaw winning the Masters in 1995 shortly after the death of his coach, Harvey Penick. But Ben had to be tough in himself and to be selfish enough within himself to say: 'I'm going to do this for Harvey.'

You have to be able to focus to get your own mind and your own body ready to do what you have to do. When it comes down to the end it is about how strong you are, how strong-willed you are, the faith you have in yourself. All those things, the confidence you have in yourself, come down to mental strength and the ability to finish a golf tournament and get the job done.

Nick Faldo had that mentality, but Tiger is a phenomenal person at grinding out what needs to be done. Was he born with that? Maybe, but he certainly had a wonderful teacher in his late father, Earl, who helped develop it into such a strong quality.

When I was growing up we played matchplay tournaments, so you learned to play in head-to-head situations. I enjoyed that – I thought it was great. When I went through most of my golf, I had Gary Player, I had Arnold Palmer, I had Lee Trevino. They won a lot and they never backed off, absolutely never.

Today it's a different game. Tiger learned how to win; he has been in those head to head situations. He won three consecutive US Amateur Championships, something no one else has done before or since. He is the toughest. Do you see him come down the stretch and fold? If he is leading on Sunday, he's going to win 99.9 per cent of the time because he has been there and learnt how to win. That's why it is so difficult for guys to challenge Tiger these days. They haven't had the experience of winning, and winning breeds winning. I had that: Trevino, Palmer and Player, all those guys had it. They had that head-to-head competition and that's why they were so tough coming down the stretch.

Only because I don't think Tiger has that competition today, I think Lee Trevino is the toughest I played against. He loved to beat me but I loved playing him because I knew he was going to be tough. I loved having great competition. The stronger the competition, the more fun it was.

One of the other things that tests a great player is the elements. I won some tournaments in poor weather but there were a lot of players better than me. Arnold Palmer was a very good player in the elements. Conditions at Birkdale were horrendous when Arnold won the Open there in 1961, and when Greg Norman won at Turnberry in 1986.

But most of my life I had trouble, especially when it got bad at the Open. I never saw Peter Thomson play, but to win as many Open championships as he did he had to be pretty good. Tom Watson, who also won five Opens, played so well in the wind, taking two or three clubs more and taking the spin off the ball. Spin is what makes the ball go right, left and up – what makes it go down is no spin. Tom played so well in so many different conditions that he would be my pick as the guy to battle the elements.

Perhaps the truest test of a player is whether you can rise to the greatest of occasions. When you are on the course you have to be able to concentrate at the right times and to think clearly at the right times. But it starts even before you get to an event: you have to be able to take your game with you and raise it up for the occasion.

Tiger has shown he can do this by winning all four majors in a row, but you have to go back to Bobby Jones. He was the ultimate big-occasion player. He won the original grand slam – the Opens and Amateur of the US and Britain – in 1930 but he didn't play very much. Even in 1930, his great year, he only played in six events and won five of them. That's pretty amazing.

---

13 DECEMBER 2006

NORMAN'S GENERATION USED MORE FINESSE

David Leadbetter

Driving

If you ever have the chance to watch film of Greg Norman in his heyday, make the most of it. Greg had a swing which was made for driving rather than iron play and he was unquestionably the best driver of a ball I ever saw. Apart from being long, he was relentlessly straight.

Greg studied Jack Nicklaus instructional books in his youth. Like Nicklaus, he had this big, wide arc, coupled with a big turn, high hands and a strong leg action. He stayed behind the ball well and he swept it away, using much the same club-head speed as Jack and hitting similarly towering shots.

When he first came to me in the late 1990s, things had gone a bit awry. His swing had become a little flat and his club was shut at the top. What we did was to study some of the old pictures and try to get him back to where he had been before. We never quite got there but we got close.

Greg was still using persimmon in those days and, although people find this difficult to believe, he hit the ball pretty much the same distance as the guys hit today. In fact, at 285 to 300 yards he would not have been middle of the road but up there with some of the longer ones. As for his straight hitting, that was down to his one-piece take-away and the fact that his hands hardly came into play.

Because persimmon was less forgiving than modern metal, the players of Greg's generation had to finesse the ball rather than hit it flat out. Today it is the other way about. With everything from clubs to balls so much more stable, the moderns can go at the ball 110 per cent.

If they are athletic, they can really use that athleticism to good advantage because the harder you hit, the more you benefit from the latest technology. Today's game is all about power. Take the following statistic from Vijay Singh: in 2005 Vijay hit fewer than 60 per cent of fairways yet he was number one in the 'greens hit in regulation' category on the US tour. To players like Vijay and Tiger Woods, it is more important to get close to the greens than to keep out of the rough. At club level, too, the harder hitter will get more out of his metal driver than his shorter hitting rival.

Yet there is one advantage which is the same for everyone. Namely, that it is not as important as it once was to hit the ball bang out of the middle of the club. You can hit it from one flank of the club face or the other and, although you will still get your hooks and slices, the great thing is that the ball is not going to curl as much as it did in the past.

Iron Play

Luke Donald is the man to watch if you want to learn a thing or two about iron play. Luke, who has won on both sides of the Atlantic, is not in any sense a power-hitter. Instead, his strength lies in a wonderfully repetitive swing allied to good tempo and balance. At the end of a shot, you will see him holding precisely the same finish every time. He knows – and you know – that the ball is heading for the target. In technical terms, Luke maintains that constant spine-angle which is so essential with iron play. Amateurs, in contrast, are apt to bob up and down as they try to lift the ball in the air and, when that happens, they have little or no chance of being in the optimum position to make a solid strike.

Throughout history, the greatest golfers of the day have tended to be the best iron players, with the key factor being how close they hit to the flag – the real strength of Jack Nicklaus' game. The player who hits shot after shot to ten feet is always going to have more single putts than someone who is 20 to 30 feet away all the time. Tiger is a superb example. When he won those six events in a row this summer, his iron shots were mostly pin high and leaving him with one short birdie putt after another. His control of distance and trajectory are nothing short of phenomenal.

Nick Faldo was the consummate iron player of his day. He maintained his posture through impact and was endlessly consistent. Both in 1987 and 1992, when he won his two Opens at Muirfield, he came from behind down the stretch and each time delivered a lethal iron to the final green. In '87, it was a five iron which paved the way for what was his 18th straight par. Nick's three wins at the Masters were similarly the result of his superb control with the irons. What with the severity of the Augusta greens, nothing less than the ultimate in precision will suffice.

Not too many people are nowadays looking for advice on the longer irons because they tend not to have them any more. Middle irons have become the long irons of the day. People prefer the more forgiving hybrid clubs and, to my mind, that makes perfect sense. There is absolutely no point in making the game more difficult than it has to be.

As I mentioned earlier, the biggest problem amateurs have with the irons is that they tend to lift or scoop the ball into the air. If you hit the ball on the up, there's very little backspin imparted and, even if you hit it well, the chances are that it won't stop when it hits the green.

In order to hit down on the shot, the hands need to be ahead of the ball at impact rather than behind – the left wrist bowed rather than cupped. The key here is to have the ball back in the middle of the stance and to focus on hitting down and through it while letting the loft of the club do the work to get the ball up. Where you have good solid contact the divot will always come on the target side.

Putting

Ben Hogan put it perfectly when he described putting as a game within a game. He would often claim that a putt should only count as half a stroke, but that, of course, is not how it is. By putting well, a man can turn a poor round into a good one and a good round into a great one. By the same token, the man who wins a tournament will in all probability be the one who has had the best putting week.

Certainly, holing birdie putts is important but, if you are going to keep a score going, it is no less important to hole the par-saving putts. This is where Tiger excels. Far more than the rest, he seems to make the putts that really matter. In fact, I think Tiger's putting is the most under-rated part of his game.

I can name a number of great putters, starting with Tiger, Ben Crenshaw, Brad Faxon and David Frost, and going back to Jack

Nicklaus and Bobby Locke, and nothing fascinates me more than that they all do it differently. It's about each player finding the technique which is right for him, not least in terms of keeping mental stress to a minimum.

Anyone who does not play the game will look at a three-footer and say it can't be very difficult to get the ball in the hole. However, every golfer knows that the short putt can spell more trouble than any other shot. Just ask Bernhard Langer. He has managed to come back from three different spells of putting yips but I don't know how many others would have the mental strength to do that. At first, Langer tried solve his problems by using a cross-handed grip. Then, after a few more variations, he switched to the long putter he uses today. Chris DiMarco resurrected his game by using the so-called 'Claw' method which was uncovered by a German scientist who was looking for the best way of keeping involuntary movements at bay.

In learning to putt, the amateur will almost certainly need to work harder on distance than direction. A lot of golfers believe that it's all a matter of hitting the long putts harder and the shorter putts more softly. Yet the truth is that it is the length of the putting stroke which should be dictating how far the putt goes. The best piece of advice for, say, an 18 handicap golfer is to concentrate on eliminating the three-putts. Most players in this handicap bracket take three putts from 30 feet many more times than not.

To me, Bob Charles, the great left-handed golfer who won the Open in 1963, is the father of modern putting. While the players before him mostly used a wristy stroke on the bumpier greens, he had an arms and shoulder stroke which was very novel. It was because he was so successful with it that others followed.

While the Europeans, in my opinion, have the edge in chipping, probably because of the variety of shots required around their greens, the Americans tend to be the better with a putter in hand. Why? Almost certainly because they are putting on slick and similar greens every week, whereas the Europeans are always having to make slight adjustments. This, of course, makes it that bit more difficult to develop a repetitive stroke.

———

MAGNOLIA MAGIC

Jack Nicklaus

From the moment I first turned into Magnolia Lane, at the age of 19, I have had a special feeling about Augusta. Away from St Andrews, there is nowhere more steeped in tradition, nowhere that resonates more with the golfing world at large. Even the most casual of fans has heard of Magnolia Lane, Amen Corner and, of course, the green jacket.

Then again, there are so many great names associated with the club, from Bobby Jones and Clifford Roberts, the founders, to a string of wonderful champions. I'm thinking of players such as Gene Sarazen, Sam Snead, Ben Hogan, Arnold Palmer and Gary Player, the last mentioned of whom is still on the go today. And then there are the new champions, with Tiger Woods and Phil Mickelson having won six times between them since 1997.

Whenever I come to Augusta, I spend as much of my time looking back as forward. I was lucky enough to win six times but, to put that list in order of preference, which people often ask me to do, is very hard. Each, in its own way, makes for great memories, though there is no question that my last win, in 1986, had it all in terms of emotion. I was the oldest winner at 46 and I had Jack Nicklaus Jnr, smartly attired in one of the caddies' white boiler suits, on the bag.

As I have often said, to be able to share the win with my eldest son was more important than actually winning. I can remember Jackie asking for a good, smooth swing before every shot and coming up with a positive, 'Knock it in!' before all the shorter putts. He also knew when to plant an idea in my head, as he did at the long 15th.

'What do you think a three would do for us here?' he asked, casually. I made him his three and we went on to win by one from Greg Norman and Tom Kite.

My wife Barbara and I have always embraced after a victory but, great supporter though she has been throughout my career, she early on figured out that it was best for a golfer's spouse to keep a low profile. She was never too excited if things were going well and never too down if they weren't. The embrace Jack Jnr and I enjoyed that day was one of those father–son moments that stays with you forever.

I was 23 when I first won the Masters. People may recall this shot and that, but my abiding memory is of what happened at the 18th on the Saturday, a miserably wet day when we had to grind all the way.

As I looked up at the leaderboard on 18, I could see quite a few players with the figure '1' beside their names. Since I am colour blind, I had to check with my caddie, William Peterson, how many of those ones were red, i.e. birdies. 'Just yours, boss,' he answered. That year I won by a shot from the late Tony Lema.

For my 1965 win, which others will often name as the best of the six, I had rounds of 67, 71, 64 and 69 to win by six from my old rivals, Palmer and Player. It was that year, by all accounts, that Bobby Jones came up with his flattering 'Jack plays a game with which I am not familiar.' When I won again the following year, I became the first person successfully to defend a Masters title, though that feat has since been repeated by Nick Faldo and Woods. I won on a play-off from Tommy Jacobs and Gay Brewer.

In 1972, I played well, though not as well as in 1966, while 1975 was far and away the most fun of the lot. Johnny Miller and Tom Weiskopf were in the final group and I was in the party ahead of them. Johnny and Tom were watching from the tee of the short 16th when I holed uphill from 45 feet for my two. As critical putts go, it was quite something.

Though there are some glorious holes on the front nine, people are not wrong when they say that most of the magic attaches to the second half. I consider the short 12th to be one of the best par threes in championship golf. As much as you hate to swallow a bogey, it was my four there in '86 which probably provided the wake-up call I needed to finish the final six holes five under par.

I see the 13th as a great natural golfing hole, the 14th as the hole with the toughest green, and the 15th as the hole which sires as much drama as any other. It was there that Sarazen made his double eagle and it was also the scene of a Jack Nicklaus eagle in '86.

But if there is a hole at Augusta which has more personal history to it than any other, it is the 16th. Aside from that long putt I made in my down-the-stretch duel with Miller and Weiskopf, I was within a whisker of making an ace in '86 to follow on from my eagle at 15.

I make no secret of the fact that I am disappointed with the extent to which they have made changes to the course, and in some ways to its identity, to counter technology and the incredible distances professionals now hit the ball. Power used to be important but the premium was still on shot-making. When they embarked on the alterations, it occurred to me that the Masters would from then on be the preserve of longer hitters such as Tiger. Then Mike Weir came along in 2003.

Besides being only moderately long, Weir hit no more than 50 per cent of the greens in regulation in an event where the winner usually catches 75 per cent. All of which tells you everything you need to know about his short game. It was a remarkable effort but, sad to say, I think that the days when a shorter hitter such as Jackie Burke or Gary Player could come out on top are gone forever.

---

17 JULY 2007

GARY PLAYER'S MAJOR PLAYERS

BEN HOGAN: CARNOUSTIE 1953

I have to include Ben Hogan's win at Carnoustie in 1953. To come to the Open just the one time and win was an extraordinary feat. Hogan was far and away the best striker I ever saw and had he lived today – with all the benefits of modern technology, along with the chance this generation has to putt on spike-free greens – he would have been every inch the superstar he was then.

Hogan did not like travelling after his car accident in 1949, but he was persuaded to make the journey to Carnoustie after winning the Masters and the US Open of that year. He arrived weeks ahead of time, which is something that no one had ever thought to do before, and in that period he got used to the small (1.62in) ball and analysed every yard of the Carnoustie course. Everyone saw him as the out and out favourite.

After opening rounds of 73, 71 and 70, he shared the lead with Roberto de Vicenzo. Then he had that last round of 68 to win by four strokes from Antonio Cerda, Dai Rees, Frank Stranahan and Peter Thomson.

Such was his accuracy from tee to green over the third and fourth rounds, which in those days were played on the one day, that the locals have always had it that his shots in the afternoon finished in the divots he had made in the morning. The 'wee ice man', as they called him, was hugely touched by the locals' joy at his win.

NICK FALDO: ST ANDREWS 1990

I have often thought that if I hadn't decided to have my ashes spread over my farm in South Africa, which I love beyond anywhere else in the world, I would have chosen either one of St Andrews or Augusta. They are two courses I absolutely love. Everyone wants to win at St Andrews.

Nick Faldo's victory over the Old Course in 1990 was the second in his hat-trick of Open triumphs, and his fourth major in less than four years. His 270 aggregate – he had rounds of 67, 65, 67 and 71 – broke the previous record for a St Andrews Open by six, and was 18 under par.

Having picked up momentum by holing for an eagle at the last on the first day, Nick – who had won that year's Masters – was level with Greg Norman at the halfway stage. However, when day three came along, he piled on the pressure to go round in 67, to Norman's 76. He was five ahead of the field going into the final round and, though Payne Stewart played well enough to be just two shots off the pace at one point on the last afternoon, he finished with that five shot lead intact.

His key shot had been a six iron to eight feet at the 15th. It was an exceptional performance and one to have the British audience swelling with pride. To my mind, they were seeing a player who, with his total of six majors – three Opens and three Masters – remains quite the best golfer Great Britain and Ireland has ever had.

SEVE BALLESTEROS: ST ANDREWS 1984

Seve was the most charismatic player Europe has ever had, and one who made a huge contribution to the growth of the game. I will never forget his win at St Andrews in 1984. He was 27 at the time and this was the fourth of his five majors. One moment he was gritting his teeth with the tension of it all, and the next there was that wonderful smile as he birdied the 18th for a final round of 69 that saw him finish two shots clear of Bernhard

Langer and Tom Watson. It was a smile the people of Scotland will never forget.

Seve had been neck and neck with Watson after 16 holes on the last day. When it came to the 17th, he hit into the left rough off the tee but went on to find the green in two for the first time that week before bagging his par four. Watson, who was playing that hole as Seve was making a birdie at the 18th, knocked his approach through the green and on to the road beyond on his way to a five.

I never like saying who is the best at this or that, but I don't mind saying that nobody was ever better than Seve when it came to the short game. If he had been a good driver, he would have won more, but the fact that he was always staging dramatic recoveries from car parks and heaven knows wherever else made him that much more thrilling to watch.

------

9 APRIL 1994

DAVIES REFRESHINGLY CLEAR ABOUT GOLFING 'PRIVILEGE'

SHE HAS NEVER HAD A GOLF LESSON, REACHING THE TOP BY MIMICKING THE TECHNIQUE OF OTHERS

Michael Parkinson

In the sometimes neurotic and obsessive world of professional golf, where beta-blockers calm the palpitating heart, where God and Sigmund Freud are called upon to soothe the mental turmoil and coaches are witch doctors casting spells to ward off the yips, it is refreshing to come across a golfer with a healthy disregard for such taradiddle.

We may draw what conclusions we like from the fact that we are reporting on a woman. There will be those who will see it as a significant statement in the battle of the sexes, and others – I have in mind several male golfers of my acquaintance – who will use it as yet further proof that there are two different games: golf . . . and the version played by the members of the ladies' section.

Laura Davies takes no part in such conjecture. What she knows is that, as the newly-crowned number one woman golfer in the world, all she has to do to face life at the top is keep reminding herself that playing golf sure beats working in a supermarket. As she says: 'Playing golf for a living isn't a real job is it? It's a privilege. It's also well paid.' At the same time as she went to number one in the ratings she passed the million dollar mark in earnings.

I am grateful to Miss Davies. An hour in her company was music to my ears. It is reassuring in the often loony world of professional sport, where half-formed youths are transformed into half-baked adults – and worse – to find someone like Laura Davies, who is both a genuine star and seemingly untrammelled by success.

For instance, she arrived a little late for the interview at the Berkshire Golf Club, not because this was her due but because she had been lurking in the car park not daring to enter the building until she was sure that someone she knew was inside.

After the interview she began her preparation for rejoining the American tour not by consulting her coach – she doesn't have one – or hitting a thousand balls on a practice range, but by playing a friendly four-ball; a fiver front and back nine and a tenner on the game.

As she teed up, our photographer asked her if she would mind the noise of a camera clicking at the top of her backswing. Certain male golfers of my acquaintance would swoon at the very thought. What Laura Davies said was: 'Go for it.'

What I am trying to convey is that Laura Davies is a pleasant and uncomplicated individual. It shows in her face, her frank and clear eyes, and is sustained by her conversation, which is straight-forward, unpretentious, nothing fancy. She is five feet ten inches tall, broad-shouldered, with big feet. I don't know what she weighs but, as my dear departed grandfather would say, she'd crush some grass.

She hits the ball a country mile. In fact, this year, she has already recorded one drive of more than 350 yards and one just short of that target. Both were wind assisted, but anyone who has seen her play knows that she is capable of starting most tournaments 16 under par because she can reach the majority of par fives in two.

She has brought excitement to women's professional golf. Wherever she appears people turn up to see her play. When she stood on the first tee at the Berkshire there was an audience of club staff and golfers standing around wondering just how far she would smite it on the par five opening hole. Can she really hit it as far as the men pros?

'I'm no Greg Norman,' she says. 'But one day I'd love to play him off the back tees just to see how my power game stood up under the kind of pressure the men play under. When I practise, I play off the back tees all the time. Length isn't a problem. On a 465-yard par four I can take a driver from the tee and then a three-iron to the green. That's what I do when I practise. What I'd like to see is if I could do it under the pressure of playing a men's tournament. Probably miss the cut, but I'd love the chance.'

She started playing golf when she was 14 because her brother, Tony, took it up. Whatever Tony did, his sister imitated. She played football and cricket. Last year, just before an event in America, she hurt her wrist playing cricket in a car park. She missed the cut.

As a child she envisaged a career as a sports teacher. As soon as she picked up a golf club she knew what she really wanted to do for the rest of her life. Her headmaster rebuked her ambition.

'You'll never earn a living playing golf,' he said. At 16 she was playing for Surrey and already creating a stir with her big hitting. Playing in a final on the Old Course at Sunningdale, she reduced the opening par five to a drive and a nine iron.

She was ready-made for an American sport scholarship. She declined. Why? 'Dunno really. Just wanted to stay at home. I played the amateur circuit for five years. Worked six months, played six months. I got a job at a supermarket, a garage and a bookmakers before turning pro. My mum and step-dad were marvellous. Made a lot of sacrifices. When I turned pro I borrowed £1000 from my parents. I missed the cut in the first tournament I played. Then I won £4000 in the second. Since then I've never looked back.

'If any young player asks me what they should do to become a professional golfer, I tell them to first of all get a job so that when they come to play golf they'll understand it's a darned sight better than working. That's my philosophy.

'I had a couple of not so hot years in '91 and '92 and I started moaning and getting miserable. Then I just took stock and remembered what I was doing before I played golf every day. Since that time if I have a bad week I don't worry. It's an absolute privilege to be travelling the world playing golf. I think we have the best of the sporting world.

'Look at all the other champions in other sports like Nigel Mansell, who say they'd really rather be champion golfers. Ours is the best life. Look at how the men can go on earning money on the seniors tour,' she said.

I asked her if she thought there would be a seniors competition for women. 'Don't think so. Maybe the men will let us join theirs. That would be a way of playing with them. But most of the girls on the tour play until they're 40 and then retire to have a family. Me? Another ten years I suppose. More if I'm still winning. Then I might think about packing up,' she said.

She is 30 years old, has won 27 tournaments and sets herself the target of 50. There are good judges who claim that Laura Davies could dominate women's golf in the next ten years like the young Jack Nicklaus once ruled the men's tournaments. The question is: will the kind of success and fame we are talking about spoil Laura

Davies? Will she be afflicted by the doubts and fears suffered by many of her male counterparts? Might she be tempted to employ a guru?

'I think that too much can be made of coaching. Look at Seve. I'm sure that if he got back to being Seve, when it was just him and his brother and there weren't all those people telling him what to do, things would be better.

'I'm lucky. I've never had a golf lesson in my life. I learned by mimicking others I saw play on the course or on the telly. I pick up more just watching the great players and copying them than I would from any teacher. You can't take your coach with you to Thailand can you? At least I can't. So if things go wrong I go to a range and start mucking about, getting the feel back. I'm more about feel than technique,' she said.

What's 'feel'? I asked.

'Shaping the ball, drawing and fading it,' she said.

Now this is highly technical. People have been trying to make the golf ball obey their command for hundreds of years. Books have been written on the subject, videos have been made, coaches have become rich by telling us how it's done. What is more, a multi-million dollar industry with space-age technology exists to design golf clubs to enable us better to master the game. So come on, Laura Davies, what's this old baloney about *feel*?

'Well, if I stand over a shot and I think I've got to hit a draw, something happens to my swing and the ball goes right to left. If I want to hit a slice then I feel myself cut across the ball as I hit it. If I want to hit a draw or a slice or make the ball go low or high, I know what to do simply by having watched the great players on telly. I learned a lot watching Seve play, and Langer.

'What I learned from Bernhard was his rhythm with the irons. Woosie gave me a couple of tips for chipping, which came in useful. But the rest is what I've picked up just watching people. With me it's all about confidence. At present I'm confident and playing well. I feel I can't hit a bad shot,' she said.

The other good question to ask Laura Davies as she faces her glittering future is: What about all that money waiting to be won? What will she do with it?

'Spend it,' she said. 'I love spending it. I've got three or four cars, bought a couple of cottages I've knocked into one next door to my mum. I don't worry too much about pensions.'

She loves a gamble. Indeed she confessed that as she passed Ascot racecourse on the way to our meeting she was tempted to pay a call. As it was she settled for a bet.

Not only bookmakers have been on the receiving end of her generosity. She didn't mention it, but others told me that when Laura Davies won her first tournament she gave part of her winnings to the amateur organisation that had nurtured her. She has helped out fellow pros who were struggling and has supported the European Tour without regard for the larger rewards that would come her way if she devoted all her time to playing in America.

When I asked her to name her greatest triumph, she said being part of the team who won the Solheim Cup from the Americans. When I asked her what she was most looking forward to in the future, she said defending the cup in America. Why? I asked. 'Because it'll be great fun,' she said.

Interesting word, 'fun'. I think the reason I liked her so is because she can use the word and still convey the will to win that all great champions possess.

———

CHAPTER 5
IT'S A TEAM GAME

7 OCTOBER 1957

REES'S IRON MEN BEAT US AT ITS OWN GAME

GREAT VICTORY ACHIEVED ON AND AROUND THE
LINDRICK GREENS

Leonard Crawley

The British Isles, led by D.J. Rees, won the Ryder Cup match at
Lindrick on Saturday by 7½ to 4½ matches. Rees himself won both
his games and played like a tiger. He has always said that he could,
and that we ought to beat the Americans over here; nor does he
disagree with the view that it is nearly impossible for any British
side to win in America. His personal contribution to the British
victory both as captain and player was immense.

Harsh criticisms had been levelled at Rees overnight by H.
Weetman, whom he left out of the singles, and cannot have
helped him or his team when they set out to tackle the severe
task before them on Saturday morning. It should be added that
M. Faulkner, the other member of the side to be left out, raced
around encouraging everyone and keeping them up to date with
scores all down the line.

Having lost the foursomes by 3 to 1 on the first day, five and a half matches were required from the eight singles, and very few people can have had much hope of a British victory. Rees had every confidence in his men and declared publicly that they could still win in spite of a disappointing first day. Rees has had a long and distinguished career as a professional golfer, having won everything but the Open championship in this country. Alas, he is now in his middle forties and cannot conceivably go on much longer, either in Ryder Cup or tournament play. It is, nevertheless, very pleasant to reflect that such a splendid, indomitable character should achieve his greatest triumph of all leading a British side to victory against America for the first time for nearly a quarter of a century.

The British Isles won six singles, halved one and lost one, and each member of the team is to be congratulated on this truly remarkable performance never previously accomplished by a British side in Ryder Cup matches. With one exception they played as a team and they played their best game on a fine, testing course against a most formidable side of American players.

After long experience of international golf I must respectfully observe that this was the first and only occasion upon which any American side has collapsed. Indeed, the American professionals themselves were dumbfounded by their failure. The view that their short preparation of eight days in England was too long is in my judgment so much nonsense.

They lost the match on Saturday on and around the greens upon which on Friday they had made almost certain of victory. It is of considerable interest that they could not make up their minds as a team whether or not to play their own slightly bigger ball or the standard size ball we use in this country. The bigger ball is far more responsive to a delicate touch near the hole, and it is strange to reflect that the world's greatest professionals can be tempted by the thought of a few paltry yards of additional length to forsake the ball with which at home they earn their daily bread. It is of further interest that the only member of the British Walker Cup who disobeyed his captain's orders to use the big ball at Minikanda was the only one to suffer a severe defeat a month ago.

A fine golfing day with a moderate south-west wind greeted the players and a positively enormous crowd when play began at nine o'clock. The wind that had appeared overnight altered every hole on the course and it was noticeable that these expert players had to think and think hard as they faced new problems.

Professionals hit the ball so straight that judgment of distance and choice of club as well as the type of shot are of paramount importance. On the whole I should say that the British players were less affected by the changed conditions, but Burke assures me that he and his side are fully accustomed to playing in stronger winds at home.

I must now touch on a delicate subject, namely the manners of a gigantic and well-marshalled British crowd. It must be obvious to any sensible person that applauding at golf requires tact and particularly on occasions such as the Ryder Cup match.

The home crowd naturally give vent to their feelings when their man wins a hole and particularly is this the case when a brave putt goes down. But when an enemy misses a short putt whether for a half or a win, the crowd is left wondering whether to shout for their man or to greet his adversary's disappointment with muffled regrets.

As I thought on Saturday, Yorkshire people with their natural intelligence and understanding of games behaved splendidly. There was never any doubt about their applause when a hole was won by our side, and personally I never saw an instance of their failure to applaud the enemy for a good shot. After some eight hours solid watching I left the scene comfortable in the knowledge that I had never felt embarrassed by the applause of the crowd.

I found it therefore very distressing to hear an American opinion that the crowd had played an important part in the British victory. This was wholly unworthy of our delightful opponents.

With the exception of Alliss, the British players made a good start all down the line on Saturday morning. Out in the middle of the course hard by the excellent vantage point of the fifth, sixth, seventh, eighth and tenth holes, where the country reminds one more of a good shoot than a good golf course, people were very soon all smiles.

The general opinion was that the news was too good to be true. But as the morning wore on and sundry score boards about the course showed that things were still going well, it was not surprising that at lunchtime the news was better than ever. Alliss recovered from three down to one down against Hawkins, Bradshaw was all smiles though one down to the American Open champion, Mayer, and O'Connor had held on tightly to the formidable Finsterwald. The rest were all up and most of them well up.

Brown, never happier than when he has a chance of putting his teeth into a tough American, was outdriving and generally outplaying the fierce Bolt. Bolt found putting difficult and smiling more difficult still. Brown got round in 71 and was four to the good.

The quite admirable Mills — making his first appearance — far from being frightened of the wonderful Burke, soon started to go ahead. Burke, who a year or two ago was described as 'the greatest putter on earth', could not get the ball into the hole, and in spite of losing the short 18th to a 4, Mills was five up.

Alliss was inclined to misjudge his distances against Hawkins, of whom the more one sees the more one admires both him and his delightful game. It looked pretty bad for Alliss when after six holes he was three down, but he got a good putt of ten feet in to win the 8th in three and minus three became all square by the 15th hole. Alas, Alliss missed a tiny putt at the 16th and so finished the round one down.

Bousfield, as happy as a skylark for the first time in a Ryder Cup match, almost impatiently got away from Herbert. Bousfield's putting, slow and rhythmical, was a joy to watch, and when he holed one from the back of the 18th green for a 2, he was five up.

Rees, in buoyant mood, pranced round as though he had springs in his boots, and the grim Furgol could do nothing about it. Rees, out in 33, was three up and, in spite of having to pack up at the 14th, a glorious 2 at the home hole left him four up with 18 to go.

Hunt faced the terrifying Ford, who has deservedly acquired the reputation of being unbeatable in matchplay. (Densmore Shute was another of the same brand from the United States 25 years ago.) Hunt, playing with infinite calm, refused to be disturbed by his adversary's reputation or by his telling and some-times cruel putts – he holed three in a row from the 7th to the 9th – but he stayed with him, and a three at the 18th left him one up.

O'Connor, who was generally considered not quite man enough for the great Finsterwald, began like a machine-gun loaded with threes, and stood three up on the fourth tee. This was a fine game to watch from the point of view of style and the hitting of a golf ball, but surely the claiming of a hole by both for petty infringement of the rules was a little childish. All square at lunch seemed perfectly fair, and here was one of the keys to the final result.

Then there was Bradshaw, the much loved and respected Harry, who has been given many fearful propositions in Ryder Cup golf. He had been put at the bottom of the list to deal with Mayer against the possibility of a close finish. Bradshaw won the first three holes, the third with a 2, popping one in from a bunker at this short hole. He was followed by a vast company of support-ers led by a good platoon of reverend gentlemen, one of whom had procured a VIP badge for inside the ropes. Mayer is a superla-tively fine performer and as was expected came back after a rough start. His putting, with a stroke of unrippled smoothness, is posi-tively frightening, and when Bradshaw finished the round one down one felt that the old fellow had met his master.

Things at half time looked very promising and in the luncheon tents spread about like Derby Day at Epsom, with hundreds of excited people talking nonsense, and asking ridiculous questions about what was going to happen, one longed to be alone in case of talking something much worse.

On the face of the score card, it appeared that short of accidents four of the five and a half points required for victory were in the bag and that the result of the Ryder Cup match then depended on Alliss, Hunt, O'Connor and Bradshaw, four truly great horses, if I may so describe them.

After lunch Brown, who has a passion for driving out of bounds, made one quite angry on two occasions, but one never had any doubt about his match. He has never let go of a tough American and he is a splendid man on Ryder Cup day.

Mills refused to give in or be frightened by a brief glimpse of the real Burke, and Bousfield, having been seven up on the unhappy Herbert, got a little jumpy for half an hour and lost three of his lead all in a row. He played a beautiful pitch to the eighth and his putt of eight feet went in for a win and so unnecessary fears of a possible collapse were now gone. This meant three for the British Isles.

Rees began 3, 3, 3, as though he wanted to eat Furgol for breakfast on Sunday morning and I was really quite thankful when at last he smiled and shook his adversary by the hand on the 14th green. Four for the British Isles.

Alliss began badly again against Hawkins but came again, as in the morning. When after becoming one up at the tenth Alliss put in a putt of five yards for a half in two to retain his lead at the 11th, one felt that he had now got control. Hawkins, with great courage, reeled off the par figures and was duly rewarded. So here at last was a point for America.

Hunt, playing magnificently, soon had the mighty Ford by the throat and, although Ford had a 2 at the sixth, Hunt left him positively groggy with 3s at the eighth and ninth holes. Five for the British Isles and now there was only half a point needed to win the cup. But O'Connor, behind playing the game of his life against Finsterwald and aided by the holing of a curious but highly skilful stroke from a bush at the eighth, sealed everything if there was anything left to seal.

There was still Harry Bradshaw in the country, with his magical scythe, his faithful putter and all his courage taking care of the great American champion. He took care of him to the very end of the round. Harry B was still looking at the floor and listening patiently for a familiar gobble by the hole on the 18th green when the vast crowd acclaimed him for another great performance.

———

16 SEPTEMBER 1985

TORRANCE PUTT BRINGS EUROPE HISTORIC WIN

Michael Williams

The Belfry

At precisely five minutes past four yesterday afternoon, Sam Torrance holed a putt across the 18th green at the Belfry that echoed around the world, for with that birdie and the defeat of Andy North, Europe, at last, won again the Ryder Cup.

Not since Lindrick in 1957 had the United States been beaten by the then Great Britain and Ireland team, but the point that Torrance brought home after standing three down with eight to play put the Europeans finally out of reach. Ahead 9–6 going into this momentous final day, they got the 5½ points they needed from the first seven singles matches and, in the end, won by 16½ to 11½, which was more comprehensive than even the most optimistic onlooker had envisaged.

Not for 28 years have there been such excitement and such scenes at a Ryder Cup, and most of the 27,500 spectators there yesterday, bringing the total for the three days to nearly 80,000, seemed to ring the 18th hole for a glimpse of the magic moment.

No sooner had Torrance's putt disappeared from sight than he was engulfed by the other team members, led by the captain, Tony Jacklin, for whom victory was every bit as sweet as it was when he won the Open championship in 1969 and the US Open the following year.

Of Torrance's finish, Jacklin said: 'You just dream about that sort of thing. It was just great to be a part of it. The team was my inspiration and it shows the world how good we really are. We have so much talent, more perhaps than even we realise.' Hardly had he spoken, as his joyous team sprayed champagne over the crowd from the roof of the hotel, than Concorde thundered low overhead, making two runs over the course and dipping its silver wings in moving salute as it did so.

The narrow defeat the Europeans suffered in Florida two years ago was a warning that the balance of power was shifting, reinforced as it was by the victories this year of Bernhard Langer in the Masters, by Sandy Lyle in the Open championship and the earlier successes of Seve Ballesteros in both. For once – perhaps even for the first time – the Europeans had nothing to fear, and all afternoon they were urged on by more huge crowds, great cheers, echoing all over the course until one knew not which way to turn.

Jacklin, an inspirational captain if ever there was one, had gambled by putting the strength of his team in the early middle order and, if the Americans were to get back into the match, much depended on their first two players, Lanny Wadkins and Craig Stadler. It was, therefore, the defeat of Wadkins, whom Jacklin regarded as the opposition's most formidable match-player of all, by little Manuel Piñero that lit the fire that will burn for a long time yet.

Piñero, twice one down, and square at the turn, had three birdies in his last eight holes, and, if there was one more important than the others, it was the chip he holed from the back of the tenth after he had laid up short of the water from the tee. Such was the strength of the north-westerly wind on an afternoon of bright sunshine that Piñero could not even reach the fairway at the 11th; but he was home with a one iron second, holed the putt for another birdie, and needed no further bidding.

Behind him, Ian Woosnam was twice ahead early against Stadler and also twice came back to square, the last time with a 2 at the 14th. But for Stadler, whose missed short putt in the last of the fourball games on Saturday to make the whole match level was so crucial, it made some personal amends.

The next victory came early from Langer, who never looked back after taking the first hole from Hal Sutton. He was three up after six holes, two ahead at the turn and won by 5 and 4, moments before another point came from Sandy Lyle.

The Open champion, out in 34 and one up on Peter Jacobsen, went two up with a birdie at the 16th, but the odds seemed that it might be back to one again when Jacobsen hit the better approach to the 16th. However, Lyle holed from the very back of the green for an audacious 3 to another great yell from those packed around the green, and the little Stars and Stripes flags, which the American wives clutched almost pathetically, drooped almost to half-mast.

Victory was close now, for ahead of Lyle, Ballesteros, who had been three down with five to play against Tom Kite, was now very much on the march while, ahead of him, Paul Way was grimly fending off Raymond Floyd.

Way had been four up after eight holes, but it was back to one when he went through the 16th green and conceded the hole to his opponent. The 17th was halved but it was Way who had the stronger nerve at the last. While his drive was perfect, Floyd's leaked into the right-hand bunker and, in risking all with a near-impossible shot to the green, the American could only thin his shot into the water. Way was triumphantly home in two and did not even need to putt.

Next it was Ballesteros, brilliantly fighting back with birdies at the 14th and 15th and not even bothering to retrieve his ball from the hole as he stalked eagerly to the next tee. He is a formidable golfing animal at such moments, never more so than as he lashed two enormous shots to the 17th green to square the match and deservedly getting the half that reflected so well on both men.

And so to the final man of the moment, Torrance, a pencil, as ever, behind his right ear, as he came back from three down against North to square at the 17th, with a birdie to have the multitude craning its combined necks at the last. His drive was an absolute monster, so bold that he needed but a nine-iron for his second. For North, the pressure was now unbearable. He dropped his head in despair as his tee-shot found the water.

The US Open champion climbed forlornly to the green, but Torrance was a hero already as he followed in the midst of an excited and exultant throng.

––––––

28 SEPTEMBER 1987

EUROPE GRIMLY HOLD ON IN CLIFF-HANGER

Michael Williams

Dublin, Ohio

After a day of almost unbearable excitement, Europe successfully defended the Ryder Cup at Muirfield Village yesterday when they defeated the United States by 15 to 13. After their handsome five point lead going into the last series of singles, it was in the end an absolute cliff-hanger, as the Americans fought to their last breath, which is so typical of them. They took the singles by six games to three, with another three halved, but this was the only one of the five series of games that they won.

Never before have the Americans been beaten at home, and the European Ryder Cup team therefore follows in the footsteps of the Curtis Cup team, which won in the States last year. It is a significant triumph for Tony Jacklin, the European captain, who has now led two successive winning teams. He arranged his batting order perfectly, for his two strongest players, Severiano Ballesteros and Bernhard Langer, came up trumps as the pack of cards was in danger of collapsing.

Ballesteros, relishing the challenge of playing Curtis Strange, America's leading money-winner, led at one point by three up, but was brought back to one with five to play. However, he took the 14th, and a 4 at the 17th closed his man out, seconds after Langer had made sure of at least a tie against Nelson. Langer had been three down with seven to play against Larry Nelson, but came back with a string of birdies and did not falter again.

Other crucial contributions came from Howard Clark and Eamonn Darcy, both of whom won, against Dan Pohl and Ben Crenshaw, while valuable half points came from Sam Torrance and Gordon Brand Jnr. But, by goodness, it was touch and go, uncomfortably so, and all credit to the Americans, whose pride very nearly tipped the scales.

Even though the Europeans had held a commanding lead going into the final 12 singles, no one expected it to be easy, and it was not long before the Americans began to show more prominently on the scoreboards.

The top match was a crucial one – and an unusual pair they made with Bean standing a good 12 inches taller than Woosnam, though off the tee there was little between them. Bean was two up at the turn, having birdies at the two short holes, a feat he repeated at the 12th. Woosnam kept going, though the short putt he missed for a birdie at the 14th was a blow. That would have made them all square, but though Bean missed from a yard for his fourth two at the 16th, Woosnam let slip another chance at the 17th, where Bean was in trouble off the tee. The little Welshman found a bunker behind the green and in the end had to work harder for his five to stay only one down and he could not summon a birdie at the last.

That was one point lost, but behind him Clark, always in close contention with Pohl, got away with a half when his opponent was in trouble all the way down the last and took six to lose the hole. Faldo had looked something of a banker against Calcavecchia, but though he was one up at the turn, he lost the long 11th and 14th to pars and there was another American point.

One hardly knew which way to turn trying to interpret the various cheers wafting across the course, and every two minutes it seemed the position kept changing. Calcavecchia was round in no better than 73 in beating Faldo, and after the hectic scoring on Saturday this was very much back to the ordinary.

Then came yet another American point, this time Stewart beating Olazábal on the home green. They had been level at the turn, but Stewart went ahead with a par at the 16th and held his advantage through the last two holes. Though Rivero had come back from two down at the turn to Simpson, the scales tipped again and birdies by the US Open champion at the 15th and 16th closed the door as the Americans took their fifth point.

However, there was a welcome bonus as Darcy, having at one point gone from three up to one down against Crenshaw, came through for his first victory in his fourth Ryder Cup match. The American recovered remarkably well after breaking his putter when thumping the ground in annoyance following a missed putt. From then on Crenshaw had to putt with his one iron and it worked so well that he had three birdies in a row from the 12th. However, Darcy came back by taking the last two holes, first with a birdie and then by getting up and down from a bunker at the last.

Meanwhile Lyle had gone down to Kite, but the saviour was Langer, who had been three down to Nelson after 11 holes. The German's answer to that was three successive birdies from the 12th, and in mounting excitement they halved the remaining holes to finish all square. Almost at the same moment Ballesteros, three up early on against Strange but then brought back to only one up, edged two ahead again at the 14th, and the safest of fours at the 17th secured the Ryder Cup.

---

27 SEPTEMBER 1997

BALLESTEROS'S HEAVEN 17TH

SPECTACULAR AMPHITHEATRE FOR GLADIATORIAL CONTEST AS THREE FOUR-BALLS GO TO THE WIRE

Mark Nicholas

Valderrama

It's a 'love it or loathe it' hole and Seve Ballesteros loves it. He's about the only one. Colin Montgomerie slags it off willy-nilly; the Americans, and most particularly Tiger Woods, gave it the no-no during the days of practice; even Robert Trent-Jones, who designed it, doesn't think much of what Seve has done to it now.

Heaven knows why. It's a ripper for the spectator. The 17th at Valderrama is 511 yards of gladiatorial delight, sprinkled with bunkers, strewn with rough, protected by water and with such a complicated green that unless you putt from below the hole, you could putt yourself down the sadistically mown bank at its front and back into the lake. Yup, it's theatre, pure theatre, and did not disappoint yesterday when it played host to three hair-raising four-balls that all went to the wire.

First up for Europe was Ballesteros's prodigy, José María Olazábal, whose drive split the fairway and who hit the kind of raking, drawn one iron that even he only dreams of. The Spaniard and the Italian, Costantino Rocca, came to the 17th all square, having gorged themselves on the eagles and birdies needed to recover the two-down problem through 12 holes.

The wind swirled and Olazabal took his time, flicking grass to the sky and testing its direction. When he settled over the ball for the second time and began that business-like take-away of the club, the world seemed to stop and hold its breath until the ball landed pin-high, spun left down the slope of the plateau and rolled gently to 15 feet. They could hold their breath no more, so they screamed their joy, the thousands surrounding the green and the thousands more jostling for space along the fairway. Olazábal marched forward as though there had never been a problem with his feet, and Rocca joined him, pleased to have recovered safely from the rough and relishing his waiting wedge shot. Should it be required. It wasn't.

Whether Davis Love relished his four iron or not, he managed to hit it so competently, so smotheringly over the flag to the back fringe of the green – about equidistant to Olazábal – that even the delirious Spaniards in the coliseum had to acknowledge his guts. Two putts each, two birdies; the hole gloriously halved.

Next up was Nick Faldo, but not before the giant screen had told the restless amphitheatre that Phil Mickleson had missed from six feet at the 18th and that the dark Latins had put one over the blond American boys. Faldo tested the wind for even longer than Olazábal. His drive had caught the up slope of one of the criticised fairway humps and rolled back into one of the criticised fairway hollows. He decided on a five wood and from a vaguely uphill lie made that extraordinarily organised and focused swing.

It was always going to be like this; it was why his captain chose him. He chose him because Faldo up the stretch is the best there is. Maybe not a tournament first round or second round certainty any more, but give him the last-ditch drama and he will give you a five wood to ten feet.

It should have done the trick, it really should, but Freddie Couples, after shouting 'great shot' across the fairway to his opponent, didn't think so. He had laid up 70 yards short of the water after driving into the unhappy rough which crosses the fairway at about the 300 marker, and now Valderrama went eerily silent as the favourite American son settled over his sand-wedge.

The hush . . . before the storm. Couples' long and lazy swing nipped the ball from the perfect turf and stopped it again two and a half feet from the hole. The storm broke. 'You're the man, Freddie', and he agreed, raising his arms and smiling. He was having such fun. Faldo slid his effort past the right edge, his putter failing him again. His shoulders slumped. Couples holed. Two more birdies, another half.

They were hanging from the bougainvillea climbing walls and invading trees to get a look. They spread for 50 yards up the bank behind the bunkers at the back of the green and were 20 deep along its sides and down to the lake. They watched the big screen as Faldo nailed his approach to the 18th and nattered away about the late afternoon foursomes pairings . . . Seve this and Seve that. Why no Woosnam, why no Clarke? The Duke of York stood to stretch and to talk with Tom Kite; Ballesteros stalked back up the fairway in search of the Swedes who were in a position to ensure that the first round of matches ended even.

They did, thanks to Jesper Parnevik, the bloke with the silly hat who has blown a couple of majors. But not here, no sir. Having driven wildly from the 17th tee and into the spectators, he wedged out marvellously down and beyond the fairway rough before hitting an eight iron to 15 feet and holing the putt. This was mesmeric golf, too mesmeric even for Tom Lehman, who is not often fazed by these things. The crowd went ballistic; Per-Ulrik Johansson, whose par 5 was not shabby considering the nature of the beast set out before him, high-fived his friend.

They can argue all they like that the spectacular 17th is an incongruous, unreasonable hole among 17 other beauties, but they'll not convince a soul who sat there, wet bottoms and all, for the magical hour yesterday which, after the depressing morning rain, put the Ryder Cup back on track.

─────

28 SEPTEMBER 1999

PASSIONATE AFFAIR AT RISK OF GROWING INTO A MONSTER

Mark Nicholas

Brookline

'You have to understand,' said Payne Stewart in the aftermath of the extraordinary events at Brookline on Sunday night, 'that this is not life or death.' Which is exactly the paradox of the Ryder Cup. In its essence it is just a game of golf, but because the United States have lost it a lot recently, it has become a matter of national importance. To Americans, this European dominance thing had become an unpalatable joke.

The joke is why things got so fruity on Sunday afternoon, why Sergio Garcia and José María Olazábal, never mind Colin Montgomerie, were heckled from the bleachers; why Hal Sutton raised those huge forearms to the galleries and urged more from them; why David Duval pranced about his winning green like no golfer can have pranced before.

'This is so big, it means so much and only the men who play in it can truly understand its enormity,' said Ben Crenshaw, and Duval (remember, he of the 'it's nothing more than an exhibition match' quote) echoed him moments later.

Well, don't expect it to get any smaller or suddenly to mean any less. The Ryder Cup is no embryo but it is not the finished article either. You can't have this increasing size of emotive, partisan occasion without an increasing amount of emotional reaction. The players are bound one day to be paid. Spectators could well join them with invasions of fairways and greens in the way that spectators invade the playing fields of other sports. Greater, more vulgar security will become an ugly necessity. Don't be surprised if the cup is sponsored some day – the Remington Ryder Cup, God forbid.

While on the subject of Remington, these really are razor-thin margins which determine the matches. A putt here, a chip there and Americans are crossing that line at the Alamo again, which apparently was the theme of presidential candidate George W. Bush's contribution to Saturday night's pep talk in the US team room. Get this: some southern drawling fella in the gents on the last evening told his neighbour that, as a comeback, the American team effort rated alongside that little number Lazarus pulled off all those years ago. Yikes, give us a break, guys.

None of this nonsense, though, detracted from the quality of the golf, which was fantastic. Because of their individual performances, the US deserve their triumph, but for their performances as a team, the Europeans deserved a mite more than they got. Europe's achievement in running it so close should not be underestimated. They were underdogs and knew it. They had four players, perhaps, who rated alongside eight of the opposition, and just one, Montgomerie, who day in and day out could live with Duval, Davis Love or Tiger Woods.

By forging an extraordinary bond which came initially from Mark James's intelligent, amusing and laid-back lead and then from the teams' response to each other and their collective sense of character, Europe were able to use the force of their personality and the depth of their passion to acute advantage. The Americans feared this. They feared the 'ham and egging', as Woods called it; 'the fronting up each time one of them has to', said Love.

Because of this team spirit, defeat will be harder to bear. Sometimes, if you want something badly for other people, it means more than wanting it for yourself, which is the conviction the Europeans cultivated and which all but won them through.

Conceivably, the team thing cost them, i.e. they forgot how to do it for themselves. Had they more golfers who were self-absorbed, more Faldos and Langers, say, they might have sneaked another win or two from the singles.

Now James's team will be sick and none more, one suspects, than Montgomerie who, in his own words, wanted to win this one so, so badly. He relished the mantle of senior pro and best player; revelled, indeed, in the responsibility. For the life of him, he can't see why American audiences have got it in for him, so he bristles with indignation. Previously, this has led him to be reactive and therefore to play into their hands. He is learning now to take the flak as a compliment and turn it in his favour, to use it as a further motivation. If his team had won, and it would have been much on the back of his own performances, retribution and vindication would have been delivered. So, in the pit of his stomach, Europe's finest will be sick.

It is a ghastly feeling and will last for days. But only days – a week perhaps, but not too much longer. Because Montgomerie and his splendid team appreciate and play by the ethic of those words surprisingly uttered by Stewart: 'This is not life or death.' Hear, hear; and with luck, the crowds for the Belfry in two years have already heard him.

———

29 SEPTEMBER 1999

BLAIR JUMPS ON RYDER CUP BANDWAGON

Robert Hardman

Tony Blair and Sam Torrance have both led surprisingly sheltered lives. In the aftermath of the Ryder Cup defeat, Torrance declared that the Americans' jubilant stampede after that crucial putt was 'the most disgusting thing I've ever seen'. Down at Bournemouth this week, Tony Blair was quick to make it clear that he agreed. 'In case you want to know, the Prime Minister agrees with Sam Torrance,' declared his spokesman. So, the man who has seen the horrors of Kosovo, Bosnia and Ulster at first hand was actually more disgusted by jubilant American golfers. Note that Mr Blair was not pressed for his thoughts on the matter. His aide was pressing them on the press. As with the Hoddle fiasco, the Prime Minister was determined to jump on whichever outrage bandwagon happened to be leaving the station.

To read most of the comments on this side of the Atlantic, it appears that the majority of Britain is convulsed with nausea at the sight of a few dancing Americans. Have we all gone barmy? I am no golfer but I am well aware of the conventions and etiquettes. They were clearly breached at a crucial moment by the American team. And it is clear that a few of the spectators behaved very badly. But this should not be used as the launch pad for the extraordinary deluge of anti-American bile.

In this country, most sports have undergone a drop in sporting standards in recent times. Rugby players bite each other, cricketers behave like footballers, footballers behave like football fans and football fans give the zoo a run for its money. Tennis fans at Wimbledon jeer anyone who has the temerity to play against Tim Henman and motor racing fans cheer as Michael Schumacher breaks a leg at Silverstone.

In each of these sports, the vast majority of players and spectators behave correctly most of the time. But sometimes they do not. We may not like it but it is, in part, a reflection of society and its standards. Golf has actually managed to remain fairly gentlemanly among players and fans but it was inevitable that standards should start to slide.

The Americans over-reacted but they had good reason. Had it been the other way round and the Europeans had been dancing over the course, I suspect we would all have expressed mild concern while putting it down to 'understandable high spirits'. Out in the crowd there were clearly some American yobs, but since when did we command the moral high ground on crowd behaviour? Because of a few oiks at Brookline, some people have been quick to write off the entire American nation as 'repulsive people', 'charmless', 'rude' and 'rednecks'. Can we complain if we are all condemned as 'shaven-headed racist psychopaths' the next time a few England football fans do their stuff?

What has been largely overlooked in all this is the speed and frankness of the American apology. Hands aloft, American captain Ben Crenshaw was in full *mea culpa* mode the following day.

In allowing ourselves to become so heated and abusive over this Ryder Cup, we are only stoking up trouble for the next one. I have no doubt that our players will behave correctly but the same will not go for the fans. Some will decide that it is only fair to spit at and distract the Americans by way of revenge.

It is ironic that so many of those who attacked the *Mirror* for its anti-German tone during Euro '96 should now be so ready to heap the vitriol on the Americans. Bad losers and sour grapes are every bit as distasteful as putting a golfer off his swing.

———

30 SEPTEMBER 2002

HAIL TO UNITED STATE OF EUROPE

Paul Hayward

The Belfry

Scene from an English autumn: a Dubliner stands in a lake up to his thighs, draped in an Irish tricolour. Three days, two teams, 28 matches, and it's all about him – which seems wrong until you notice the champagne spraying, the bear-hugging, the tear-wiping and the arm-thrusting elsewhere on the Belfry's 18th green. On the water, an oblivious flotilla of four ducks glides away from the noise.

The mythical being rising from the lake is Paul Noel McGinley, and the dunking is his reward for sinking a nine-foot putt which seals Europe's victory in the 34th Ryder Cup. Elsewhere, you might read that McGinley 'won' the cup for his continent, which is only partially true. McGinley was simply the executioner. Equal credit could be taken on this blissful English Sunday by Colin Montgomerie, who scythed down a succession of American opponents; by Bernhard Langer, the indomitable elder statesman of the most compelling tournament in golf; by Padraig Harrington, who destroyed Mark Calcavecchia 5&4, and by Phillip Price, the one time 'Pontypridd Man of the Year' who throttled Phil Mickelson, who defers only to Tiger Woods in the official list of the world's best players.

By all the Europeans, in fact. Sam Torrance's team earn less, make fewer gung-ho predications and miss out on the major tournaments more. They are, in other words, the poor relations of the corporate honeypot otherwise known as the American PGA Tour. So this was nothing less than a triumph for the collective spirit: the 'we' ahead of the 'I'. So heavily bonded were the Europeans they could have passed for an upmarket stag party hugging and cajoling each other through some epic celebration of manhood.

How much can crowd psychology alter the course of history? On this evidence — a lot. Given the temptation to revive the poisoned spirit of Brookline, this was one of the most civilised audiences assembled in sport. 'I said we could end up playing the crowd as a 13th man,' Curtis Strange, the American captain, said. 'And this week we played one of the fairest and most honest 13th men I've ever seen.'

Europe's non-participating team-mate cheered anything with a European star on it, turned every fairway into a gun barrel of soul-lifting noise and fixed their affections to the home side's mast without hating or trying to demean the other side. When Sergio Garcia was coming apart on the 18th fairway in his match against David Toms, a woman called out to him and his mother: 'Well done, Sergio, you gave us a lot of pleasure. Don't worry, mum, he'll be all right.'

From this pit-stop of maternal solidarity, we swept on to the 18th green to observe the denouement. First: Darren Clarke and David Duval. Clarke lumbers on to the great stage as his chip stops eight inches from the hole. Duval has a ten-foot putt to halve the match. He sinks it. Ducks waddle up the front of the lawn and settle as if nesting. Roars and gasps can be heard through the trees as the shadows lengthen. Paul Azinger and Niclas Fasth approach.

The Pressure, part one: Pontypridd, as Bill McClaren might say, is in ferment as the radio announces that Price is finishing off Mickelson 3&2. Garcia's dad, Victor, punches the air. Two women police officers unroll a sheet of plastic to kneel on. In this foaming amphitheatre, the gap between audience and performer has dissolved. Involvement is obligatory, even for the police.

Here comes Fasth to finish it off. And off go the ducks again. Too much noise. But there's a kink in the script. Azinger's desperate 11-yard chip from the greenside bunker trickles beautifully into the pot. Azinger shares seven high-fives with his caddie and then throws his wedge to the ground. The gauntlet is down. Impaled by genius, Fasth misses a 30-footer from above the pin and loses the hole to halve the match. Europe: 14 points. A half still needed.

Pressure, you might argue, rightly, is working nights in a hospital ward for terminally ill children. This side of life and death, nothing, in sport, at any rate, can singe the spirit quite like the endgame of the 12 Ryder Cup singles. In the moments that push the outcome this way or that, the players are alone again. The captain, the players' wives and girlfriends and their team-mates are jammed into the greenside gallery, out of reach. Jim Furyk, McGinley's opponent, chips his own exquisite bunker shot a foot past the hole. So there the executioner is. Irish, European, human being – whatever he is, McGinley's job is to force a little white ball along a nine foot expanse of grass and into a hole.

The catharsis comes when the object of golf's frustration is rendered invisible. As the ball drops, so Europe rises, cascading onto the green as Garcia first pogoes toward the main stand and then cavorts back down the 18th fairway to embrace Pierre Fulke, who is trying to finish his match with Davis Love. Realising the show is over, Fulke and Love pick up, though Woods and Parnevik are still rolling and reeling towards the end of a torrid round.

Back on the 18th, Strange gets down from his buggy and starts hugging American wives, gently, as if squeezing too hard might make them break. 'Everybody did his job,' Thomas Bjorn is saying in someone's ear, as he accepts his own embrace. Montgomerie's voice booms above the love-in. 'They [Woods and Parnevik] are still playing the hole. Can you please sit down?' Hero of the struggle one minute, steward the next. We all sit down. The golf resumes.

Woods, who putts like a broken man, will never look less like a god. The Ryder Cup has dwarfed him. The crowd's eye is drawn at last to Torrance reviving the Churchillian salute he patented on this same green as a player in 1985, and McGinley being bundled into the lake, which was amply replenished by Torrance's tears. After three years, we'd forgotten it could be this good.

———

16 SEPTEMBER 2004

EUROPEAN UNION GIVES SHOWDOWN GLOBAL APPEAL

'IF YOU LOOK AT THE PAST 10 YEARS, EUROPE HAVE HAD THE EDGE'

Jack Nicklaus

I like where we're at with the Ryder Cup. It has grown into a truly great contest since it changed to become Europe versus the United States in 1979, while two years ago at the Belfry you could not have asked for more in the way of sportsmanship. It was more like the spirit of the relatively new President's Cup. The way things should be.

It was back in 1977 that I realised the match was suffering from not being sufficiently competitive. The contest had been a US versus Great Britain and Ireland affair since it started in 1927, but gallantly though the British side had fought across the years, they had only won twice and drawn once in 21 starts. I myself always felt it an honour to be chosen, but as Ken Schofield, the head of the Eurpean tour, suspected, there were Americans for whom the main challenge was one of making the team. After that, they were apt to lose a bit of interest.

It was on the last night of the '77 match, after America had won by 12½ to 7½ at Royal Lytham & St Annes, that I approached Lord Derby, the president of the British Professional Golfers' Association, at a function at the Clifton Arms Hotel in Southport.

'John,' I said, 'now that you have a successful European Tour, maybe we should think about expanding the Ryder Cup to include Europe. I think that would make it more competitive.' Lord Derby responded: 'Leave it to me, Jack.'

The rest, as they say, is history. It was a good decision. Since 1979, the Americans have won six times and Europe five, with one match halved. However, over the past ten years Europe have had the edge, winning three of the last four contests. There have been plenty of people to suggest that improved European techniques made the difference, but from where I stand it has more to do with a thriving European Tour. The level of competition in Europe is better than it ever was, while the courses and tournament conditions are superb.

If you look at the Europeans of today, the difference between where they are now and where they were, say, in the 1960s, is as night and day. The other thing I have noted, apart altogether from the quality of their golf, is the quality of the young men themselves. They have brought class, sportsmanship and a respect for the game's traditions.

I would like to give Luke Donald a mention here. Like Charles Howell, he is on my Royal Bank of Scotland team. I've gotten to know Luke well in the last couple of years and will be taking a special interest in his progress this week. He is a talented young man, who is playing well now and promises more for the future. He has the skills, the tools and the head to perform. This Ryder Cup will provide a great experience in his golfing development, one which he will remember all his days.

I captained the American team twice – in 1983, when we won, and 1985, when we lost. My favourite memory from '83 came when Lanny Wadkins stiffed his pitch at the last to halve his match with José María Cañizares and ensure an American triumph. On the spur of the moment, I picked up Lanny's divot and gave it a kiss. I find myself smiling every time I think about it.

Two years ago, Sam Torrance and Curtis Strange played a big part in restoring order to the match after things had got a bit out of hand at Brookline in 1999. But while I believe the captains have an influence on the overall tenor of the match, I'm not sure that it's the most important one. It's my belief that the media play the bigger role on that front, with no good coming of all the hype which started when Europe began to win. Brookline apart, it was bad at Kiawah Island in 1991. The hype and war mentality we saw there was ridiculous and wholly out of keeping with what the Ryder Cup is meant to be about.

As I said, I always felt it was an honour to play in the Ryder Cup but today, with the contest having become so big in world terms, it's an event everyone wants on his CV. I'm sure we're in for another great contest and I wish all 24 players the best of luck.

---

20 SEPTEMBER 2004

MONTGOMERIE THE TOAST OF EUROPE

Lewine Mair

Oakland Hills

Who else but Colin Montgomerie scored the crucial point as Europe defeated the United States to win their fourth Ryder Cup in five starts. With Europe having started the day with an 11–5 lead, the 40-year-old Montgomerie had a magnificent one-hole win over David Toms to give the Europeans an unassailable haul of 14½ points. 'It wasn't for me, it was for the team,' said the elated Scot of the three-footer he had to make on the home green.

Montgomerie, who had needed a wild card after a year in which he suffered the traumas of a divorce, had got the match off to the perfect start on Friday as he and Padraig Harrington beat none other than Tiger Woods and Phil Mickelson. Yesterday, against Toms, he was never down but the match could not have been more demanding.

One up playing the 18th, Montgomerie caught the green in two to Toms' three, but he had left himself in something of a fix. Ahead of him lay the most difficult of downhill and turning putts you ever saw. To the glee of his team-mates who, to a man, had wanted him to get his wild card, he read it to perfection. The moment he holed the resultant short putt, the whole of the European team were embracing on the back of the green, their faces wreathed in smiles after an afternoon of more tension than anyone would have believed possible.

In the match in front, Lee Westwood had ensured that the match could not be lost when he staged a brilliant comeback against Kenny Perry. Two down after six, he was one up going down the last and succeeded in holing a wicked three-footer to bag his point.

If Montgomerie and Westwood both played a massive role, so, too, did Sergio Garcia. Of the first five Europeans who fell behind one after another, the Spaniard, playing second, was the first to turn his match around. Two down after eight, he made three birdies in a row from the ninth, with his putt at the tenth, a 40-footer, one to remind the European fans that all could yet be well.

Garcia, who will have been earmarked as a captain of the future, grabbed his point at the 16th as Mickelson hit into the water to complete a Ryder Cup he will never forget. The American – criticised for changing his equipment and for going his own way when the rest were practising – picked up just one point.

Bernhard Langer had said on Saturday night that he would be surprised if he did not win two matches out of the first three. The matches in question were Tiger Woods versus Paul Casey, Phil Mickelson versus Sergio Garcia and Davis Love versus Darren Clarke.

The only time Woods was at a disadvantage against Casey was when he hit into the rough at the first and Casey bisected the fairway. Though Casey delayed the process by holing a handful of good six-footers, he was two down at the turn on his way to losing by 3&2.

Garcia, of course, did his bit to make Langer's prediction correct, and Clarke nearly did. Two down with four to play, he chipped in from off the penultimate green to draw level. Up the last, Love drove into thick rough and, when he took three to reach the green to Clarke's two and failed to make his par, Clarke had a three-footer to win the match. The putt swung round the edge of the hole and he had to be content with a half.

Langer had never mentioned 1999 at Brookline when the Europeans went into the last day with a 10–6 lead before losing the match by the odd point. He sensed that they had all heard enough of that disaster over the past five years. They had, and they had come to their own conclusions. Luke Donald, for one, had put it down to the way in which there were rookies who had not been given an outing before the Sunday. Here at Oakland Hills, all five rookies had had one or more outings before yesterday, with David Howell and Casey the first newcomers to win in tandem in 25 years.

Mercifully, what happened yesterday turned out to be nothing of a repeat of the Saturday morning panic when it had looked as though the Americans would win all the four-balls by way of a reply to Europe's 6½–1½ first day lead.

Howell and Casey, in the third match, were fully aware of the danger – and even more acutely so when Chad Campbell, who had done nothing all day, suddenly holed a 30-footer to put the Americans one up with one to play. After the Americans had both overshot the green at the short 17th, Howell hit to 6 feet. Howell holed for the birdie to get back to square and, as they left the green, so they learned that Westwood and Garcia had grabbed half a point up ahead.

When Howell caught the right rough off the 18th, Casey was ready to take centre stage. He smote his drive up the middle, caught the green in two and, after a long and swirling putt, signed off with a winning par.

———

25 SEPTEMBER 2006

EMOTIONS RUN HIGH AS CLARKE FULFILS HIS DESTINY

Mark Nicholas

The K Club

It began for real at the tenth green, in front of the house that Dr Smurfit built. Right there, not even a pitch from the creator of the K Club's garden gate, Darren Clarke holed the most wicked right-to-left, swinging 30-foot putt to go three up on his opponent, Zach Johnson. The young American knew then what destiny had in mind; his eyes betrayed him. So did Clarke and so did the people who had begun to gather from all parts of the course and roar their appreciation of this remarkable Northern Irishman.

About an hour and a quarter later, the destiny was fulfilled. Clarke and Johnson shook hands on the 16th green and from that moment on, emotional pandemonium broke out. Clarke wrapped his arms around his caddie, the faithful Billy Foster, before raising them to salute the enormous crowd whose hearts he had touched. Next, with the River Liffey reflecting beneath them in the gorgeous late-afternoon sun, Tom Lehman came to hold and to hug and Clarke finally caved in, the salvation of his own heart under way.

A little over a month ago, this man lost his wife. Yesterday he won the Ryder Cup. To have competed was something; to have so dominated was something else again. He has been stripped to the bone and come through it with extraordinary inner strength. Think of his children at home, two broken-hearted young boys glued to their television screen, now so inspired by their father.

After Lehman came Ian Woosnam for more of the same, more flooding emotion from hard-bitten Celts who have seen both sides of the tracks. They gripped each other so tight you wondered how they might breathe, but it was the air of redemption they somehow sucked in and the sweet air of victory that made them giddy. Many others appeared at Clarke's side – players and caddies from both teams, family and friends – tears flowing in part for him and in part for the joy that overtook them. Thousands upon thousands lined the Liffey and thousands more rose from the damp ground in the temporary stands that housed them, wiping their eyes too.

These were the jaw-dropping moments that only sport can bring, unique for the understanding between performer and spectator of all that it takes, physical and emotional. Two of the most famous men alive were part of this unforgettable scene. One, in black jeans and scarlet T-shirt, was former president Bill Clinton, whose aura was matched only by the other, Tiger Woods, whose father had passed away late this last spring. Clinton kept a low profile, shaking some hands but realising the attention belonged elsewhere. Woods bided his time, wanting a private moment in this most public place. When it came, he took Clarke to his chest and they clung briefly to the memory of their respective losses before separating and smiling a little – the victor and the vanquished in a golf match, drawn closer still by the most cruel certainty of life.

Truly, Clarke had been too good for Johnson, as Europe have been too good for the United States. The Irish have played their part and so has the weather, which lengthened the course and shortened the visitors' patience, but the better players collectively and their unbreakable spirit were beyond the reach of even Lehman's fine leadership.

Having holed from 30 feet at the tenth, Clarke ripped the guts out of Johnson at the par three 12th. He hit a poor tee-shot a couple of feet off the fringe of the green. He laughed at the incompetence, a genuine light-headed laugh, and lit another cigar. When he got to the ball it was lying well but in the clammy first cut. He chose to putt rather than chip, across the first cut onto the green and down the ridge from top tier to bottom, towards the lake that waited a further ten feet beyond the target.

At a conservative estimate the flag was 70 feet away. Outrageously, he holed it. Ridiculous. Everyone went crazy, really wild, but Johnson barely bothered. He just picked the ball out of the hole, lobbed it back to his tormentor and grinned a defeated grin. Neat and tidy, slim and preppy, young Mr Johnson had worked out this storyline two holes back, if not two days back. Yes, that was it, the irresistible force that was the European golf team in County Kildare gave us no chance, thought Zach – fancy imagining anything else.

By now, the crowd following Clarke had doubled, trebled even. Hordes of golf fans had wound their way to the soul of this team and wanted to walk him home. They sensed, as he sensed, that he would lose himself soon and that they could help.

Clarke has much appreciated the support. It has come from every corner and every nation that has a part to play, sometimes vociferously, always mentally. He felt it during the practice days, then at the opening ceremony and most touchingly on that electric first tee on Friday morning, when he choked a bit on his heartache but hung on.

It was shrewd of Ian Woosnam to pick Clarke's great buddy, Lee Westwood, to stand alongside him for the week. Such challenges are made easier by the presence of friends. In the end, though, Clarke achieved this himself, riding the wave of emotion with an amazing show of self-control and playing some memorably skilful and enterprising golf.

The next week or so will test him again but in a different way, for it will be so empty. Asked about the role of the Ryder Cup in his healing process, he said simply that time would heal, nothing else. Perhaps it has begun the process, though, showing him that there is much about life in which he can still rejoice.

Darren Clarke is the man of this Ryder Cup. Good luck to him and his boys.

————

CHAPTER 6
THE 19TH HOLE

---

7 APRIL 1988

THE OPEN IN UGANDA

Brian Oliver

The United States Masters at Augusta and Uganda's Western Open, which starts this weekend at Fort Portal, have only one thing in common:they are played at exclusive clubs. Membership of the Augusta National is regarded by some as the ultimate status symbol in America. Nobody applies to join the club. The membership of about 250 is invited.

That is more than ten times the figure at the Toro Club in the shadow of the Mountains of the Moon at Fort Portal, Uganda. The reason is not a committee bent on exclusivity; it is the difficulty of finding golf equipment and a monthly subscription of 3000 shillings, about £30 at the official exchange rate, which restricts membership to 20.

Tomorrow Dennis Kigoya, a garage owner, and a few dozen dedicated club golfers in Uganda will begin play for the Western Open at Fort Portal. When Kigoya drives off he will do so with two tees tied together with a nine-inch length of string. Like all the Fort Portal golfers he places the ball on A, sticks B in the ground too – and thereby ensures that A plus B means you never lose a tee.

He tries desperately hard never to lose balls either. If he does, he cannot rely on the Ugandan postal service to deliver replacements from the capital. He must drive to Kampala – the only place in the country where he can buy balls – and that means a ten-hour journey each way on a series of pot-holes interspersed with the occasional stretch of road.

On a trip to Uganda last month I played two rounds of the nine-hole course with Kigoya and, despite hitting the tropical deep rough (the equator is only 50 miles away) at least half a dozen times, I did not lose a ball. One of the expert barefoot caddies – average age ten – would tread down ferns taller than himself, occasionally stepping on a toad, until he found it.

The field for this week's tournament, for which sponsors were being sought to provide the rare luxury of scorecards and some semblance of a prize, would think nothing of travelling for a day to reach Fort Portal.

This sort of dedication has helped to keep the golf clubs going. There are a dozen or so clubs in Uganda, built in the days of British colonialism, and only Kampala can boast top-class playing conditions, because they have many wealthy members from embassies and big businesses.

Upkeep is a serious problem elsewhere, not surprising in a country still recovering from 20 years of civil strife. The Western Open will be played on well-kept fairways (providing diesel is available for the club's one mower) but the Toro Club mower is not suitable for greens and here the grass is too long. Instead of pins there will be tree branches.

The members have adapted. None of them has had a coaching lesson, some play barefoot and they use old clubs begged, borrowed, bought years ago or left behind by European aid or United Nations workers. The three members I went round with had handicaps of 11, eight and seven and played to them.

The course is not well manicured, yet it is a sight to behold, surrounded by a huge tea plantation and the Ruwenzori Mountains (Mountains of the Moon). Tropical trees, flowers and ferns complete the picture. Ian Woosnam will never play here, but if any Europeans fancy a holiday with a difference, golfing in Uganda does have a certain ring to it. And do not forget the string.

---

13 JULY 1992

CANNY CADDIE WHO IS MORE THAN A BAG-MAN

Robert Philip

Arthur James Balfour, prime minister and sporting nobleman, hooked his umpteenth tee-shot deep into Turnberry's waist-high rough. Alexander 'Sandy' McIlwam, caddie and misanthrope, watched its wilful flight through the driving rain with his customary jaundiced expression.

Turning to the small, drenched figure in galoshes, cloth cap and belted trench-coat, the belted earl demanded: 'What should I take now?' The reply was spoken so softly the long curve of ash on the sodden Woodbine wedged firmly between his lips scarcely twitched. 'Hoo aboot the 4:45 back tae London?' In an era when computerised yardage charts, satellite weather forecasts and high-tech equipment have turned the caddie's art into a science, Willie Aitchison may be the very last of the old school. Muirfield will be his 40th Open – the past 25 of which have been spent as Lee Trevino's sidekick.

But as he contemplates retirement – 'Lee insists he won't be back after this year and I honestly can't envisage carrying for anyone else' — the other memories remain suffused in the hazy glow of golden summers past.

'I've been incredibly lucky considering I was a petrol tanker driver in Glasgow,' says Aitchison. 'I've walked up the 18th three times with the Open champion, I've stayed in a VIP suite at the George V in Paris, I'm on first name terms with Sean Connery, I turned down Jack Nicklaus and never regretted it and Lee has become one of my closest friends. The man's unique.' A hard act to follow? 'Bloody impossible. Who else but Trevino has ever been able to make spectators gasp and laugh at the same time?'

On his impoverished beginnings: 'At five, I was working in the fields. I thought hard work was how life was meant to be. I was 21 before I discovered Manual Labour wasn't a Mexican.'

On partnering Chi Chi Rodriguez and Homero Blancas in the first round of the Masters: 'We must have looked like a civil rights march.'

After a particularly miserable round: 'I was in more bunkers than Eva Braun.'

'Name me a player today with the charisma of Trevino or Palmer,' challenges Aitchison. 'And the old-fashioned caddie is also gone forever. Jimmy Dickson or Tip Anderson could stand in the middle of the fairway and sniff the wind and rain to come as accurately as Ian McCaskill. And I could measure a course by the length of my stride better than any fancy machine.'

Indeed, Aitchison was the last man to 'eyeball' a British Open in 1967 when he guided De Vicenzo around Hoylake without the aid of a yardage chart as detailed as an AA route map. 'I remember striding up the 18th on the last day and the tears were streaming down Roberto's face. He couldn't see his own feet, never mind the flag. "Willie," he says, "pass me whatever club I need to reach the green." I handed him an eight iron and he knocked the ball to within 12 feet. That was a magic moment.'

Tall, slim and weather-beaten to a rich shade of Eldorado brown — and with the wiry tungsten-steel muscles of a Pickford's removal man – Aitchison refuses to disclose his age. 'Though I will tell you I have seven children, nine grandchildren and two great-grandchildren. I'm glad to be getting out now. I don't mean any disrespect when I say that the new generation aren't caddies at all – they're bag carriers, pure and simple.'

As a descendant of the legendary 'Fiery' John Carey, Old Da' 'Pawky' Corstorphine, Lang Willie, Tweedly Sweenum and 'Daft' Willie Gunn, Aitchison is well versed in the folklore of the original caddies.

Gunn, a notorious but harmless eccentric, accepted tips in the form of clothes. However, his peculiar idiosyncrasy was to wear them all at the same time, which is why he bestrode Carnoustie in four tail-coats, five pairs of trousers and a leaning tower of tartan bunnets and top hats.

Lang Willie cared nothing for such sartorial elegancies as he teetered around the Old Course. His taste ran only to whisky. Caddie to a classics lecturer at St Andrews University, Willie was rightfully disdainful of the professor's prowess with a five iron: 'Ach, Latin an' Greek's wan thing, but ye need brains to be a golfer.'

And, finally, Willie's all-time most popular joke from the caddie hut: Jackie Gleason to Bob Hope after shooting a 172: 'What should I give the caddie?'

'Your clubs.'

———

12 JULY 1993

'GATE-CRASHER' STILL SETS SIGHTS ON BEING INVITED TO THE PARTY

LEWINE MAIR SEES 12 BALLS DISAPPEAR IN A ROUND WITH
THE SCOURGE OF THE R&A, MAURICE FLITCROFT

You cannot, it seems, get the top names to go anywhere these days without travelling expenses and appearance money. Maurice Flitcroft, who first hit the headlines in 1976, when he took 121 in the first of the Birkdale Open's qualifying rounds at Formby, is no exception. A little reluctantly, the man who has gate-crashed as many as five Opens, settled for lunch and a round of golf, though at the end of our game he moved the goalposts. He would be invoicing the *Daily Telegraph* for lost balls (12, as it turned out).

Because he has been banned from the courses around his home in Barrow-in-Furness for 'bringing the game into disrepute', we were granted permission to play at Windermere, a gloriously-sited course ablaze with rhododendrons.

Flitcroft, now 63 but still aiming his game at the Open, albeit not this year, or so he says, felt a little rushed at the start. He and his son Gene, acting as chauffeur-cum-caddie, had taken a few wrong turnings and arrived only a minute or so before our 11:25 starting-time. Then, when we were about to tee off, one of the club's assistant professionals had spotted that Gene, below his long and rumpled brown locks, was not wearing a collar and was therefore breaking Windermere's dress rule.

Just as Mrs Flitcroft, when asked about her husband's performance at Formby, had silenced the critics with an emphatic 'Well, he's got to start somewhere', so Gene is admirably supportive of his golfing father. He was not going to make a fuss. Without further ado, he ran off to the car and found himself the top of an old England World Cup shell suit. That, apparently, made things all right.

With Gene, a part-time disc jockey, explaining to the world at large, 'He's not as bad as everyone thinks,' Flitcroft shaped to his opening tee-shot. It was, indeed, unexpectedly good. A little high and a little left, but entirely respectable. To his unmistakable glee, he began with nothing worse than a bogey.

At the second, there was a notice warning of vehicles on the adjacent road. By the time Gene had finished drawing our attention to it, there was no question as to where his father would hit.

Flitcroft has a tendency to lift the club back rather than swing it and, in this instance, the added dimension of danger had him operating at twice his normal speed. The ball careered over the wall and down the little country lane. Eventually, it came to rest on the far grass verge. In the son's eyes at least, the shot was not without its redeeming features. 'It's pin-high, dad!' he cried, delightedly.

The fourth was a bad hole. Having announced that he would 'slosh' his drive, Flitcroft knocked it into the ferns on the left, never to be seen again. We let someone through. Flitcroft then dropped another ball on the fairway and, a couple of shots later, that, too, had disappeared. Patience was wearing a little thin when, finally, ball number three arrived on the green's apron.

Flitcroft took out a wedge, but Gene wanted him to use a putter. 'I know what I'm doing,' said Flitcroft. 'You don't,' returned the son.

Flitcroft, an erstwhile crane driver and high-diving stuntman, started hitting golf balls in a field – the same field where he plays 99 per cent of his golf today – in the winter of 1974. He learned the basics of the game from a series of instructional articles by Al Geiberger – and one suspects that that former US PGA champion would not wince overmuch, if at all, at his student's stance or overlapping grip.

As luck would have it, the Open of 1976 was to be played in Flitcroft's neck of the woods. He duly wrote off to Peter Alliss at the BBC to ask for an entry form. With no reply forthcoming, he tried the R&A who, if unwittingly, were rather more helpful. The form, however, presented some problems. Was he an amateur or a professional? Since he was not a member of a club and did not have a handicap, he would have to call himself a professional.

The great day arrived, with Gene's overriding memory of the occasion one of pulling up at Formby with 'the car loaded to the brim'. One did not like to digress but what, precisely, was in the car? 'Clubs and things,' explained Gene.

'On the tee: Maurice Flitcroft,' came the starter's call. Flitcroft's knees began to quake.

He says himself that his opening drive was a poor one; he skied it. And so began a round in which he was, in every sense, at sixes and sevens.

His playing companions, meantime, were 'dour' and 'silently critical'. They congratulated him when he pinned down his only par but, at the end of the day, they made it clear that their own golf had suffered. That oft-repeated complaint – that their father has ruined the chances of others – is something his offspring have never been able to fathom. Gene and his twin brother were disco-dancing champions and they always drew strength from seeing fellow competitors in a spot of bother.

Having posted his 121, Flitcroft pulled out of the 1976 Open. He felt that his chances of qualifying had receded somewhat, while the fuss from the media and officialdom was such that he had had 'a bellyfull' by the end of the day.

He gave the Open a miss the following year but, by using a pseudonym, succeeded in teeing up again in 1978 and 1979 for pre-qualifying at South Herts. In neither instance did he get beyond the first few holes, the R&A asking him to withdraw as soon as they realised who he was. In 1983, at Pleasington, he did rather better, getting nine holes under his belt – he was 63 for that first half – before they found him out.

Then there was Ormskirk in 1984 where he felt he had never been in with a better chance. He began with a double bogey and followed it up with a bogey. At the third, he hit a fine drive and was 'looking at a par' when an R&A buggy screeched to a halt in front of his ball. Flitcroft remonstrated with the driver, asking that he be allowed to finish the hole. The R&A man would not hear of it. Nor, for that matter, would they return his £60 entrance fee.

It has all taken its toll in terms of how Flitcroft views golf's officials. He sees them as so many 'berks'. Gene, for his part, will tell you that golf clubs, with their rules, regulations and hierarchy, are like 'little schools'.

Even if Flitcroft is giving the St George's Open a miss, he has it in mind to go to the Belfry for a fortnight. He did not say anything about playing in the Ryder Cup, but he did talk of taking lessons from a Belfry professional and of getting a handicap in the process. If that worked out, he would be able to play in his next Open as an amateur. And that, he said, would make all the difference. He is sick and tired of the pressures inseparable from playing under an assumed name.

To date, he has never had an official lesson, though Gene, it has to be said, had a perfectly plausible explanation as to why his angle of attack, for the purposes of his woods, is all wrong. In walking the family Alsatian along the beach at Barrow, he apparently takes with him a club and a ball. Without so much as slowing his stride, he belts the ball for the amusement of the dog.

'That,' says Gene, who reckons that he himself could play to a 16 handicap were he given half a chance, 'gets him out of the habit of turning his shoulders'.

Father Flitcroft, heartened at having hit a handful of good seven irons in our game together, was not wholly convinced. 'My swing's just a fraction out,' he maintained. Oddly enough, those were precisely the words which Nick Faldo had used to describe his own action a few days earlier.

Nor was that the only thing these two golfing luminaries had in common. Faldo, though he failed to make quite the same impact, started his major championship campaign at that Open in 1976.

---

27 AUGUST 1993

MINDING THE TEES AND QUEUES IN JAPAN'S BUNKER MENTALITY

A ROUND OF GOLF AT THE WORLD'S MOST EXCLUSIVE CLUB, WHERE MEMBERSHIP IS £2.75 MILLION

Robert Philip

Tsuyoshi Miyauchi hopped from one foot to the other with inordinate glee, pointing manically into the near distance and yelled: 'Bun-kaah!' It was a moment so delicious he could not but share it. 'Bun-kaah!' he hollered again, turning his beaming smile upon the great semi-circle of amused faces at our back awaiting their turn. They smiled in unison, nodded excitedly and concurred. 'Bun-kaah,' agreed 50 or so voices, though not without a detectable and welcome trace of sympathy here and there.

It was 6:45 on a misty morning, there was a hint of drizzle in the air and I was some 6,500 miles from home with my ball in a bunker not 65 yards removed from where I was standing.

Koganei Golf Club, on the southern outskirts of Tokyo, is the most exclusive stretch of par 70 greensward in the world, with a minimum initial membership fee of £2.75 million, and an annual subscription of around £50,000. As I stood on the first tee, watched by the biggest gallery of my life, I was fully aware that even a divot was out of my price range.

Hole one: 467-yard par four. Teeing the ball up at near as damn knee-height to protect the priceless turf, I cravenly reached for the putter. Tsuyoshi, writer, broadcaster and man of honour, shook his head imperceptibly. A five iron? He scowled threateningly. I compromised with a three iron, though out of the corner of my eye I could see mine host frenziedly waving a driver, a device which unfailingly assumes a mind of its own on the occasions when I am ill-advised enough to attempt 'a John Daly'.

But even my faithful three iron had entered the conspiracy; the ball flew spitefully from the tee, described a hideous sideways parabola and arced unerringly towards the 18th green and into what the local members colourfully refer to as Jaws . . . a bloody great bun-kaah.

While St Andrews will forever remain the spiritual home of golf, Tokyo is now the habitat of the ancient game's most passionate practitioners, the *kichigai* (golf nuts). For those able to afford the prohibitive membership costs of a club near the centre of the city, untold luxury awaits, even if you have to arrive on the first tee before 6 a.m. to be certain of beating the crowds.

Velvet fairways, flawless greens, an open air spa bath by the ninth green, computerised mini-monorail systems to whisk your clubs along the edge of the fairways, moving walkways to speed those weary limbs on to the next elevated tee, and the finest food and sake. Such is life at the likes of Koganei.

Fifty miles to the north of Tokyo lies Narita, a nasty little course where anyone can play for a hundred quid. The first tee-off time is generally 4.30 a.m., which explains why long queues start forming at two hours after midnight on Saturday and Sunday mornings.

Those unable to afford the time – almost everyone in Tokyo can afford the £100 involved – must make do with one of the many thousands of golf ranges which cover the country. It is estimated that fewer than one in six of Japan's 15 million regular golfers has ever set foot on an actual course. How very wise.

The three-tiered Shiba range on the outskirts of the sprawling capital has space for 240 golfers, an Olympic sized pool, a sushi bar, two restaurants, massage parlour, sauna, beer garden, wine bar, ten-pin bowling and a professional's shop. With land precious in the city centre, ranges are constructed on the roofs of department stores and surrounded by 150 foot-high netting.

But why venture outdoors on a dank morning? Among the table lamps and coffee tables on the sixth floor at Seibu – Selfridges with sukiyaki – kichigai can while away the hours on a glass-enclosed practice green complete with real grass and real 'bun-kaahs'. I am reliably informed there is even a brothel in the Shinjuku area called the Hole-In-One with a putting green in the waiting room.

Koganei offers diversions of other kinds to take one's mind off the occasional sliced drive. After nine holes, which took over three hours because of the chaotic congestion on the course at that ungodly time, Tsuyoshi insisted we stop for lunch, which comprised seven courses, several beers, countless flasks of sake and a plunge in the hot tub.

It can also lay claim to the most remarkable caddies' hut to be found in golf, a band of seemingly fragile women all capable of toting four bags around 18 holes, estimating yardages to the inch without a plan of the course, and who come prepared with mobile phones so that on misty mornings such as this, they can call ahead to a colleague in order to determine whether the next green is clear.

The one thing you must not do is shoot a hole in one. For as well as the traditional round of drinks for everyone in the club-house (a small beer costs £10 and there might be 200 in attendance at any given time), the lucky golfer is also expected to complete the following rigmarole: engraved clocks noting the course, hole and date for close friends and relatives, cigarette lighters similarly embossed for his workmates, a generous tip for the caddie, a new cherry blossom tree for the club.

30 AUGUST 1993

'TIGER' READY TO BEAT THE BIGOTS

Robert Philip

When Puerto Rican Chi Chi Rodriguez was drawn to play in a threesome with Mexico's Homero Blancas and Calvin Peete, the last black golfer to win a US Tour event, at a tournament in the deep south some years ago, he commented wryly: 'The members will think it's a civil rights march out there.'

Eldrick 'Tiger' Woods is still too young to use Rodriguez-style wit to demolish the vile hatred he attracts, but if he finally forces American golf to confront the issue of racial prejudice, future generations may come to consider him as influential a figure as Michael Jordan is to basketball and Arthur Ashe was to tennis.

When he made his US Tour debut as the only black player in last year's Los Angeles Open, Woods, then just 16 years and two months old, had to walk the course in the company of several security guards after a series of threatening telephone calls. That he shot a first-round one-over-par 72 (he missed the cut following a distracted 75 on day two) proved that not only is he possessed of a precious talent but that he is blessed with a streak of defiance which will serve him well in battles to come.

Rick Hartmann, a regular money-winner in the United States and a frequent visitor to Europe, stepped from the practice tee at Hubbelrath last week and offered the opinion: 'Hey, anything can go wrong, we've seen it happen before. But this is one kid who's got it all. There's no way you can predict anything in golf, but he sure has what it takes to become the star of the show. That's going to upset quite a few folks, but I guess they'll just have to live with that.'

Those who feel less than comfortable at the prospect of a young, black superstar will also have to live with the intimidating and high-profile presence of Earl Woods, a former lieutenant-colonel in the Green Berets who first put a sawn-off putter into his son's chubby fists when the mite was ten months old. According to legend, the two-year-old Tiger (named in memory of a South Vietnamese officer beside whom Earl Woods fought and who is still listed as 'missing presumed dead') covered the outward nine of the Navy Golf Course at Cypress, California, in 48 strokes.

Though this tale is undoubtedly apocryphal, what is beyond dispute is that the toddler won a televised driving contest with Bob Hope at the age of 27 months and, at eight years, spread-eagled the opposition in the World Under-10 Championship. 'From the first time I ever laid eyes on him, I just knew he was going to be the Wolfgang Amadeus Mozart of golf,' recalled his original tutor, Rudy Duran, with suitable hyperbole. 'When he becomes the next Nicklaus I will take great delight in telling the world "I told you so".'

The next Nicklaus? Maybe not, though earlier this month Woods won an unprecedented third successive US junior amateur title, whipping the other American wonderboy, Ted Oh, 4&3 in the semi-finals. 'Now I want the senior US amateur, then the Walker Cup, then my Tour card, then a major, the Masters preferably, then a crack at this Ryder Cup thing,' Woods told his television audience with the brash confidence of youth.

While he will not be in contention for a Ryder Cup place in 1995, Woods may well be to the fore by the time of the '97 contest. By then he should be on his way to achieving his ultimate ambition of 'becoming the best golfer in the world . . . not the best black golfer, simply the best golfer'.

If life were only that simple.

———

7 FEBRUARY 1994

BLACK DAY WHEN PRINCESS ALMOST BECAME A CADDIE

HOW I NEARLY MADE MY MARK AT GLENEAGLES, FEELING
ANCIENT IN FRONT OF A ROYAL

Michael Parkinson

The other day a chap called doing a survey for a golf magazine. Wanted to know what were my outstanding memories of the last 12 months. He didn't want the obvious moments, like Greg Norman winning the Open or Nick Faldo smiling (and such a nice smile too). Rather he wanted my personal recollections of the season, those times when I strode down the fairway convinced that had I played golf from an early age, they would never have heard of Arnold Palmer.

It was a good time to ask. All I have done of late is stare out of the window watching the wind and rain buffet the bare trees. What I noticed as autumn lengthened into winter was the decreasing amount of foliage in the landscape being matched by a corresponding increase in the amount of clothes worn by the wife as she prepared for a round of golf.

(While on the subject, I was recently taken to task by a reader who objects to my use of the term 'the wife'. I am criticised for being at best patronising, at worst demeaning by addressing her in this fashion. All I can say is that she regularly calls me 'the old man' when in conversation with others and I have not yet felt the need to write her a solicitor's letter. What is more, she is called something far more colourful than 'the wife' when she sinks a 15-foot left-to-right putt to take my money – as she often does.)

Anyway, the wife (for it is she) is nowadays wearing so much clothing that, combined with her overloaded golf bag, she becomes a danger to bridges weakened by structural damage. I envy her determination and fortitude. I am made of softer stuff. I cannot abide golf in cold and inclement weather. It is not that I am namby-pamby, rather I suffer from a medical condition known as Digitus Pastinaca, or, to give it a common name, Parsnip Fingers. This disability means that whenever it gets cold, my fingers take on the anaemic colour of parsnips.

I have tried all the remedies. Those sheepskin-lined mittens seemed the answer, until a friend pointed out I would play better if I removed them before I hit the ball. What I really require is a warm golf club. Surely it cannot be beyond the wit of modern man to invent a set of centrally heated clubs?

What a revolution that would bring about. Golf in the Arctic Circle, the Reykjavik Open, a skins in Murmansk, the next Ryder Cup in Alaska. Instead, what the boffins have come up with are musical socks. These play your favourite tune as they are slipped on the feet. It might not sound much but I believe the invention could have real significance for the game of golf.

Disciples of the Holloway Musical Golf Swing method (as devised by my friend and golfing partner Lozza Holloway, pianist, composer and smooth swinger) will need no explaining how these socks could be programmed for their benefit. Instead of humming the opening bars of the Blue Danube as we swing (Da-Da-Da-Da-Dum) we could rely on our socks to do the job for us. It would be an immense load taken from minds already burdened with good advice.

I digress. Back to my golfing year. It started at Gleneagles in May. We were invited to play in the Monarch's Challenge, the tournament officially opening the new Monarch's course designed by Jack Nicklaus. Gleneagles is one of my favourite places on this planet. The glen is inspiringly beautiful, the hotel sumptuous without being awesome, the courses landscaped by man but with a lot of divine intervention.

We went to bed the night before the practice day in high expectation. It had been a lovely day in mid-May. When we awoke it was to a perfect winter's morning. There was six inches of snow on the ground and the Ochil Hills looked like they were made of icing sugar.

Jackie Stewart, who was organising the event, sent for supplies of wet-weather gear and thermal underwear. The wet gear arrived safely but the thermal underwear was stuck on Shap Fell where the driver was no doubt much consoled by the load he was carrying. It was not, by any stretch of the imagination, a propitious start.

Overnight, the rain washed most of the snow away and the big day dawned with the Ochil Hills black with cloud and Mr Nicklaus's baby submerged in flood water.

Our team included Commander Tim Laurence, whose wife, the Princess Royal, decided to come along for the walk. This meant that we were followed by a large gallery including many photographers. Now it is one thing teeing off in front of a crowd, quite another when that crowd trails around with you. Normally, after the first tee, you can forget the spectators and display your incompetence in private, which is how it should be. Not this time.

On the first hole I hit my second shot into a bunker. This greatly intrigued Princess Anne, who asked me if there was a particular technique for playing out of sand. I told her what I remembered from the *Gary Player Book of Bunker Play*. When I put it into practice the ball stayed in the trap. 'Mr Parkinson knows what to do but the ball doesn't,' Princess Anne told her husband.

It was an ordinary start and it didn't get any better. Neither my humour nor my reputation was helped by the fact that my wife was playing ahead of me. Wherever we turned up someone would remind me that Mary had just passed through and had made par net birdie against my double bogey.

'Can I take it Mrs Parkinson is a better golfer than you?' the Princess Royal asked. I was tempted to say that the Queen Mother was probably a better golfer than me on present showing. Instead I nodded miserably. Looking back I think at that moment I touched the Royal heart, and precipitated the extraordinary event that followed.

After we had driven off on the next tee a squall raced down the glen bringing high wind and sleet against our backs. I went to put on my wet gear and discovered that I had left it at the clubhouse. My caddie was sent in a buggy to collect it before the dreaded parsnip syndrome took over my whole body.

I sloshed my way down the fairway to where my drive had landed. With the wind behind I had hit a good shot of 200 yards or more. Looked like a three wood second shot. It was then I realised I had left my bag on the tee. I squelched all the way back and by the time I returned to my ball there were about three gallons of water in the bag and the woes of the world were on my shoulders. In the meantime my fellow golfers, who had been awaiting my second shot, had played on.

I took my three wood from the bag and found the grip had all the purchase of a greasy pole. The club spun in my hands and the ball sliced down the fairway into yet another bunker. I was about to curse when I was aware of someone standing behind me. I turned and there was the Princess Royal. She gave me the sort of look you see on the face of animal lovers when they visit Battersea Dogs' Home. 'Would you like me to carry your golf bag?' she asked.

Had it been the wife I wouldn't have thought twice. 'You couldn't possibly,' I replied. Now Princess Anne is the wrong person to tell she mustn't do something. 'We'll see about that,' she said and bent to pick up my bag.

At that moment, my caddie came aquaplaning down the fairway in the buggy. Had he not done so I am perfectly convinced I would have walked towards my next shot with a royal bag-carrier.

Imagine the photograph in the papers; think of what it might have done for my standing at the Royal & Ancient; picture, if you are able, me standing at the clubhouse bar telling the lads: 'As I was saying to my caddie, the Princess Royal, only the other day . . .'; contemplate, if you will, the television pictures beamed into every household, and my Auntie Madge in Chesterfield saying: 'Who's that woman carrying our Mike's bag?'

When it comes to who has the best golfing memory of 1993, I rest my case. One further point of interest for royal watchers the world over: if you are ever approached by someone called Tim Laurence for a game of golf and he tells you he has a handicap of 18, play for fun, not money.

---

18 APRIL 1998

GOLDEN BELL TOLLS FOR HEROES AND HACKS IN THE PRIVATE WATERWORLD

RAPIDLY SHIFTING WINDS CAN TURN THE PERFECT SEVEN IRON TEE-SHOT INTO ANOTHER GOLFING NIGHTMARE

Martin Johnson

Augusta

Standing on the 12th tee, coming off – as they say in America – double bogey at 11, it was something of a relief that there was less of an audience than there had been for Mark O'Meara the previous day. Even so, the mind conjured up disturbing images of the CBS commentator chuntering into his microphone. 'Martin Johnson . . . trying to stop the bleeding.' Or a variation on that familiar cry from the gallery as the ball hobbled off the clubface: 'You're not the man!' Then there was the grave voice of the CBS summariser, intoning, in the way that CBS summarisers tend to do, 'You don't try and get cute with Amen Corner on a Monday afternoon. Just take your triple bogey and get out of there.'

There was certainly enough time for all these ghostly apparitions to be flitting around inside the head, as there was a 25-minute log-jam on the tee while a succession of club-handicap golfers did battle with one of Augusta National's most buttock-clenching holes. On the one occasion every year that the world's most private golf club opens its doors to a small selection of media representatives, there were three four-balls waiting to hit off, while the group up ahead had encountered a variety of problems. Two of them were taking penalty drops from the water, another was barely visible up among the azaleas on the far bank, and the fourth was busy removing most of the sand from the back bunker.

The hole is known as the Golden Bell, and two years earlier it had tolled for Greg Norman against Nick Faldo as the Shark made an involuntary contribution to the highly profitable industry known as American Lake Balls. There is water all over Augusta's back nine, but none so treacherous as here in front of the 12th, where the turtles can barely recognise their eggs among the collection of submerged Maxflis.

The wind shifts so often and so quickly here that what began as a perfect seven iron when it left the tee can either turn out to be two clubs short or two clubs long by the time it gets up above the pines. However, as the wait continued, my caddie did his best to break the tension. 'Ever heard of Clifford Roberts?' 'No, don't think so.' 'Well, he was co-founder of the Augusta National with Bobby Jones. Shot himself in the head. Right here on the 12th hole.' Very cheery. When you ask your caddie for a weapon at the 12th, you're not sure whether he's going to hand you a six iron or a six shooter.

We were also playing to the same pin placements as the likes of O'Meara and Fred Couples the previous afternoon, and this one, set tight to the right, positively invited a watery grave. Not surprisingly, valour fought an extremely brief and losing battle with discretion, and a hoicked seven iron to the back left fringe was followed by a duffed chip, a nervous prod with the putter from 25 feet, and a seven-footer which wriggled in by the side door. Given that a bogey here feels like an eagle, I strutted to the

13th tee wondering what sort of score poor old Clifford Roberts had racked up before reaching for the revolver.

Playing the same course (albeit from slightly forward tees) as the final round Masters competitors tends to have a limiting effect on ambition, and mine was simply to make a better fist of my first ever shot at Augusta than Ignacio Garrido made of his. On the opening day, the Spaniard had brought joy to every hacker who has ever played by topping his tee-shot off the first and being comfortably outdriven by the 96-year-old Gene Sarazen.

However, apart from the water on the back nine, the only really nerve-racking aspect of Augusta National is putting, a point that was reinforced even before setting out when I lost a ball on the practice green. An eight-footer downhill turned sharp right, and when it finally came to rest, it was unidentifiable among another clutch of balls 45 feet further away.

I had asked the caddiemaster if Joe Collins was available to carry the bag, but Colin Montgomerie's man had, not surprisingly, failed to show up for work after pocketing his 10 per cent of Monty's $89,000. I ended up with Jimmy Briscoe, flat rate $50 but with the promise of a large bonus if I managed a lower score than the highest recorded in Masters week, Doug Ford's 86 in the opening round. I missed a ten-footer for an 85 at the 18th, and Jimmy looked so sad that he got his bonus anyway. Coincidentally, Jimmy had carried Doug Ford's bag in the 1976 Masters (it was not until 1983 that the players were allowed to use their regular caddies here) and I asked him how Ford had played. 'Just terrible,' he said. Poor old Jim. First Ford, then me.

I offered Jimmy several reminders of Doug Ford on the way round, not to mention one or two impersonations of Gerald Ford as well, who inflicted almost as many injuries on American pro-am galleries as Spiro Agnew. As things turned out, I was lucky to get Jimmy, not so much because he was the local equivalent of Pete Coleman, but in that he was refreshingly honest in his appraisal of a lousy shot. The other three caddies in our group had each graduated from the 'have a nice day' school of American sincerity, and their gushing comments bore less relation to the quality of the stroke they had just witnessed than the size of the tip they were hoping to get.

The most oleaginous of them all was Russ, who spent most of the round attempting to convince an American golf writer named George that the Augusta National was a touch too easy for a man of his talents. George certainly scored pretty well, thanks largely to a method that involved playing at least two balls on every hole, and discarding the one he didn't much care for.

His opening tee-shot was a heeled scuttle on to the ninth fairway, which he immediately abandoned in favour of hitting another, this time holing out with three shots and two putts. Russ, without so much as blinking, said: 'Nice five, George.' Neither did George look the slightest bit embarrassed about claiming the honour on the second tee.

Russ offered further encouragement on the 16th tee, where George appeared a little uncertain about the club that Russ had thrust into his hand. 'Trust it, George, trust it,' said Russ, and when George's ball barely made it halfway across the water before splashing into oblivion, Russ was able to reassure him that only a capricious change in the wind had thwarted what might otherwise have been a hole in one.

John, an American freelance reporter, was not quite so gullible as George, and when his caddie decreed that bad luck had been responsible for his tee-shot at the 18th – sharp left into the trees, a ricochet into the back of the spectator stand around the 17th green, and an eventual resting place behind a water fountain – John's attempt to bury his driver ten feet into the tee bed suggested that he might not entirely have shared this view.

More than once during the BBC's Masters coverage, Peter Alliss has suggested that decent club golfers would struggle to break 100 around the Augusta that the Masters field is obliged to play, entirely due to the speed of the greens. And he'd be right. The ones we putted on had had 24 hours of growth, and were merely like waxed linoleum rather than, as someone once suggested, attempting to stop a marble on a car bonnet.

At the 14th, on in two, I nudged a 15-footer for birdie 12 feet past, tapped the next one four feet past, and was grateful to escape with a five. At the 16th, aiming for the right of the green and away from the water, I pulled it slightly, and finished three feet from the pin. The wrong side of the pin. I didn't so much putt it as breathe on it, and it rolled three feet past. In fact, Augusta is so finely manicured you'd have trouble stopping a putt on the tees never mind the greens.

The penalty that the members have to pay for Augusta's greens is not being able to play between May 17 and October 10. That's how long the course is closed every year to prevent the bent grass from frying in the Georgia heat. If you managed to get past the security guards for a peek at the course in mid-summer, and saw the greens being watered and sheltered under shaded tents, you'd probably think you'd wandered into a garden centre.

However, what Alliss failed to point out is that the course is actually easier for the professionals. You have no real definition behind most of the greens when there are no spectators, and, of course, no spectators means that there is no one to stop your ball if you hit it too hard. In all modesty, I have to say that a gallery behind the bunker at the second might well have turned my eight into a pleasing seven.

As for my six at the 11th, I only put my second shot into Larry Mize country in the interests of research, and can authoritatively state that what Mize did to Greg Norman in 1987 by chipping in is not possible. I can also confirm that most of the fairways – I never saw the 15th, but played the 17th twice in opposite directions – are immaculate enough to eat your dinner off. In fact, all you have to worry about after playing Augusta is coming home and attempting to make your next dozen putts travel further than two inches.

————

24 JULY 1999

DOWN IN THE JUNGLE SOMETHING STIRRED

MARTIN JOHNSON DISCOVERS THE FULL HORROR OF
CARNOUSTIE'S OBSTACLES

If you thought Jean Van de Velde was a sand-wedge short of a full set when he rolled up his trouser legs and clambered into the Barry Burn on Sunday, you should try doing it when the course is open to genuine hackers. In the interests of research, I had a go two days later, and was more in need of a hard hat than the workmen dismantling the adjacent spectator stand. It was like being at the wrong end of the firing range at Bisley. Splash, splosh, sploosh.

I had only been in there half a minute before coming under mortar attack, and began to wonder whether the crazy Frenchman had decided to come back for another go. However, instead of several cries of 'Mon Dieu!', a succession of agonised 'Ah sos!' floated across on the Carnoustie wind, and it turned out to be – on the golf course from hell – a Japanese four-ball from hell.

None of them felt inclined to climb down and pursue the option of playing the ball as it lay, and only when you're down there can you fully appreciate just how completely Van de Velde and the plot had parted company. There is a minimum of four inches of water lying on top of a bed of slippery rock and if Jean had gone ahead with the most ill-conceived French strategy since the Maginot Line, there would have been so much twisted metal that his caddie would have eventually been forced to hand him the putter.

It was not an unusual sight in itself to see a Frenchman playing golf with his trousers rolled up, as anyone who has played in France could testify. Over there, they play in jeans, culottes, skirts, high heels, you name it, and it is by no means unusual to find yourself stuck behind a seven-ball – not including the dog, the grandmère and grandpère, and the baby in the pushchair.

Jean's wife, Brigitte, therefore, would be well used to curious sights on a golf course, but when the television cameras picked her up watching her old man disappearing into the burn, she looked as though she was about to give birth to a litter of kittens. No wonder. Mentally, she'd probably been around Harrods at least twice with the £350,000 winner's cheque.

When Inspector Clouseau was back on the 18th tee, it looked as though he could have played the hole with his umbrella and still become Open champion. Or indeed played it with one arm, as my own caddie, Alex Wilmott, has done thousands of times without racking up anything as nasty as a seven. Alex, who lost an arm in a butcher's mincing machine at the age of 14, has won the British one-armed golf championship no less than seven times. At his peak, he played to a handicap of eight, which, around this course, is no mean achievement even for someone who is able to get two hands on the club. Now 67, Alex said that he had never seen anyone attempt to play out of the burn at the 18th in more than half a century of playing here.

'That's how the Frenchie should have played it,' said Alex, as I laid up short of the water, not so much out of common sense as (having dunked my drive deep into a bunker) necessity. A chip, a putt and a routine par four later and I was thinking: 'That could have been me holding the auld claret jug.' Well, it could have been if you discount the 81 strokes required to get to the 18th tee on a course set up 950 yards shorter and with no higher penalty for making a Clouseau of it than having to buy the drinks for my opponent. This was the New Zealand Olympic yachtsman Russell Coutts, who himself made a four on a day when the wind would certainly have filled the spinnaker on his America's Cup defenders' boat next January.

So what was it like to play a course that left so many professionals apparently in need of counselling? On a blustery day to boot, and with the head green-keeper yet to take a lawnmower (or, more likely, a combine harvester) to the rough in case any of the Open competitors had yet to find their way out of it. Nothing much to it, actually. I still have the same ball, a little battle-scarred admittedly, but nonetheless the same one. And the closest I came to losing it was on the tee at the par-three 16th when it momentarily got jammed inside the ballwasher.

In fact, at four strokes better than Sergio Garcia's first round 89, it was a minor disappointment to find that the press centre had all but been dismantled. I would have been more than happy to grant Dougie Donnelly an interview. Neither was there any wimping that boring American Tiger Woods. Nothing but the driver, which, when it was really middled, would occasionally have been within 100 yards of Woods' two iron. It is a slightly different game when you find yourself playing the downwind par four 15th with a driver and a seven iron and realise that Woods – from 47 yards further back – played it with a six iron and sand-wedge.

In the knowledge that Van de Velde had twice overruled his caddie on the 18th, I had no hesitation in leaving club selection to my own man, especially as Scottish caddies traditionally have a nice line in deflationary wit. On the card-wrecking, par five sixth, Hogan's Alley, I ventured a tentative: 'Driver, Alex?' 'Aye,' he replied. 'Then another driver, and maybe a driver for the third.' A par at the second yielded a 'good four there', followed by – lest I got carried away – 'any four is a good four round here. Even on the par threes'.

On the fourth tee, it was slightly puzzling when a horrific slice met with Alex's instant approval. 'Great shot,' he said. 'Ye've hit it so far right, that'll be on the 15th fairway.' And so it was. A birdie at the par-three, 145-yard crosswind eighth ('eight iron to 15 feet, holed the putt' as I would have said at the press conference) got us out in a semi-respectable 41, but on the back nine I would happily have traded in the eight iron for a machete.

A Clark Gable off the tee at the 11th ('gone with the wind', explained Alex) found one of those lies which gave Greg Norman apoplexy, and a ferocious swing advanced my ball a few inches, from a horrendous lie into a merely horrible one. Another purple faced lunge moved us a further three feet on to a spectator path and, joy of joys, behind a TV tower. Nothing gives an amateur so much pleasure, or makes him feel more like a pro, than getting a drop for line of sight relief.

The best shot of the day was a four iron to the back of the green at the par three 16th, 223 yards downwind compared to 250 for the Open. Again, Alex did not allow this to go to my head. Casting his mind back to a duff off the fairway at the 12th, Alex said: 'Aye, ye're a hard man tae club. Ye're either hittin' a four iron 245 yards, or hittin' it ten feet.'

Finally, it was the triumphant walk down the 18th, where the noise from the gallery (i.e. two blokes hammering away in a deserted grandstand) was deafening. It was only polite to give them a wave. 'How many shots harder than the Old Course is this one?' I asked Alex. He replied: 'At least seven.' Which is how many Van de Velde took down the 18th. The Frenchman could, in fact, have been the subject of one of Carnoustie's more celebrated caddie stories when an American, who had spent all day fishing his ball out of the course's signature feature, asked for the best route back to his hotel in St Andrews.

'Up tae Brechin, across tae Troon, doon tae Edinburgh, across the Forth Bridge, and on tae St Andrews,' said the caddie. 'Are you sure that's the quickest way?' asked the Yank. 'Well it's no actually the quickest,' said the caddie. 'But I guarantee ye'll nae have tae cross the Barry Burn.'

Carnoustie comparison: Martin Johnson v Sergio Garcia

Hole	1	2	3	4	5	6	7	8	9	10	11	12	13	14	15	16	17	18	Total
Par	4	4	4	4	5	4	3	4	4	4	4	4	3	5	4	3	4	4	
M Johnson	5	4	4	5	5	6	5	2	5	5	6	6	4	5	6	3	5	4	85
S Garcia	7	4	4	5	5	5	4	4	6	6	5	6	3	4	5	5	5	6	89

The Open course measured 7,361 yards, par 71. The members' course is 6,405 yards, par 70. Martin Johnson plays off a 9 Handicap.

31 DECEMBER 2000

BALLESTEROS FINDS BALANCE AMID DECLINE

PASSION FOR GOLF DRIVES LEGEND ON DESPITE FALL TO MORTALITY DURING DARK YEARS ON TOUR

Martin Johnson

San Roque

As the members gathered round for a lesson at the Seve Ballesteros School of Natural Golf in San Roque on Saturday, they probably weren't too sure what kind of tips the great man was about to impart. 'Always carry a machete for getting through the undergrowth,' perhaps, or: 'Remember, the tracker dogs may not always be able to find you out there. So don't leave home without a compass.'

There was a time when Ballesteros could charm the birds from the trees with his golf swing, but nowadays he's more likely to send them squawking out of the branches with a snap hook off the tee, propelling his drive into areas where only the buzzards circle overhead. His descent into golfing mortality involves the kind of gradient normally experienced only by Olympic downhill skiers, and grateful though the punters were for his nuggets of advice, the most powerful wish down on the range was for the physician to heal himself.

When Ballesteros won the 1979 Open at Royal Lytham, he was dubbed – somewhat unfairly at the time – the car park champion. Nowadays, however, there is every chance of seeing him playing his second from the back seat of a Land Rover – doors ajar under the line-of-sight relief rule – and it is only his unrivalled ability to conjure up a par from a tricky lie on the leather upholstery that offers him any hope of competing at all.

Saturday's clinic was exclusively devoted to the bunker shot, which Seve was demonstrating to an assortment of high handicappers busy removing plenty of sand, but very few golf balls. 'Not too tight with the hands on the club,' he exhorted a middle-aged American lady with a grip like the Boston Strangler, and who was causing a high degree of pandemonium with a series of low shanks.

'You see, this is not a difficult shot,' he said, feathering the ball over a steep lip to about three inches from the cup, and indeed it isn't for a professional golfer wielding a 60-degree sand-wedge. Ballesteros, though, was using a three iron, something that Jack Nicklaus was not able to do, despite seeking tuition when he came across the Spaniard in a bunker during a practice round at the Tournament Players' Championship in America.

'Jack said to me: "why would you need this type of shot anyway?" but I was just having fun. I learnt it when I was nine, when all I had was a three iron. Having only one of something was not very unusual in my village. There were 300 people living there, and we only had one telephone.'

Ballesteros now has more telephones than that in his bathroom, but the last ten years or so have been such a dark period for his golf that the numbers in his personal directory probably include one for the Samaritans. He's tried everything else – gurus, psychologists, swing doctors, you name it – but while Seve remains the man you'd most likely call up to make a par for your life, you'd die of a heart attack anyway watching him make it.

'I know what is wrong,' he says. 'It is very simple. I am bad physically with my back, and also my right shoulder. I think I hurt my back when I was 13, when I used to do boxing with my friends, and the shoulder may be from picking up my seven-year-old daughter. But there are other things. As you get older you lose some strength, some flexibility, and [tapping at his forehead] a little bit in here, too. The desire to compete is not quite as great, it is harder to leave your home and family behind, to be dedicated, and concentration is more difficult, too. These are a lot of things, yes?'

And yet he keeps going, like a former Ferrari driver attempting to keep up with the boy racers in a battered Trabant. Why? 'Listen, I am no different to any golfer. I am still motivated because I like the game, and we all have one or two shots in a round that make us feel happy. So we keep coming back.

'The worst thing for me is not playing well. You don't enjoy it. You know you can do it but, for whatever reason, it goes. I say to myself a lot after a bad round: "No more of this. No more." But this frustration, it only lasts a minute. Then I try again.

'Golf is a game that makes you humble, and the biggest thing of all is that it needs patience. It is the best education for life of any game I know, and it makes you become an addict. I practice hard by myself, searching for things, but I also like to play social golf as well. With my family, with my friends, and anyone I want to, whether they are good players or not. You can learn a lot from players who are not as good as you are, believe me.'

Ballesteros also enjoys helping other golfers, even if he finds it hard to help himself, and that familiar flashing smile is most often seen nowadays when he's playing in the pre-tournament pro-ams. 'It is a good feeling helping someone play better,' he said.

He will perhaps never regain the cutting edge which made him one of the world's greatest players, and beyond any doubt, the world's greatest match player. It is something he himself recognises. 'I still have goals, but they are realistic ones. Like Gary Player, who wanted to be the oldest player to make the cut at the Masters, and who in ten years' time might want to become the oldest player to make four pars in a row at the Masters. Goals are always changing. People ask if I will carry on to play on the Seniors Tour in six years' time when I am 50. Perhaps I will. Perhaps not. Who can say?

'My biggest goal, I have already achieved. I wanted to get married, and have a family, and make sure they were healthy and received a good education. So I will educate my children at a

British boarding school when the time is right, because Britain has the best education system I think.

'One of my sons may be a professional golfer, he is very good already, nine handicap, and the other one may be a soccer player. He wants to play for Real Madrid. They both play golf, and I make them go out with just one club. Maybe a seven iron one day, or a nine iron another. It is good for teaching imagination.'

Sadly, it is perhaps stretching imagination too far to think that Ballesteros will emulate Nicklaus, who won a major championship at the age of 46, but typically he refuses to acknowledge that it is totally out of the question. 'Ian Woosnam almost won the Open this year aged 44, so who is to say it cannot be done. There is difficult, and there is impossible.' He smiled. 'To walk all the way to the moon – that's impossible.'

***

31 MAY 2003

SOME HACKER ALWAYS TURNS UP WITH A SACK OF BATS, DRESSED IN A MILLWALL SHIRT

PRO-AM ETIQUETTE

Jasper Carrott

I cannot think of any other sport where the rank amateur can play against or with his professional heroes, at the most famous venues, on more or less level terms. Pro-am golf gives you this opportunity.

On Wednesday, at the Marriott Forest of Arden, Thomas Bjorn, Darren Clarke, Justin Rose *et al* will be chaperoning 21-handicap postmen and lawyers round the intricacies of a testing course. What the professionals think of these obligatory days is kept very much under wraps, but the official line is that they enjoy themselves and appreciate the chance to meet their public.

There's not an amateur playing in the event who doesn't think that given the time and instruction they couldn't be up there with the best of them, and believe me they will be out there trying to prove it.

Certainly their equipment will be on a par. They will have the latest plutonium driver with the moon-rock core that will add 40 yards to their drive, the new Zynthane-covered ball that gives extra length and even the new tee that guarantees at least ten per cent to your distance. In theory they should hit the ball some 500 yards – the problem is connecting club with ball. On the other hand, some hacker always turns up with a 'sack of bats' that belonged to his dead aunt, dressed in borderline jeans and a Millwall shirt.

However, the pros are forever patient and I have to give credit to them when playing with the amateurs. They suffer braggarts with resilience and rabbits with good humour and in my experience they are more than happy to give advice on swings, rules and etiquette providing you don't turn it into a personal lesson.

A pro told me a story he swears was true about a player coming up to ask him for advice. The player told him he had taken an air shot, at a ball that wasn't his, using a friend's wedge, and who should he see? 'An optician,' said the pro.

There are certain niceties that should be observed when playing alongside the golfing gods. If you have a late tee-off be careful of the freely obtainable hospitality – drink can affect one's demeanour. On one occasion a well-known actor arrived at the tee dribbling brandy from all orifices. On removing his driver from its sheath he proclaimed to the ball in a rather affected thespian tone: 'I shall smite thee poor Yorrick unto the realms of Hades.' He swung the club, smote a 3-lb divot straight into the starter's coffee and promptly toppled into the resultant hole.

It is important to remember when accompanying said gods that you realise they are earning their living. They might be top of their profession but they are still capable of scuffing a 20-foot bodge shot into a spectator's duffle bag. Informing them you do that on a regular basis and your mates let you take it again does not go down too well.

And whatever you do, don't mess with the pro's equipment. They hate players pulling out one of their clubs and swishing it through the undergrowth to test what it feels like. I heard that one idiot, having examined his pro's club, had pulled the lead tape off the club head and said: 'No wonder you can't hit the ball, look at the crap you had stuck on the end.'

I have been fortunate to play in many of these events and am always considerate of whom I am playing with. However, even I can get it wrong. In Jersey one time I was playing with a Spanish professional who couldn't speak English. I have a rudimentary knowledge of Spanish and was trying to converse with him – not easy when your vocabulary is limited to ordering food and drink and Real Madrid. On the 14th hole he carved a shot way into the undergrowth with no way of recovery.

I tried to think of some way of telling him his ball was lost. The only word that came to mind was 'Basura!' It is Spanish for rubbish. 'Rubbish! Rubbish?' I hollered at him as he turned and gave me a look that made me feel Gibraltar was my fault. He walked off spitting some Spanish invective in my direction that, roughly translated means, 'one who makes love on his own'.

The best vantage point at any pro-am is the first tee. Here you can see what nerves do to a golf swing. Many an amateur player is reduced to trembling plasma as several hundred voyeurs look on in anticipation as competitors try to get the ball away. Air shots, for some reason, are the funniest thing since Norman Wisdom.

Pete McGovern, director of golf at the Belfry, has a hilarious video of first tee nerves. The variations on such a simple thing as a golf swing beggar belief. You can see golfers who should be at the Royal Ballet as they pirouette on the tee, to lumberjacks whose swing would fit into a telephone box. One chap hits the ball with his back directly opposite to the direction he wants it to go, claiming it cures the dreaded slice; believe it or not, it works.

Sadly, I will not be there on Wednesday, but if you can get along you'll see some unbelievable golf, skilfully executed and a wonder to behold. The pros aren't bad either.

———

5 MARCH 2004

EVERY SHOT ENDS UP IN THE SAND AT AL GHAZAL

Martin Johnson

Abu Dhabi

When Nick Faldo, Ian Woosnam and several other big-name European golfers drive up to the Al Ghazal Course here on Monday, the long road up to the clubhouse may not quite evoke memories of Augusta's Magnolia Drive. One look at the landscape and they will probably be wondering why they are sitting in the back of an air-conditioned limousine rather than on the back of a courtesy camel.

There is not much that Faldo and Woosnam have not seen or done in their careers, but the Gulf Air-sponsored World Sand Golf Championship will be a novel experience. Apart from the giant privet hedge sculpted to advertise the golf club owners, Abu Dhabi Duty Free, there is not a blade of grass on the entire course, and caddies will be checking their yardages from the burrows (known as dhubs) dug by desert lizards.

The reward for hitting the fairway, which is defined by a line of wooden stakes, is the privilege of hitting your next shot off a piece of portable Astroturf, and the penalty for missing it, even by a couple of inches, is the kind of lie Alan Shepard had for his six iron on the moon. Here in the Middle East, it is a mat if you are on the fairway and a prayer mat if you are not.

Not even the greens are green. The 'browns', as they are known, are a mixture of sand and oil, pioneered in the late 1940s by a group of ex-pats working for a Saudi Arabian petroleum company in Dhahran. The browns are a long way short of Augusta on the stimpmeter, but there are no spike marks or bumps to contend with, as an assortment of large sweeping-brushes are on hand to give you an unblemished line to the hole. The tournament is being televised on Sky, and viewers are unlikely to mistake it for the Sunningdale Foursomes.

The one-day pro-am tournament has managed to attract the likes of Faldo, Woosnam and Padraig Harrington by dint of dropping it in between the Dubai Desert Classic and the Qatar Open, and has avoided the label of 'just another routine tour event' by not being staged on either of Abu Dhabi's two championship grass courses. These are sustained by a daily dose of 2½ million gallons of water, whereas the head green-keeper at Al Ghazal can comfortably get by on a couple of buckets.

The course record of 65, at a club with a mixture of 350 local and ex-pat members, will almost certainly come under threat, although the chances of anyone taking it apart will be substantially reduced by the capricious desert winds and the different technique required for the approach shots. And if you get one a bit heavy from the wrong side of the fairway pegs, the penalty is not only a shot that goes nowhere, but more sand in your clothing than you would bring back from a family outing to Skegness.

I was partnered by the British golfer Yasin Ali, 22, whose helpful hints were largely wasted on someone who, by the time we shook hands on the 18th, resembled a haggard survivor from Rommel's Afrika Corps.

Like most young pros nowadays, Yasin gives the golf ball such a fearful thump that he eschewed his driver off the first tee to remain short of a ditch 280 yards away. He plucked out a two iron, so I casually inquired how far he normally hit it. 'Oh, about 240,' he said, whereupon the arrival of a slight following breeze persuaded him to switch to a three iron.

Later on, he flew through the back of a brown with a five iron from 220 yards, while I was away on another Saharan expedition, being chaperoned by Mohamad Mounib, club member and managing director of Abu Dhabi Duty Free. Mohamad was a bit anxious about my proximity to an ancient desert burial ground which has been known to swallow errant golfers. It is one of the more unusual sites for a 'Ground Under Repair' notice, although the likes of Faldo need not worry too much, largely because it is about 150 yards wide of where he will be aiming.

Neither should it represent too much of a hazard for spectators, as the desert sand tournament, uniquely, will usher the galleries onto the fairways rather than behind a crowd-control rope. The pros will have their patience severely tested with spectators wandering about behind them, and it is not entirely out of the question that the ancient burial grounds might be in for a few more modern customers.

Yasin had two contrasting highlights to his round, the first when I nearly took him out with a seven iron as he sat in what he foolishly regarded as a safe spot to park his buggy, and the second when the beep from his mobile phone turned out to be a text message from Faldo asking if he would care to join him in a practice round for the Dubai Classic.

'He kind of knows me from his Junior Golf Academy,' said Yasin, who was runner-up in the 2000 Faldo Series grand final at Hoylake, 'but, phew, I never expected this.' Yasin got into the Dubai tournament by winning a local qualifier, having failed – by a single stroke each time – to win a regular place on this season's European or Asian tours. Born in Kenya and brought up in Britain, he has now relocated to Dubai as a touring pro attached to the floodlit Nad Al Sheba course there.

There is a lot to be said for golf in the Gulf, which is only about six and a half hours away, has plenty of high-class championship courses, and is a good bit cheaper and less crowded than Spain and Portugal. And in the case of Al Ghazal, there are three surefire guarantees: it'll be different, you'll always get a perfect lie on the fairway, and, for hay fever sufferers, there's the bonus of a sneeze-free round.

———

6 MAY 2004

PLAYING PRO-AMS WITH ARNOLD PALMER WAS A PRIVILEGE

HE WAS MR GOLF

Jimmy Tarbuck

In every man's life there are a handful of people he will never forget. His parents, the teacher who gave him a hard time at school, the first girl who did not say 'no', his wife and children, and the golf professional who gave him his first lesson, a handicap, and a purpose in life.

No wonder I was elated when a letter arrived informing me that I had been invited to play in a pro-am. Asking me to play in yesterday's *Daily Telegraph* Damovo British Masters pro-am was almost as good as an invitation to play in the Augusta Masters. You cannot have a stand at Lord's with Ian Botham, you cannot run out at Wembley with David Beckham, and you would not want to be tackled by anyone at Twickenham. But what you can do is play a round with the professors. It is glorious seeing the professionals up close. It is golf, but not as we know it.

Of all the people that I have partnered in pro-ams, I have the fondest memories of Arnold Palmer. He was 'Mr Golf'. He revolutionised the sport. What was fantastic about spending time with Arnold was that he was a hero who lived up to what you wanted him to be. He was a real man's man. You played your round, and there was always a drink afterwards at the 19th hole. It was a great experience to be swapping stories with Arnold over a beer or two.

I remember once playing with Arnold in a nine-hole television match, on the BBC programme *Celebrity Golf* that I used to feature on regularly. We were up against Gary Player and 007 himself, Sean Connery. Arnold said to me: 'Jimmy, can you handle the big fella?' 'Sure,' I said, 'he can't beat me.' Arnold birdied three of the first four holes, I made a net three on the fifth, and we beat them 5&4. It was all over and I was elated.

I saw the producer striding out on to the course. It looked like he was going to congratulate us. 'Thank you very much,' the producer said, 'You've f***** up our programme.' It was lovely. Sean was wonderful in defeat as always. 'You lucky bastard,' he said.

I once played with the great Tony Jacklin in his pomp. It was at the Southport and Ainsdale, and we were paired with Dr David Marsh, who was a local hero after winning the Walker Cup. Jacklin asked me what the line was on his putt. 'Ask David, it's his home course,' I said. 'No,' Jacklin replied, 'I want you to tell me.' So I crouched down on to the green. I was very nervous, there on Marsh's home course, with several hundreds of eyes looking at me.

I took my time. Jacklin crouched beside me. 'I think,' I ventured, 'that it comes in from the right.' He replied: 'I know that, but look at the knockers on the bird in red over there.' And he was quite right. I had fun on the course, but I always remembered to keep my mind on the job.

The camaraderie is what I enjoy. Ronnie Corbett once tripped in a divot. He was so embarrassed. Ian St John could not get out of a bunker. He got the ball out, but he could not get out. They had to help him out with a rake. Everyone used to exchange views on each other's professions, especially if a famous sportsman had brought his clubs.

What came across from all the guests was the sheer joy at winning at their particular profession, whether it was sport, politics, show business, whatever. But with all these top names on the course, and with the pros showing me how to hit a shot, or just watching them striking an improbable three iron from the bunker, I have always found it difficult to control my nerves at a pro-am. It is sheer, childlike excitement.